An Arab
Common Market

PRAEGER SPECIAL STUDIES IN
INTERNATIONAL ECONOMICS AND DEVELOPMENT

An Arab Common Market

A STUDY IN INTER-ARAB TRADE RELATIONS, 1920-67

Alfred G. Musrey

FREDERICK A. PRAEGER, Publishers
New York · Washington · London

The purpose of the Praeger Special Studies is to make specialized research monographs in U.S. and international economics and politics
available to the academic, business, and government communities. For
further information, write to the Special Projects Division, Frederick
A. Praeger, Publishers, 111 Fourth Avenue, New York, N.Y. 10003.

FREDERICK A. PRAEGER, PUBLISHERS
111 Fourth Avenue, New York, N.Y. 10003, U.S.A.
5, Cromwell Place, London S.W.7, England

Published in the United States of America in 1969
by Frederick A. Praeger, Inc., Publishers

Library of Congress Catalog Card Number: 69-14573

Printed in the United States of America

To
Ummi

ACKNOWLEDGMENTS

I wish to express my deep gratitude to Professor Charles Issawi of Columbia University for his constructive criticism and many helpful suggestions; to extend my appreciation to Doris Riley, Patricia Libbey, Dorothy Berkowitz, and the other members of the Tariff Commission library staff for their assistance and co-operation on so many occasions; and, above all, to thank my wife, Carol, for her editorial suggestions and typing of the manuscript, and my daughters, Christina and Dana, for being good little girls.

The views expressed in this volume are those of the author alone and are not intended to reflect in any way the views of the governmental agency with which he is associated.

CONTENTS

LIST OF APPENDIX TABLES

ABBREVIATIONS AND SYMBOLS

BSL   Banque de Syrie et du Liban

EEC   European Economic Community

GATT   General Agreement on Tariffs and Trade

I.D.   Iraqi dinar

J.D.   Jordanian dinar

K.D.   Kuwaiti dinar

L.E.   Egyptian pound

L.L.   Lebanese pound or Libyan pound

L.P.   Palestinian pound

L.S.   Syrian pound

U.A.R.   United Arab Republic

$ United States dollar

INTRODUCTION

As in other parts of the world, there was in the Near East during the first half of the 1960's a movement toward the formation of a regional trading bloc. Measures were adopted and implemented to create a common market and effect economic integration. Such measures, however, involved only a few of the Arab countries, and there was a noticeable reluctance by the remainder to become associated with the undertaking.

On June 6, 1962, representatives of five of the Arab countries—Jordan, Kuwait, Morocco, Syria, and the U.A.R.—signed an Economic Unity Agreement in which they stated that their goal was to establish among themselves complete economic unity and in which they promised to undertake certain general measures at an unspecified future date in order to achieve that goal. Iraq and Yemen became signatories to the agreement in December 1963, and on April 30, 1964, the agreement came into force for Iraq, Kuwait, Syria, and the U.A.R. following the deposit of their instruments of ratification. Shortly thereafter, Jordan also ratified the agreement.

Pursuant to the agreement, an Economic Unity Council was established in Cairo to determine the measures necessary to implement the agreement in stages. On August 13, 1964, the Council adopted a resolution that provided, pending the drafting of schedules containing more favorable treatment, for the removal, in stages, by January 1, 1974, of the customs duties and other restrictions on trade in domestic products between the countries that had ratified the Economic Unity Agreement. This resolution was subsequently ratified by Iraq, Jordan, Syria, and the U.A.R., and the initial tariff reductions and exemptions from quantitative restrictions provided for in the resolution were placed into effect by these countries on or as of January 1, 1965. Kuwait did not ratify the resolution, and the remainder of the Arab countries were not eligible to participate in the common market undertaking without first ratifying or adhering to the Economic Unity Agreement.

The limited participation in the common market undertaking reflected a number of political and economic factors. Politically, relations were strained between many of the Arab countries and a civil war was in progress in Yemen in which both sides were supported by other Arab states. Economically, there were, among other things, differences within the region in economic systems, levels of industrial development, trade and exchange controls, and patterns of international trade that acted as deterrents. Lebanon, for example, with a laissez-faire economy, had long been an advocate of free inter-Arab trade but was reluctant to participate in an economic integration scheme involving three socialist Arab countries for fear that such participation would compromise the nature of its economy, which tended to be heavily dependent on trade and other services and on the inward flow of capital. Kuwait, Saudi Arabia, and Libya, with large annual supplies of foreign exchange in the form of oil royalties but with a virtual absence of an industrial base, likewise manifested a reluctance to participate in an undertaking that probably would have entailed eventually the imposition by them of a comprehensive system of trade and exchange controls, with consequent restrictions on their capital movements as well as alterations in their patterns of trade. The prospect of the utilization of their oil revenues and of uneconomic trade diversion within the framework of a common market to aid industrialization in the U.A.R. and in some of the other Arab countries found little support in these oil states. Algeria, Morocco, and Tunisia also found themselves in an economic position that militated against their participation in an Arab common market. With their trade and economies oriented toward France, in particular, and the European Economic Community (EEC), in general, these countries were in the process of effecting closer economic ties with the EEC and were exceedingly reluctant to jeopardize the negotiations in progress by participating in any regional scheme.

Not only were there a number of political and economic factors that acted as deterrents to the participation of the aforementioned Arab countries in the common market undertaking, but, in addition, there were within the common market framework a number of factors that cast doubt on the undertaking itself, notwithstanding its limited composition. Only two of the four participating countries—Iraq and the U.A.R.—had what could be called amicable political relations with each other. The Baath regime in Syria was virtually on nonspeaking terms with the U.A.R. and Iraq, and political relations were far from friendly between Jordan and the other member Arab countries. Moreover, three of the four member countries—Iraq, Syria, and the U.A.R.—were pursuing a policy of state socialism, so that the common market resolution constituted in essence an attempt to effect a common market in name only. Planned trade through state agencies acting within the framework of an over-all economic plan had replaced or was gradually replacing tariffs and specified quantitative restrictions as the regulator of access to and of exports from these socialist countries.

Within the political and economic milieu in the Arab world, the potential benefits from a regional approach to economic development involving the creation of a wider market for Arab industrial products, the mobilization and utilization of regional resources for regional purposes, and the functioning as an economic entity vis-à-vis the rest of the world did not constitute a sufficient incentive for most of the Arab countries. Such an approach would have required a wide community of interests and aspirations due to the many measures needed to be adopted and implemented, the accompanying compromises and adjustments, and the requisite institutional structure. But this was the very ingredient that was lacking among the Arab countries. These countries were for the most part neither politically nor economically oriented toward each other.

It is the purpose of this study first to place the recent Arab common market undertaking in its proper perspective by considering the developments in inter-Arab trade relations leading up to that undertaking and then to evaluate Arab economic integration by considering the economic difficulties involved therein and the economic benefits that could be derived therefrom. As will be seen, the common market undertaking constituted, in one very important sense, more an attempt to arrest Arab political and economic disintegration than a step in the direction of further political and economic integration. Moreover, this disintegration process had extended over a rather long period of time so that Pan-Arabism or Arab nationalism as a moving force in the Arab world was not sufficient to counteract the forces of political and economic nationalism that had evolved in the area.

The period commencing with the termination of World War I has been selected as the starting point in considering the developments in inter-Arab trade relations. Arab economic disintegration had started well before that time, but there did exist as late as 1914 a customs union between most of the Arab countries as a part of the Ottoman Empire, which did create at least a semblance of Arab economic unity, albeit under foreign domination.

This customs union had been in existence for many years. In accordance with the capitulations concluded by the Ottoman Empire with European countries during the seventeenth century, a rate of duty of 3 percent ad valorem had initially been applied to imports into and exports from the Empire.[1] This rate was subsequently increased to 12 percent ad valorem for exports pursuant to the Anglo-Turkish Commercial Convention of 1838 and subsequent similar conventions with other European countries.[2] Then, during 1861 and 1862, treaties of commerce and navigation were concluded with Great Britain, France, the United States, and a number of other countries which provided for an increase in the import duty to 8 percent ad valorem but a decrease in the export duty to 1 percent ad valorem by 1869.[3]

Included within the Ottoman customs union in the 1870's were the territories which today consist of Iraq, Israel, Jordan, Kuwait, Lebanon, Libya, Saudi Arabia, Sudan, Syria, Tunisia, the United Arab Republic (Egypt), and Yemen. Morocco had never come under Ottoman suzerainty, and Algeria had become a French colony in 1830 and a part of France in 1848.[4]

Although this customs union as it existed in the 1870's did not constitute what could be regarded as a regional market due to the absence, among other things, of adequate transportation facilities, it did constitute an area with a common tariff and in which goods could generally move free of customs duties and quantitative restrictions.[5] However, it was essentially a customs area to facilitate the trade of certain of the European countries with the Ottoman Empire rather than one to facilitate the movement of domestic products within the Empire. The Ottoman Empire was a "sick man" not only politically but also economically, and very little industrial development had taken place within the Empire during the nineteenth century.[6] Consequently, Great Britain, France, and other European countries that had undergone an industrial revolution prior to the 1870's supplied the bulk of the manufactured products that were consumed within the Empire. Great Britain, through the East India Company, had practically a monopoly in the seaborne trade with Mesopotamia (Iraq) and the Persian Gulf territories;[7] and Great Britain and France had developed trade relations with the Arab countries in North Africa and with Syria,[8] whereby British and French manufactured articles were exchanged for Arab foodstuffs and for Arab raw materials used by the British and French industries.[9] These two countries (especially Great Britain) had the shipping tonnage and financial and other connections that enabled them to establish such patterns of trade with most parts of the Ottoman Empire.

This customs union was subjected to a number of alterations during the period from 1870 to 1914, but it remained essentially intact. The alterations that occured involved for the most part the Arab countries in North Africa. Tunisia became a French protectorate in 1881 and its economy was gradually integrated thereafter with the French economy; and Libya became an Italian colony in 1912.[10] In addition, there were alterations in the form of trade relations between Egypt and the Sudan and the remainder of the Ottoman Empire. In December 1890, the Administration of the Indirect Taxes of the Ottoman Empire and the Egyptian Customs Administration entered into an arrangement which provided that henceforth articles produced or grown in other parts of the Empire and imported into Egypt would be subjected to the Egyptian tariff of 8 percent ad valorem, and articles produced or grown in Egypt and imported into other parts of the Empire would be subjected to the Ottoman tariff.[11] In 1907, the Ottoman rate was increased from 8 percent to 11 percent ad valorem, except for Egyptian products, which continued to be subjected to the lower rate.[12] In the Sudan—which had in effect been a province of Egypt since 1821 but which had remained nominally under Ottoman suzerainty—a rebellion occurred during the 1880's, and it was not until 1898 that the country was finally reconquered by British and Egyptian forces. On January 19, 1899, Great Britain and Egypt concluded an agreement between themselves that provided for Anglo-Egyptian condominium over the Sudan.[13] In accordance with Article 7 of the agreement, there was free trade between the Sudan and Egypt in all products, whether of domestic or foreign origin,[14] and the Sudan applied the Egyptian rate of duty of 8 percent ad valorem to products imported from other countries.[15]

Except for these alterations, there was virtually no change in the composition of the Ottoman customs union. Moreover, a certain amount of railroad, road, and port construction had taken place within the Empire toward the end of the nineteenth century and during the early part of the twentieth century, so that by 1914 some of the producing areas in the Empire were connected with the larger cities and ports by either railroad or road or both. There was, however, an absence of railroad connections between Syria, Egypt, and Iraq. Most of Syria's trade with Egypt was carried on by sea, with some use being made of the old coast road via Gaza and Rafa, and most trade with Iraq was over the two caravan routes from Damascus and Aleppo to Deir al-Zor to Baghdad.[16]

With this customs union essentially intact and with Egypt and the Sudan still nominal parts of the Ottoman Empire and applying a rather low import duty, there was by 1914 a semblance of a regional market in the Near East. And notwithstanding the virtual absence of industrialization in the area prior to World War I, inter-Arab trade accounted for a rather sizable portion of the trade of certain of these Arab territories. Available statistics indicate that in 1910 about 45 percent of Syria's exports of approximately 2.8 million pounds sterling from the ports of Alexandretta, Beirut, and Jaffa went to Egypt and other parts of the Empire.[17] These exports included such products as barley, millet, sheep and other livestock, dried apricots, legumes, wine, eggs, samn (butter), oranges, lemons, pistachio nuts, melons, skins and leather, wool, tobacco, soap, silk textiles, and cotton textiles.[18] About 11 percent of Egypt's average annual imports during the five-year period from 1909 to 1913, inclusive, came from other parts of the Empire;[19] trade between the Sudan and Egypt was a substantial part of the Sudan's total trade;[20] and trade between the various administrative divisions of Syria appears to have been rather substantial. Cereals, for example, were sent in large quantities from Homs and Hama to Aleppo, Tripoli, and Beirut; from the Hauran to Damascus and Haifa; and from Gaza and Beersheba to Jerusalem and Jaffa. Fruits, vegetables, vegetable oils, soap, textiles, and leather were also important articles of distribution.[21]

Although the aforementioned percentages probably reflected substantial quantities of reexports of European products—mainly British and French—and although the patterns of trade of the Arab countries continued to be predominantly those that had been established by the European countries with these countries, inter-Arab trade in agricultural products and certain handicrafts was nevertheless significant. The Ottoman and Egyptian and Sudanese rates of duty were too low to result in any significant industrialization in the Arab countries and in changes in their patterns of trade with the European countries; but, on the other hand, these rates apparently did not constitute impediments to the exchange of agricultural products between Egypt and the Fertile Crescent countries[22] nor apparently did they constitute impediments to agricultural production within the region. In effect, what existed in the Near East by 1914 was a tariff framework that perpetuated the international patterns of trade of these underdeveloped countries and at the same time facilitated the regional exchange of agricultural produce while impeding regional industrialization.

It is from this point that the more recent process of Arab economic disintegration begins. In the chapters to follow, an attempt will be made to trace, from 1920 through 1963, the deterioration in the inter-Arab trade relations of the Fertile Crescent countries, the Arabian Peninsula countries, and Egypt and the Sudan. The Maghreb countries—Algeria, Libya, Morocco, and Tunisia—had, as indicated, virtually ceased by 1914 to have any economic ties with the remainder of the Arab countries. Moreover, no attempt was subsequently made by France, Spain, or Italy to establish such ties while these countries were under their control.[23] Accordingly, only passing reference will be made to these countries until Chapter 5.

1

ARAB POLITICAL AND ECONOMIC DISINTEGRATION: THE INTERWAR PERIOD (1920-39)

DECADE OF THE 1920's

Dissolution of the Ottoman Empire in Asia

Following World War I, the Ottoman Empire in Asia was dissolved. The region in the Empire that had been referred to as Syria prior to the war was divided between Great Britain and France: Palestine and Transjordan became a British Mandate, and the remainder of the region, which included the State of Syria, the State of Greater Lebanon, and certain other territories (and which hereinafter in this chapter will be referred to as Syria), became a French Mandate.[1] Iraq also became a British Mandate, while Egypt, which had formally become a British protectorate in 1914, was declared an independent state in 1922. Yemen likewise became independent following World War I, as did the Arabian Peninsula territories of Hejaz, Asir, Hail, and Nejd. The first three of these territories were subsequently conquered by Nejd during the 1920's, resulting in the establishment of the Kingdom of the Hejaz and Nejd and later of the Kingdom of Saudi Arabia in September 1932. Kuwait continued after the war to be in effect a British protectorate,[2] while the Sudan remained an Anglo-Egyptian condominium.

With the complete dissolution of the Ottoman Empire in Asia, separate customs territories with different units of currency evolved in the Fertile Crescent and in the Arabian Peninsula during the 1920's. In Syria, the official currency became in 1920 the Syrian pound, which was equal to 100 piasters and which was tied to the French franc. The import duty that was applied to most products continued until 1924 to be the old Ottoman rate of 11 percent ad valorem. In that year, Syria's normal rate[3] was in-

10

creased, with certain exceptions, to 15 percent, and a maximum rate of 30 percent was instituted. In 1926, these rates were increased to 25 percent and 50 percent, respectively. However, from 1928 to 1930, a number of products were subjected to lower rates of duty or were exempted from duty. The increases in Syria's import duties during the 1920's were generally for the purpose of acquiring revenue rather than for the purpose of furnishing protection to local industrial or agricultural establishments.[4]

In Palestine and Transjordan, the unit of currency became in 1927 the Palestinian pound, which was equal and tied to the British pound sterling.[5] Palestine applied a rate of duty of 12 percent ad valorem to most articles during the early 1920's, but subsequently subjected many articles to specific rates of duty and exempted many other articles from import duties.[6] Transjordan's import duties and exemptions were for the most part the same as Palestine's.[7] Great Britain had recognized the existence of an independent government in Transjordan on May 15, 1923, but Transjordan remainded closely tied economically to Palestine during the entire mandatory period.

In Iraq, the official unit of currency became the Indian rupee. The Ottoman rate of duty of 11 percent ad valorem was increased in 1921 to 15 percent ad valorem for most manufactured products and for various other products, including fruits and vegetables. Increases to 20 percent ad valorem, as well as some decreases and exemptions from duty, were subsequently made, but most products remained dutiable at 11 or 15 percent during the 1920's.[8]

As for the Arabian Peninsula countries, the tariffs imposed by them on the relatively small amount of merchandise that they imported continued for the most part to be rather low.[9] In the Hejaz and Nejd, the silver riyal became the official currency in 1928,[10] while in Yemen and Kuwait the currency was polyglot with no definite monetary unit in use.[11]

Inter-Arab Trade Agreements

Although separate customs territories with different units of currency were established in the region, the mandatory powers and other members of the League of Nations recognized the existence of economic ties between certain of the Arab territories and made provision for the maintenance of such ties. Consequently, the dissolution of the Ottoman Empire in Asia did not significantly affect inter-Arab trade relations during the 1920's.

Provisions were contained in the Mandates for Palestine, [12] Syria, and Iraq—as exceptions to the general provision in those Mandates that there could be no discrimination with regard to imports from countries that were members of the League of Nations—which authorized the conclusion of certain inter-Arab preferential trade agreements. The Mandate for Palestine provided that special customs agreements could be concluded by Palestine with "any State the territory of which in 1914 was wholly in Asiatic Turkey or Arabia." Article 11 of the French Mandate for Syria provided in part: "The mandatory, or the local Governments acting under its advice, may also conclude, on the grounds of contiguity, any special customs arrangements with an adjoining country." And the Treaty of Alliance of October 10, 1922, between Great Britain and Iraq—which treaty, as amended, constituted during the 1920's the British Mandate for Iraq under Article 22 of the Covenant of the League of Nations—contained a similar provision. Article 16 of the 1922 treaty provided: "So far as is consistent with his international obligations, His Britannic Majesty undertakes to place no obstacle in the way of the association of the State of Iraq for customs or other purposes with such neighbouring Arab States as may desire it." [13]

Syria-Palestine Agreements

In accordance with these provisions, agreements were concluded by the mandatory powers providing for free trade between Palestine, Syria, and Transjordan. Trade relations between Palestine and Syria were governed during the 1920's by trade agreements concluded in 1921 and 1929. The 1929 agreement, [14] which was very similar to the 1921 agreement, [15] provided that goods—other than tobacco and tombac in all their forms, pure alcohol, spirituous liquors, salt, matches, and any other goods which may be agreed upon by the contracting parties—which

(a) are wholly produced in Palestine or Syria; or
(b) are manufactured from local produce and have not undergone any process of manufacture outside the country of origin; or
(c) are wholly manufactured in Palestine or Syria from foreign materials; or

(d) are wholly manufactured in Palestine or Syria in part from
   foreign materials and in part from local products
shall be admitted to the other territory free of import duty. [16]

Goods wholly of foreign origin, other than the aforementioned
exceptions, were when imported into Palestine or Syria and then
reexported to the territory of the other contracting party within a
twelve-month period to enter the latter country free of duty if the
import duty levied on the commodity was the same in both
countries. If the duty was higher in the country to which the
merchandise was reexported, then that country would impose an
import duty equal to the difference between its import duty on
the commodity and the import duty levied by the reexporting
country. If its duty was lower, then the reexporting country
would refund to the consignor in the reexporting country the
difference. The reexporting country would turn over to the other
country the duties it collected on reexported foreign merchandise,
except for the amounts refunded to the consignors when the duty
in the country to which the merchandise was reexported was
lower. [17]

There were also rather elaborate provisions in the agreement
dealing with goods of foreign origin passing in transit through the
territory of one contracting party to the territory of the other
contracting party, and with domestic products of one of the contracting parties passing in transit through the territory of the other
contracting party destined for a third country. [18]

Transjordan-Syria and Transjordan-
Palestine Agreements

Trade relations between Transjordan and Syria and Palestine
were governed by the trade agreements concluded by Transjordan
with Syria in 1923[19] and Palestine in 1928.[20] The provisions of
these agreements were very similar to the provisions of the 1921
trade agreement between Syria and Palestine. All articles, with the
exception of tobacco, alcohol, and spirituous liquors, which were
the product of or manufactured in the territory of a contracting
party were exempted from customs duties upon importation into
the territory of the other contracting party.

The agreement between Transjordan and Palestine confirmed
the form of trade relations that had been in existence between the
two territories since March 1, 1920.[21] No customs duties were

payable on goods of any description, foreign or domestic, traded between Palestine and Transjordan, with the exception of the aforementioned products, on which full customs duties were payable. Under the arrangement provided for in the agreement, customs duties which were collected on products imported into either country and subsequently exported to the other country were paid to the latter country. This arrangement amounted to a fixed yearly payment by Palestine to Transjordan, which was revised from time to time in the light of the import and export statistics. [22]

Other Trade Agreements

In addition to the free trade agreements between Palestine, Syria, and Transjordan, there were other attempts to maintain and develop economic ties between some of the Arab countries. In accordance with Section 12 of the Transjordanian Customs and Excise Ordinance of 1926, products of the Hejaz and Nejd were exempted from duty when imported into Transjordan, and Syria and the Hejaz and Nejd concluded a customs convention on March 19, 1926, which provided for the application by each country of a schedule of low duties to certain animals and animal products imported from the other country. [23]

No preferential agreements, however, were concluded on behalf of Iraq with the other Fertile Crescent countries, [24] nor were any preferential agreements concluded by the Fertile Crescent countries with Egypt. Egypt concluded provisional most-favored-nation agreements with Syria and Palestine in 1928, [25] but these agreements did not and could not involve the granting of preferences. Egypt's hands were tied by the trade agreements that it had entered into during the latter part of the nineteenth century and early part of the twentieth century, and under the Mandates for Palestine and Syria preferences could not be granted by Syria and Palestine to Egyptian products.

Inter-Arab Trade

With free trade arrangements in effect between most of the Fertile Crescent countries and between Egypt and the Sudan, with the low Ottoman rate of duty of 8 percent still in effect in Egypt, and with rather low rates of duty in effect in the remainder of the Arab countries, inter-Arab trade during the 1920's constituted a substantial portion of the total trade of most of these countries. Over one-third of Syria's exports went to Egypt, Palestine, Transjordan, Iraq, and the Hejaz and Nejd, with Egypt and Palestine being Syria's most important Arab customers; and about one-tenth of Syria's imports came from Egypt, Iraq, Palestine, and some of the other Arab countries. Over two-fifths of Palestine's total trade was carried on with Egypt and Syria, and most of Transjordan's small amount of exports went to Syria, Egypt, and Palestine. About one-fifth of the Sudan's imports came from and about one-tenth of its exports went to Egypt. About one-tenth of Iraq's exports went to the Arabian Peninsula countries and Syria. And although only about one-twentieth of Egypt's exports and imports went to and came from other Arab countries, Egypt did purchase a substantial amount of the exports of Palestine, Syria, and the Sudan, and, in turn, sold to those countries a substantial amount of its exports other than cotton.

On the other hand, Iraq, notwithstanding the completion of the transdesert route from Beirut to Baghdad in 1923, obtained a rather small amount of its imports from other Arab countries, and the Sudan carried on little trade with Arab countries other than Egypt. Moreover, many of the export figures cited above included reexports of articles produced in countries outside the region and exports from one Arab country to another that were ultimately destined for reexport to countries outside the region; and many of the import figures included imports from countries of consignment or shipment rather than from countries of origin, as well as imports of products that were ultimately destined for export to countries outside the region. [26]

As indicated, the economies and trade of the Arab countries had over a rather long period of time become geared to and oriented toward the economies of the mandatory and occupying European powers—Great Britain and France. The formal framework for such trade continued to be nonpreferential, but there were many other factors, including tied currencies, foreign investments, and foreign control, that channeled trade to and from these European countries.

During the latter part of the 1920's, over one-third of Egypt's exports went to and about one-fifth of its imports came from Great Britain, while over one-third of the Sudan's imports came from and about two-thirds of its exports—mainly cotton as in the case of Egypt—went to Great Britain. Likewise, in the Fertile

Crescent, about one-half of Iraq's imports and exports came from and went to Great Britain and British India. France was the leading exporter to and a good customer for Syria, accounting for about one-sixth of Syria's imports and exports. And Great Britain, in addition to being the supplier of a substantial amount of the imports of Palestine and Transjordan, was the leading customer for Palestinian products, purchasing over one-third of the exports of that country. A large percentage of the imports of the Arabian Peninsula countries also emanated from Great Britain, British India, and other parts of the British Empire. [27]

However, notwithstanding that the Ottoman Empire had been dissolved and most of the Arab countries were under the control of and tied to Great Britain or France, there was still a semblance by 1930 of a regional market in the Near East, which constituted an important outlet for the foodstuffs and some of the other agricultural commodities produced in the region, as well as for some of the small number of industrial articles produced in certain of the Arab countries.

DECADE OF THE 1930's

High Tariffs and Other Trade Restrictions

It was during the 1930's that this regional market was substantially narrowed by the depression and by tariff, trade, and monetary developments in the Arab countries. Economic nationalism, which heretofore had not been a significant factor in inter-Arab trade relations, began to assert itself, and one of the tools that was used was the high tariff.

Egypt

In 1927 Egypt had given some indication of the type of tariff policy some of the Arab countries were to follow during the decade of the thirties when it appointed an international committee to prepare a new tariff aimed at materially increasing the revenue derived from import duties and affording protection to existing and potential domestic industries. [28] The new tariff thus prepared was made operative on February 17, 1930, the day following the expiration of the commercial treaty between Egypt and Italy, which was the last of the commercial treaties of the old era to expire. [29]

Whereas prior to 1930 the general rate of duty was 8 percent ad valorem, under the new tariff the rate of 15 percent, or specific rates more or less equivalent thereto, became applicable to many products. Some goods were dutiable at 20 or 25 percent or even at a higher rate. Nevertheless, the rates set forth in the 1930 act were relatively low compared with those that were to be established when Egypt began to feel the effects of the world depression. Within a few months after the 1930 act became effective, Egypt made further increases,[30] and it continued to raise throughout the decade its import duties on many industrial and agricultural products.[31]

By the second half of the 1930's Egypt was well on its way toward achieving its aforementioned goals. A report of the British Government on Egypt published in 1937 described what had occurred in the following terms:

Many tariff changes have been introduced since February 1930, and both objects of the experts responsible for the new framework of the tariff may be held to have been fully attained, for approximately 50 percent [compared with 39 percent in 1928] of Egypt's total revenues are to-day derived from customs duties, whilst many local industries would collapse immediately if the individual protection now afforded them by the tariff were removed. [32]

In addition to imposing high import duties, the Egyptian Government also extended funds, through the Bank Misr,[33] to encourage the establishment of new industries and the expansion and modernization of old industries, and it purchased carpets, footwear, leather goods, cotton clothing, and various other articles from Egyptian producers only.[34] With such government aid, significant economic progress was made by Egypt during the 1930's. But, as will be seen, equally significant was the effect that Egypt's high tariffs and its "Buy Egyptian" policy, two facets of economic nationalism, had on its inter-Arab trade relations, especially those with Palestine and Syria.

Iraq

Iraq, like Egypt, pursued during a part of the 1930's a policy of increasing its customs revenue and of affording protection to its industrial and agricultural establishments. On April 1, 1932, the Iraqi dinar, which was equal and tied to the British pound sterling, replaced the Indian rupee as the unit of currency in the country, and in October 1932, the British Mandate was terminated. On April 29, 1933, a new Iraqi tariff was enacted, which incorporated earlier increases and provided for new increased duties on various items. [35]

The Iraqi Government tried during the 1930's to foster a national movement for the development of domestic manufactures on modern lines. The objectives of the movement were to make the best use of "Iraq's agricultural produce, to reduce the import of manufactured articles, and to divert to Iraqi pockets the profits taken by foreign traders." [36] Under the Encouragement of Industry Law, which was passed in 1929, companies formed for industrial purposes were exempted from income tax for a period of six years; they were allowed to import their raw materials free of duty; and they received tariff protection ranging from 25 to 50 percent for their products. In addition, loans to new industries were granted under the Capital Works program, and the government followed, whenever possible, a "Buy Iraqi" policy by purchasing locally manufactured products. [37] However, after some progress during the first half of the 1930's, when a number of textile and cigarette factories and modern brick kilns were built, the program lost its momentum, and there was little industrialization during the latter half of the decade. [38] By the end of 1938, the rates of duty initially provided for in the Customs Tariff of 1933 were still in effect for most articles. [39]

Syria

In Syria, import duties were raised substantially on many articles during the early 1930's. [40] Further adjustments, including various decreases, were made during the following years as the High Commissioner for the Mandate tried to balance the interests of Syrian producers, exporters, importers, and consumers. Then, in September 1936, the Syrian pound, which was tied to the French franc, was devalued, and additional devaluations followed at intervals during 1937 until at the end of that year the real value of the Syrian currency had depreciated by about 50 percent. [41] In October 1936, shortly after the September devaluation, Syria increased most of its specific import duties by 15 percent, [42] and in May 1938 it increased them by an additional 20 percent. [43] Inasmuch as many ad valorem rates of duty had been replaced by specific rates during 1934, 1935, and 1936, these two increases applied to many products, and they constituted a substantial rise in the pre-devaluation rates of duty.

Palestine

Palestine's tariffs on various industrial and agricultural products were likewise increased during the 1930's. There was during that period a rapid development of industry, which consisted for the most part of small establishments, [44] and increases in the customs duties were made to afford a measure of protection for some of the domestic producers, including the producers of silk fabrics, furniture, certain wearing apparel, and certain leather articles. [45] A "Buy Palestine Products" movement was also instituted to assist domestic establishments, [46] and the import duties on wheat, barley, and other cereals, and on certain other agricultural products were increased to protect the domestic growers. In addition, the importation of certain cereals was subjected to restrictive licensing at various times when crop conditions were good. [47]

Transjordan

Transjordan, which had few industries to protect and which was dependent to a large extent on imports for its needs, did not make any wholesale increases in its import duties during the 1930's. A new customs tariff became effective during the latter part of 1936, but it was enacted mainly to establish a classification for imports and exports based on the League of Nations Standardised Nomenclature, and there were few important changes in the prevailing import duties. [48] It was estimated that customs duties collected during 1938 represented about 18 percent of the value of dutiable goods. [49] Transjordan did, however, prohibit the importation of wheat, barley, and millet on August 15, 1935. [50] This prohibition lasted until the latter part of 1936 when it was replaced by quotas under which imports were allowed after permits had been obtained from the Director of Customs and Trade. [51]

Other Arab Countries

As for the tariff policies of the other Arab countries, Saudi Arabia applied a number of rather high specific and ad valorem rates of duty during the 1930's, whereas the Sudan, Kuwait, and Yemen continued to apply low import duties. [52] The Sudan, which like Egypt had imposed during the 1920's an import duty of 8 percent ad valorem on most products, did not make during the 1930's the many tariff changes that were made by Egypt. Consequently, its tariff structure became very different from Egypt's. It increased with regard to most products the 8 percent rate to 10 percent, and that rate remained in effect during the period preceding World War II. [53]

Inter-Arab Trade Relations

Within the tariff frameworks that evolved during the 1930's, few attempts were made to perpetuate or develop regional economic ties. With the exception of the free trade relations between Egypt and the Sudan, no preferential treatment was extended by Egypt, the Sudan, Iraq, or the Arabian Peninsula countries to each other's products or to Palestinian, Syrian, or Transjordanian products; the free trade relations between Transjordan and Syria were seriously threatened during most of the period under consideration; and those between Palestine and Syria were terminated in 1939.

Inasmuch as similar agricultural commodities were produced in most of the Arab countries and similar industries tended to be established or expanded, the use of tariffs as a means of protection had a very significant impact on inter-Arab trade in the absence of preferential treatment. In addition, the monetary dichotomy existing in the Near East—with some of the Arab currencies tied to the British pound and others to the French franc—also adversely affected inter-Arab trade. First the British pound was devalued during the early 1930's, which affected exports from the Arab countries with currencies tied to the French franc, and then the franc was devalued numerous times during the second half of the 1930's, which affected exports in the other direction.

Egypt

The most significant deterioration in inter-Arab trade relations that occurred during this period involved Egypt and Syria and Palestine. Whereas the absence of preferential trade agreements between the latter countries and Egypt did not significantly affect their trade relations during the 1920's, it had, along with the depression, a very adverse effect during the 1930's.

Shortly after Egypt's new tariff went into effect in 1930, the mandatory powers concluded on behalf of Syria and Palestine, as well as Transjordan, most-favored-nation agreements with Egypt in order to prevent the imposition of a surtax by Egypt on imports from those countries.[54] By virtue of Article 2 of Egypt's new customs tariff act, a surtax equal to the amount of duty set forth in the act was to be applied to goods originating from countries with which Egypt had not concluded customs agreements.[55] These agreements, however, gave the parties only a respite before they proceeded to increase their duties on a number of articles produced by each other.

Within six months after it concluded its agreement with Syria, Egypt raised its duties on oranges, apples, grapes, and other fruits, and later on household soap, artificial silk products, and various other articles, and, in addition, devalued its currency in 1931. Syria retaliated by increasing its duty on rice and by setting the official value of rice for customs purposes at twice its former value, as well as by increasing the duties applicable to various other articles produced in Egypt.[56] In February 1933, following further tariff increases by Egypt, Syria denounced the agreement.[57] On April 30, 1933, Egypt imposed a surtax of 100 percent on imports of Syrian products,[58] and on August 16, 1933, Syria subjected imports of Egyptian products to its maximum duties, which were usually twice the normal rates.[59] This state of affairs lasted until October 21, 1934, when a new provisional most-favored-nation agreement, concluded on October 11, 1934, went into effect.[60] In an exchange of notes annexed to the agreement, Syria promised not to increase its duties on lemons and hulled rice, and Egypt promised not to increase its duties on lemons, pistachio nuts, and certain fruit pulp.[61] Shortly thereafter, Egypt's duties on oranges entered during a certain period, lemons, limes, grapefruit, and watermelons were decreased, as were Syria's duties on certain articles produced in Egypt.[62] However, as indicated, Egypt increased many of its import duties during the second half of the 1930's, and Syria did likewise while devaluing its currency.

Trade between the two countries decreased substantially. Syria lost the Egyptian market for most of its traditional exports, and the developing industries in both countries had little opportunity, in view of the tariff and monetary developments, to sell their products in each other's market. Prior to 1931, Egypt was one of Syria's best customers. During 1929 and 1930, approximately 17 percent of Syria's exports in terms of value went to Egypt, whereas during the remainder of the 1930's only about 5 percent of its exports went there.[63] Imports (excluding specie and gold bullion) into Egypt from Syria decreased in absolute terms from about L.E. 700,000 annually during the second half of the 1920's to about L.E. 200,000 in 1937 and in 1938.[64] During the 1920's, Syria had exported to Egypt in fairly substantial amounts a variety of articles, including a number of agricultural and animal products, as well as various textiles.[65] By 1939 the only textile that was being imported by Egypt in any significant amount was natural silk yarn, and imports of agricultural and animal products had decreased substantially both in value and volume.[66]

Egypt's exports to Syria also decreased during the 1930's but not to the same extent as Syria's exports to Egypt. Syria had depended much more on the larger Egyptian market than Egypt had on the Syrian, and Syria had exported a wider variety of products to Egypt than it had imported from there. Egypt's main agricultural product by far was cotton, which was exported mostly to Great Britain and the other industrialized European countries. Its main export to Syria had been and continued to be rice, which constituted about 50 percent of its total exports to Syria during the 1920's and 1930's. Egypt's exports of that product to Syria remained substantial during the 1930's notwithstanding the changes in Syria's import duty and the devaluations of the Syrian pound. However, exports of certain other Egyptian products which were rather substantial during the 1920's fell off noticeably during the 1930's.[67] Moreover, although Egypt had established and expanded quite a few industries during the 1930's, hardly any of the products of those industries was being exported to Syria. Exports from Egypt to Syria amounted to a little over L.E. 200,000 in 1937 and in 1938 compared to about L.E. 400,000 in 1928 and in 1929.

The deterioration in trade relations between Egypt and Syria was paralleled by the deterioration in Egypt's trade relations with Palestine. Duties were substantially increased by Egypt on most of Palestine's main exports to Egypt, and Palestine, in turn, increased its duties on various articles produced in Egypt and prohibited or subjected to quantitative restrictions various other Egyptian articles. During the first part of the 1930's, Palestine prohibited, ostensibly for health reasons, the importation of such Egyptian products as figs, bananas, carrots, green beans, tomatoes, egg-plants, citrus fruits, mangoes, pomegranates, mulberries, guavas, sweet sops, and quinces, [68] and subjected to restrictive licensing the importation of unrefined olive oil, acid or offal oils, flour, semolina, and wheat. [69]

On August 18, 1936, the two countries, by an exchange of notes, concluded an additional trade agreement, but this contained only a few tariff concessions, and the concessions that were granted did little to arrest the deterioration in trade relations between the two countries. [70]

Like Syria's exports to Egypt, Palestine's exports decreased substantially in both absolute and proportional terms during the 1930's. In 1929 and 1930, over 20 percent of its exports went to Egypt, whereas during the second half of the 1930's only about 2 percent of its exports went there. [71] In absolute terms exports decreased from approximately L.P. 400,000 in 1929 and in 1930 to less than L.P. 100,000 annually during the second half of the 1930's. [72] Egypt was one of Palestine's three best customers during the 1920's, the other two having been Great Britain and Syria. Following World War I, the Egyptian pound had become the unit of currency in Palestine and remained so until 1927. This common unit of currency facilitated trade between the two countries during the 1920's, as did the absence, generally speaking, of high tariffs and quantitative restrictions on such trade. Palestine's chief exports to Egypt during that period included such items as household soap, watermelons, oranges, lupines, raisins, almonds, grapes, leather, wine, and olive oil. In 1938 the only imports into Egypt from Palestine that exceeded L.E. 5,000 were household soap and olive oil, and imports of household soap had decreased substantially during the 1930's. [73]

Egyptian producers also found it difficult to penetrate the Palestinian market. About 60 percent of Egypt's exports to Palestine in 1938 consisted of only three products—rice, sugar, and specie (British sovereigns). Moreover, about 90 percent of the 1938 exports of approximately L.E. 400,000 consisted of those products plus fish, eggs, onions, raw cotton, molasses, asphalt and similar petroleum products for roads, and books, newspapers, and periodicals. [74]

The effects of Egypt's tariff and trade policies on its relations with Iraq, Saudi Arabia, and Transjordan were much less significant than the effects of such policies on its relations with Syria and Palestine since Egypt had carried on with the former countries only a very small amount of its trade during the 1920's. However, what opportunities there might have been during the 1920's for developing such trade virtually disappeared during the 1930's. By 1939 Egypt's inter-Arab trade, excluding its trade with the Sudan, constituted less than 3 percent of the total value of its trade.

The one exception to Egypt's nonpreferential trade policy during the 1930's was its trade with the Sudan, which continued to be conducted within the free trade framework of the Anglo-Egyptian condominium. This trade involved a wide variety of agricultural and industrial products and constituted a substantial portion of the Sudan's total trade. In 1938 about one-fifth of the Sudan's total imports of approximately L.E. 6 million came from Egypt and about one-eighth of its total exports of approximately L.E. 5.5 million went there. Moreover, about two-thirds of the Sudan's exports other than cotton, cottonseed, gum arabic, and gold went to Egypt during that year.[75]

Iraq

Iraq continued during the 1930's the nonpreferential trade policy that it had followed during the 1920's. It conducted negotiations with Syria and concluded with Transjordan a Treaty of Friendship in 1931, which provided that everything should be done to facilitate with the least possible delay the conclusion of agreements relating to commercial, customs, and similar matters,[76] but apparently no preferential trade agreement was concluded with either country. It concluded a nonpreferential trade agreement with Egypt in 1938[77] and a trade agreement with Palestine in 1936, which involved a number of tariff concessions by Palestine, but none by Iraq.[78] Iraq's only commitment under the 1936 agreement was to maintain up to the Transjordanian border the road from Baghdad to Haifa. A modern harbor had been completed at Haifa in 1933, and Palestine was attempting to increase the transit traffic through that port to and from Iraq and Iran by diverting such trade from Beirut. The Palestinian Government realized the potential importance to Haifa of this transit trade and undertook various measures, including the conclusion of the trade agreement, to encourage Iraqi importers and exporters to use the Baghdad-Haifa land route, which was still under construction at the time the agreement was signed. [79]

Iraq, like Egypt, carried on during the 1930's only a small part of its import trade with other Arab countries—mainly Egypt and Syria. Most of the imports from Egypt consisted of one product— refined cane sugar—and imports from Syria, which decreased substantially during the 1930's, [80] also consisted of a small number of products. [81] Less than 5 percent of the total value of Iraq's recorded imports in 1939 came from other Arab countries. [82]

Iraq's exports to other Arab countries constituted a greater proportion of its export trade than imports from such countries of its import trade, [83] but this export trade, except for exports to Palestine, was quite small. [84] Exports to Palestine, which had been small during the early part of the 1930's, increased substantially following the conclusion of the 1936 trade agreement between the two countries, as greater use was made of the Baghdad-Haifa route. [85] These exports consisted of such products as hard wheat, poultry, sheep, lambs and other livestock, fish, dates, butter, and eggs. Iraq had found a good market in Palestine for such products, since Palestine customarily relied on imports of most of these commodities to fill domestic requirements. [86]

Arabian Peninsula Countries

The inter-Arab trade relations of the Arabian Peninsula countries, which had begun to deteriorate during the 1920's, further deteriorated during the 1930's. No preferential trade agreements were concluded by these countries with the other Arab countries or with each other, and the tariff concessions that had been accorded in some cases during the 1920's were terminated. Moreover, as a result of various factors, there was at times a virtual halt in the trade of some of these countries with each other and with some of the other Arab countries.

Trade between Saudi Arabia and Transjordan, for example, practically ceased during the early 1930's due to the political friction and insecurity that prevailed in the desert areas separating the two countries. It was not until the garrisoning of a security force in the desert and the conclusion in 1933 of the Treaty of Friendship and Bon Voisinage between Transjordan and Saudi Arabia that trade caravans began to again cross the frontier. [87]

Trade was also disrupted between Kuwait and Saudi Arabia during a part of this period. The rulers of the two countries had a dispute as to the collection of import duties on goods passing from Kuwait into Saudi Arabia, and, as a result of this dispute, an embargo was placed by Saudi Arabia on all goods from Kuwait.[88]

Likewise, restrictions were imposed by Saudi Arabia on imports from Syria, which led to the termination in 1930 of the trade agreement that had been concluded by the two countries in 1926. The agreement did not provide for the application of low rates of duty to most textiles, which were Syria's chief export to Saudi Arabia, and when obstacles were placed by Saudi Arabia in the path of the importation of Syrian textiles, Syria terminated the agreement.[89]

As would be expected, the inter-Arab trade of the Arabian Peninsula countries was very small during the early 1930's. It increased somewhat during the latter part of the 1930's, but continued to constitute a very small percentage of the recorded trade of the other Arab countries.[90] The primitive economies of the Arabian Peninsula countries—oil had not yet become a significant source of income for these countries—did not enable them to buy or sell very much from or to the other Arab countries, and the tariff and trade policies of Saudi Arabia did little to facilitate the development of inter-Arab trade.

Palestine, Syria, and Transjordan

What semblance there was of a regional market in the Near East during the 1930's was limited to trade between Palestine, Syria, and Transjordan, as the free trade relations that had existed between these countries during the 1920's were continued. However, during the second half of the 1930's both Palestine and Transjordan expressed their dissatisfaction with their relations with Syria. They maintained that the balance of trade had been constantly in Syria's favor and, in addition, that they wished to protect some of their existing and contemplated agricultural and industrial establishments and to increase their customs revenues.[91] Transjordan notified Syria in July 1938 of its desire to terminate their 1923 agreement as of the end of February 1939. This notice, however, was subsequently withdrawn as World War II approached.[92]

Palestine, on the other hand, carried out its intention to terminate its 1929 agreement with Syria and to establish a new basis for trade. In November 1939, following the outbreak of World War II and after negotiations had been in progress for over a year, two agreements were drafted to regulate trade between Palestine and the states of Syria and Lebanon within the French Mandate. (These states were in the process of obtaining their independence when World War II started.) The two agreements, which were practically identical, came into effect on December 1, 1939, and substantially altered the form of trade relations that had been in effect.[93] Each agreement provided that certain enumerated articles produced or manufactured in the territory of one contracting party and imported directly into the territory of the other contracting party would be admitted free of customs duty, certain other articles would be subject to the normal duties imposed on similar articles of foreign origin, and all other articles produced or manufactured in the territory of one contracting party and imported directly into the territory of the other contracting party would be subject to duties equivalent to two-thirds of the normal rates. The duty-free list included, with a few notable exceptions,[94] most of the agricultural commodities produced in the territories of the contracting parties. It was, however, practically devoid of articles that were being produced in significant quantities by their industries.[95] The normal-duty list contained such articles as alcoholic beverages, perfumery, petroleum and certain petroleum derivatives, tobacco and tombac (including cigarettes and cigars), salt, matches, mechanical lighters, and playing cards. All products not specified in these two lists were, as indicated, to be subject to preferential rates of duty only one-third less than the normal rates.

With regard to quantitative restrictions, the agreements provided that trade between the contracting parties was as far as possible not to be impeded by any import or export prohibitions or restrictions. However, insofar as prohibitions and restrictions might be enforced on the importation or exportation of any goods, articles produced or manufactured in the territory of one contracting party and imported into or exported to the territory of the other were to receive treatment in all respects as favorable as that accorded to the like articles produced or manufactured in, or exported to, any foreign country. The agreement specified that the foregoing provision was in particular to apply in respect to any import or export licenses that might be required and in respect to the conditions under which such licenses would be issued.

Although this break in free trade relations between Palestine and Syria occurred too late to have any effect on their trade with each other during the 1930's, it was probably the most significant development in inter-Arab trade relations during that period due to the size and composition of the trade involved. The bulk of inter-Arab trade during the 1930's, with the exception of the trade between Egypt and the Sudan, consisted of the trade between these countries. During the second half of the 1930's, for example, about one-third of Syria's exports of domestic products, in terms of value, went to Palestine, which was by far Syria's best customer, and about one-tenth of Palestine's exports went to Syria, which was Palestine's second best customer. [96] Political developments in Palestine had resulted in a sharp decrease in 1938 in this trade, but it was still quite substantial and involved a wide variety of agricultural and industrial products.

While Transjordan's free trade relations with Syria and Palestine continued in force, such relations were much less significant than those that had existed between Syria and Palestine. Transjordan had a very weak economy, and its trade with Syria and Palestine was, except for Transjordanian exports of wheat to Palestine, quite small in size and composition.

SUMMARY

By the end of 1939, the process of Arab economic disintegration was well advanced, but it had not yet run its course. The Maghreb countries had long since been effectively integrated into the French, Spanish, and Italian economies and carried on very little trade with the other Arab countries; Egypt, Iraq, and Saudi Arabia were following nonpreferential trade policies within tariff frameworks that restricted inter-Arab trade; Yemen and the Sudan (except for its ties with Egypt) were geographically, politically, and economically removed from the other Arab countries; Kuwait had few economic ties with Arab countries other than Iraq; and Palestine had terminated its free trade relations with the French mandatory states of Syria and Lebanon (hereinafter referred to as Syria and Lebanon).[97] However, there still remained the tenuous free trade relations between Transjordan and Syria and Lebanon; the free trade relations between Syria and Lebanon within the French Mandate, between Egypt and the Sudan within the Anglo-Egyptian condominium, and between Transjordan and Palestine within the general framework of the British Mandate for Palestine;

and the substantially modified preferential trade relations between Palestine and Syria and Lebanon. With the exception of Egypt's trade with Palestine and Syria and Lebanon, inter-Arab trade during the interwar period had consisted essentially of the trade carried on by these countries. Hence, although there was little semblance of a regional market in the Near East by the end of 1939, there were still some significant Arab economic ties. Moreover, most of the Arab countries had still to achieve their independence. Trade negotiations for many of these countries were conducted during the interwar period by the British and French within the framework of the Mandates, and, as indicated, these Mandates did not permit the granting of preferences to Egyptian products. In addition, although attempts had been made by the mandatory powers during the 1920's to maintain economic ties between certain neighboring Arab countries, no attempt had been made by these powers to effect economic integration within a broader, regional framework. The process was one of perpetuating the patterns of trade that had developed rather than the undertaking of measures that might have resulted in alterations in these patterns.

With the outbreak of World War II, however, this regional concept was to acquire a greater importance due to wartime economic conditions. Consequently, as will be seen, there was to be a hiatus in Arab economic disintegration.

CHAPTER **2** SEMBLANCE OF REGIONALISM:
THE WAR YEARS (1940-45)

Most of the Arab countries imposed import, export, and exchange controls shortly after the outbreak of World War II, but their trade with each other was not significantly affected until 1940. During the latter part of that year, however, the Near East was split: Palestine, Transjordan, Egypt, the Sudan, and various territories in the Arabian Peninsula were under British control, whereas Syria and Lebanon were under Vichy French control. Under such circumstances, the amount of inter-Arab trade decreased substantially.

The decrease in the trade of Syria and Lebanon with the other Arab countries was especially noticeable. Except for a few small barter transactions with Palestine, Iraq, and Egypt, chiefly of foodstuffs, Syria and Lebanon's trade with the Arab countries during the latter part of 1940 and the first part of 1941 was practically nil.[1] Commercial activity was complicated by the uncertainty over the Syrian-Lebanese pound, which was tied to the French franc, and emergency restrictions rendered it virtually impossible to obtain import licenses and foreign exchange for "non-indispensable" goods.[2] The British economic blockade and the lack of transportation facilities also contributed to the steep drop in the trade of Syria and Lebanon with the other Arab countries, as well as with countries outside the region.

However, at the same time that a large portion of inter-Arab trade was coming to a virtual halt, rather substantial quantities of civilian products, including various luxuries, were being imported into Egypt (mainly by the Red Sea route)[3] and into some of the other Arab countries from countries outside the region. Such imports were causing the ports of these Arab countries to become congested and were thereby hampering the movement into the region of military supplies and foodstuffs that were needed by the

British for their operations in the Mediterranean area. Consequently, in order to regulate the flow of civilian imports into the
region as a part of the strategy of the Middle East theater of war,
the British established the Middle East Supply Center in April
1941.

Shortly thereafter, the Vichy French forces in Syria and
Lebanon capitulated,[4] and on July 15, 1941, the two territories
entered into a relationship with the sterling bloc, whereby the
movement of goods and capital funds was to be permitted between Syria and Lebanon and the sterling bloc countries.[5] Subsequently, in November 1941, the official exchange rate of the
Syrian-Lebanese pound in relation to the pound sterling was
established at 8.83125 Syrian-Lebanese pounds equal to 1 pound
sterling, and this rate constituted the basis for the rates of other
foreign currencies.

THE MIDDLE EAST SUPPLY CENTER

With the entire Fertile Crescent and Egypt and the Sudan either
in the sterling bloc or associated with it, the British were in a
position to attempt to regulate the external trade of the region
and to effect concomitantly closer regional trade and economic
relations. This twofold task of regulating and reducing imports
into the Middle East from outside the region and increasing production and trade within the region was undertaken to ensure, on
the one hand, that there would be available adequate transport
and quay space for incoming war materials and, on the other hand,
that the civilian population in the Middle East countries would be
provided with those supplies which were considered essential for
their livelihood during the war. As indicated, this task was assigned
to the Middle East Supply Center, which, in a general sense, was to
become a regional planning agency for the Arab countries within
an international wartime framework and was to effect a semblance
of functional integration among the Arab countries.

The aforementioned functions of the Supply Center—which be-
came a joint, Anglo-American agency in 1942—were carried out
during the war years in the following territories: Egypt, Iraq,
Lebanon, Syria, Palestine, Transjordan, Sudan, Libya, Saudi
Arabia, Aden, Sheikhdoms on the Persian Gulf, British
Somaliland, Cyprus, Eritrea, Ethiopia, French Somaliland, Malta,

and Iran.[6] Various procedures were established to regulate imports from outside the area and to increase intraregional trade, and various programs were undertaken and different kinds of assistance were extended to increase production within the area.

The Supply Center, which had its headquarters in Cairo, concerned itself for the most part with the planning and direction of the volume of trade into the region by working in conjunction with the relevant supply agencies in Washington and London and with the Middle Eastern countries involved. Lists of requirements were made about every six months by each of these countries in consultation with the Supply Center. The lists were then combined and sent by the Supply Center to London or Washington where a preliminary allocation of supplies and transport facilities was made to fill as much of the requirements as possible upon receipt of import licenses issued by the Middle Eastern countries and approved by the Supply Center.

A commodity index were prepared to give some guidance to the Middle Eastern countries regarding the available sources of supply. The commodity index listed the sources on which the Middle Eastern countries could draw for the various commodities which they wished to purchase. One of the underlying principles involved in constructing and revising the index was that if the merchandise in question could be secured within the Middle East, then shipping and supplies should not be used to transport it thousands of miles.[7]

The special system of licensing that was established to control imports from overseas territories and their distribution supplemented the licensing systems that had been applied in most of the Arab countries to practically all imports and exports since 1939. Individual licenses for imports from overseas territories were issued by the Middle Eastern country concerned, subject to approval and grading (according to the degree of urgency) by the Supply Center in Cairo. Such items as cereals, sugar, fertilizers, hides and skins, tea, coffee, cocoa and cocoa beans, canned milk, oil seeds, copra, crude rubber, coal, coke, motor vehicles, and tin plate were often purchased in bulk by the United Kingdom Commercial Corporation at world prices, then supplied to a pool stock in the Middle East from which allocations to the governments in the individual territories were made by the Supply Center and executed by the Commercial Corporation.[8] This method constituted an attempt to ensure governmental control of the prices and distribution of these commodities in the countries concerned.

Private trade, however, continued to account for a large portion of the imports and exports of the Middle Eastern countries. Individual transactions passed through their normal channels, but were subject to licensing, whether they involved intraregional trade or trade with countries outside the region, in order to ensure that essential goods would be given priority. [9]

While this plan of operation was being used to channel trade into and within the region, the Supply Center was also concerning itself with the utilization and coordination of the resources of the region. In conjunction with the Middle East governments involved, the Supply Center assisted in shifting acreage from cotton to wheat, in cultivating additional acreage, and in numerous other ways to increase regional production of various agricultural commodities.[10] The Supply Center also assisted in the establishment or expansion of various industries in the Arab countries. Specialists were made available to assist in the setting up and running of new plants; facilities were provided to train persons for work in certain industries and repair shops; and the Supply Center helped some industries obtain equipment and materials needed by them. However, although there was a need for some industrial products which could have been made in the Middle East, a good deal of care was taken by the Supply Center not to aid in the establishment or expansion of industries which it regarded as likely to become uneconomical after the war when supposedly the manufactured products of the industrialized nations would once again have access to the Middle East markets.[11] With the aid of the Supply Center in some cases, and in spite of it in others, various industries were established or expanded in the Arab countries during World War II. Most of this industrialization took place in Palestine and Egypt. [12]

The Supply Center also assisted in converting Middle Eastern railroads (mainly in Egypt) and plants to oil, which was available in the Middle East. These conversions resulted in a substantial reduction of coal imports into the region.[13]

Over-all figures cited for the World War II period indicate that the main objective of the Middle East Supply Center was achieved. Imports into the principal Middle Eastern countries from outside the region decreased from about 6 million tons in prewar years to about 1.5 million tons in 1944. [14]

With regard to the Supply Center's economic contributions to the Middle Eastern countries, it appears that its main contribution was to help these countries obtain various products from Great

Britain, the United States, and certain other countries, which they might not have obtained without the help of the Supply Center, and to coordinate the demands of the Middle Eastern countries for products from outside the region in order to achieve a more equitable distribution within the region. But this contribution, to the extent that it involved an attempt to increase production within the region, was rather limited, since many of the products that the Arab countries could have used—including agricultural and industrial tools and machinery and parts, fertilizers, and industrial raw materials—either were obtained in small or substantially reduced amounts or were not obtainable at all. As a result, the increases in industrialization that occurred in Palestine and Egypt were based mostly on the greater use of the raw materials and machinery existing or available in the region and on the transfer of machinery from the production of one article to the production of another. Moreover, although increases in the production of various fruits and vegetables occurred during the war, due mainly to favorable crop conditions and increased demand, the production of cereals in most of the producing Arab countries was about the same, or lower, than prewar production.[15] Notwithstanding favorable crop conditions in many of the Arab countries during most of the war years, the shortage of fertilizers and farm machinery and parts impeded any significant increase in the production of cereals. Cereal production, however, as well as that of various fresh fruits and vegetables, might have been lower were it not for the help rendered by the Middle East Supply Center in averting locust attacks, introducing better farming techniques, and effecting a greater use of the farm machinery that was available in the region or that the Arab countries (notably Syria) were able to purchase from the United States and other countries.

INTER-ARAB TRADE

As for trade between the Arab countries during the war years, it would appear that the Supply Center was very successful in its endeavor to increase such trade. The trade statistics of most of these countries show substantial increases in absolute and proportional terms in the value of inter-Arab trade.[16] However, such figures are not good indicators of the volume of inter-Arab trade, nor do they indicate what the composition of that trade was. As will be seen, the increases and changes in inter-Arab trade during the war years were not as significant in most cases as would appear by reference simply to these figures.

In the first place, a substantial portion of the increase in the value of inter-Arab trade reflected the rather severe inflation in the Arab countries during World War II [17] and the very substantial rise in the unit values of most of the products involved.[18] Moreover, a large part of the increase consisted of exports of crude petroleum from Iraq to the refineries in Haifa in Palestine and Tripoli in Lebanon [19] and of exports of gasoline, kerosene, and solar, mazout and diesel oil from Haifa to mainly Egypt and Syria and Lebanon among the Arab countries.[20] About 97 percent of the total value of Egypt's imports from Iraq (via Haifa) in 1944 consisted of petroleum products; over 70 percent of the total value of Palestine's imports from Iraq during the same year consisted of crude petroleum; about 85 percent of the total value of Palestine's exports to Egypt in 1943 and a comparable large percentage of the total value of such exports in 1944 consisted of petroleum products; and about 65 percent of the total value of Palestine's exports to Syria and Lebanon in 1943 and a comparable large percentage in 1944 consisted of such products.[21]

In addition, the increases in inter-Arab trade often reflected increases in trade in only a few other items. For example, about 75 percent of the total value of Egypt's exports to Palestine in 1944 consisted of raw cotton, cigarettes, wheat, rice, and certain other cereals. About 70 percent of the total value of Egypt's imports from Syria and Lebanon during the same year consisted of walnuts, liquorice root, dried apricots, apricot paste, potatoes, olive oil, caraway and certain other seeds, and natural silk yarn. About 80 percent of the total value of Iraq's exports (excluding petroleum) to Palestine and Transjordan (mainly Palestine) during 1944 consisted of one item—barley. And about 90 percent of the total value of Iraq's exports (excluding petroleum) to Syria and Lebanon during the same year consisted of bovine cattle, sheep, goats, dates, barley, hides and skins, and raw wool.

There were, however, some sizable increases in the composition of inter-Arab trade during World War II. Various industries were expanded and certain new industries were established in Palestine during the war, and a number of these industries were selling their products in some of the other Arab countries. Imports into Iraq from Palestine increased from I.D. 14,586 in 1939 to I.D. 583,676 in 1944 and I.D. 828,734 in 1945, and most of these imports consisted of manufactured articles. These imports included in fairly substantial amounts such items as medicinal preparations; fruit juices; tanning extracts; paints; cosmetics; floor and furniture polishes and waxes; matches; sole leather; cardboard; footwear and other manufacturers of leather; socks, stockings, underwear, and certain other wearing apparel; glassware; stoves and heaters; razor blades; buttons; games and toys; chairs; and batteries. Likewise, many of the foregoing products, as well as chocolates and other confectionery, wines, fountain pens, and brushes, were exported to Egypt. In addition, Palestinian orange growers exported substantial quantities of their product to the Egyptian market that had been practically closed to them during the 1930's. Imports of oranges into Egypt from Palestine increased from 64,603 kilograms valued at L.E. 708 in 1938 to 13,558,590 kilograms valued at L.E. 160,775 in 1944.

Syria and Lebanon also increased their exports of manufactured products to Iraq. Whereas before the war Iraq imported most of its cotton fabrics from Japan, during the war Syria and Lebanon and India supplied the Iraqi market with the bulk of its cotton fabrics. Total imports into Iraq from Syria and Lebanon increased from I.D. 155,970 in 1939 to I.D. 2,312,587 in 1944, and approximately 55 percent of the 1944 imports consisted of cotton fabrics. Imports of such fabrics from Syria and Lebanon increased from 100,754 square meters valued at I.D. 1,540 in 1939 to 2,191,961 square meters valued at I.D. 1,263,776 in 1944.[22] In addition, Syria and Lebanon exported to Iraq substantial quantities of matches, artificial silk fabrics, and various other products.

Syria and Lebanon also sold substantial quantities of their cotton, artificial silk and woolen textiles, as well as various agricultural commodities and certain other manufactured products, to Palestine, and purchased in return fairly substantial amounts of wearing apparel, leather articles, cosmetics, glassware, razor blades, medicinal preparations, and various other articles. However, although Palestine and Syria and Lebanon, following the practical cessation of their trade during the latter part of 1940 and the first part of 1941, resumed being good markets for each other's products, there was, notwithstanding the rise in the unit values of such products, no increase in the value of their trade (excluding petroleum products) with each other during 1943, 1944, and 1945 when compared to their trade during the late 1930's. Likewise, trade between Jordan and Syria and Lebanon registered no significant increase in value during the war years.

Egypt's inter-Arab trade, except for its increased imports from Palestine, also showed few significant changes. Only a few of the products of Egypt's new and expanded industries were exported to Arab countries other than the Sudan. Trade between the Arabian Peninsula countries and the other Arab countries increased somewhat over the small amount of such trade during the 1930's, but it was still relatively insignificant. [23] And the Sudan's trade with Arab countries other than Egypt was also of little consequence even though it also increased somewhat during the war years.

QUANTITATIVE RESTRICTIONS AND TARIFFS

The limited developments in inter-Arab trade during World War II reflected, in addition to various other factors, the absence of any undertaking to effect an over-all transformation in the form of inter-Arab trade relations so as to create a regional market for inter-Arab trade. Within the regional framework established in part by the Middle East Supply Center, there were prohibitions on trade in various articles with non-Arab countries that were not applied to inter-Arab trade in such articles,[24] but the Arab countries were still functioning and developing for the most part as separate economic entities rather than as an economic unit. Export and import licensing, which was not imposed by the Arab countries on a broad scale during the 1920's and 1930's, was imposed in most cases by these countries during World War II not only on trade with countries outside the region but also on intra-regional trade. When domestic demand exceeded domestic supply with regard to a particular commodity, it was often difficult to obtain an export license even for exportation to another Arab country. Likewise, the importation of various products from any source, including other Arab countries, was subjected to quantitative restrictions. In addition, since the World War II period was a highly inflationary period in the Arab countries and since customs duties constituted an important source of revenue for such countries, many of these countries increased their customs duties during that period. Egypt, for example, increased its specific duties by 100 percent from 1941 to 1943;[25] Syria and Lebanon, in 1942, made similar increases by substituting a large number of ad valorem rates for specific rates; [26] and Palestine, in 1944, imposed, with certain exceptions, an additional duty of 10 percent on goods subject to specific duties and an additional duty of 5 percent on goods subject to ad valorem duties. [27] Although import duties on various articles were suspended during the war years, [28] rather high duties were still being imposed by the Arab countries on many products.

However, even though there was no over-all transformation in the form of trade relations within the region in the manner indicated, what did change significantly were the conditions of supply and demand due to the war and the presence of allied forces. Import duties in many cases ceased to have the restrictive effects that they had during the depression years, and licensing requirements with regard to inter-Arab trade were in many cases more restrictive as to exports than as to imports. Due mainly to wartime conditions and in part to the efforts of the Middle East Supply Center, producers and consumers in the Arab countries were starting to look to each other as buyers and suppliers of products formerly purchased from countries outside the region. As a result, there were some significant, albeit limited, increases and changes in inter-Arab trade. Nevertheless, the basic changes in the Arab economies and in the form of their trade relations that were necessary to effect a large expansion in their trade with each other and to give some permanence to the limited alterations in their patterns of trade did not occur during the war years, and, therefore, the Arab countries began to revert to their prewar patterns even before the end of World War II.

TERMINATION OF SUPPLY CENTER

When World War II ended, so did the Middle East Supply Center. [29] It was a piece of functional machinery imposed from without which had served its immediate primary purpose of decreasing the volume of imports into the Middle East from overseas countries so as to facilitate the exportation of war materials to and through the region. Although the British were willing to maintain the Supply Center in some form during the postwar period, the United States and the Arab countries wanted it dissolved as soon as possible. The United States regarded the Supply Center as a wartime expedient and favored the restoration of trade with the Arab countries which would not be subject to the wartime restrictions and controls that the United States associated with the Supply Center. The Arab countries naturally favored the dissolution of an Anglo-American organization that had been set up in the region primarily to assist the allies in winning the war. Moreover, the Arab countries had established in March 1945 their own machinery for cooperation in the form of the Arab League.

CHAPTER **3** THE SYRIAN-LEBANESE CUSTOMS UNION: EARLY POSTWAR PERIOD (1946-51)

During the early postwar period, there was a virtual absence of Arab bilateral or multilateral economic cooperation, notwithstanding the attainment of independence by the Fertile Crescent countries and notwithstanding the establishment of the Arab League. Political and economic developments within the region were such that although lip service was paid to Arab economic integration, hardly anything was done to bring it about. In fact, as will be seen in this and the following chapter, the semblance of such integration created by World War II was to constitute only a pause in the gradual process of Arab economic disintegration.

One significant attempt, however, was made during the early postwar period to achieve a degree of economic cooperation and coordination. Syria and Lebanon, as independent countries, sought to preserve the economic ties that had existed between them during the Ottoman and mandatory periods by establishing a customs union. Since this customs union constituted the only significant endeavor by the Arab countries to integrate economically during the early postwar period and since it was in fact to become the prime symbol during that period of Arab economic disintegration, it will be considered in some detail before proceeding in the following chapter to a consideration of what took place in the region as a whole.

CUSTOMS UNION FRAMEWORK

Although the loose Ottoman economic entity was dissolved shortly after World War I, there continued to exist an economic union between Syria and Lebanon involving the free movement of capital, labor, and goods and the application of a common tariff.

The common tariff for the two territories was made and administered by the French; their common unit of currency was linked to the franc and issued by the Banque de Syrie et du Liban, a French controlled bank with its head office in Paris;[1] and various administrations, which regulated and administered activities considered common to the two territories, were under French supervision.

The authority to make and administer the common tariff was vested in the French High Commissioner for the Mandate. In performing this function, he was assisted by French officials and by commissions in which the strategic posts were likewise held by French citizens. The native governments of the states of Syria and Lebanon and the native Chambers of Commerce served in an advisory capacity, and Syrian and Lebanese officials performed the routine work of administration under the supervision and control of a few French officials.[2]

In 1941 Syria and Lebanon were proclaimed independent states, and after elections were held during the summer of 1943 and national governments had taken office, the two countries entered into discussions concerning their future economic relations. These resulted in the Agreement signed in Damascus on October 1, 1943, which provided for the establishment of a customs union between Syria and Lebanon and for the assumption of control by both countries of some of the administrations theretofore under French supervision.[3]

Article 4 of the Agreement provided for the establishment of the customs union in the following terms:

> Syria and Lebanon will become a single customs area with a single tariff schedule. The transportation of goods will be guaranteed complete freedom without any customs duty or customs tax. On this basis, the two countries will possess a single customs administration, and this administration will perform its work within the framework of a single customs plan.

A joint council named the Superior Council of Common Interests was to be formed to supervise the common customs administration, the administration charged with regulating the tobacco monopoly in existence in Syria and Lebanon, and the administration which regulated certain concessionary companies that operated in both countries.[4] The Superior Council was to consist of three delegates from each country; each delegation was to be permitted one vote; and the agreement of both parties was to be necessary for the adoption of any resolution.[5]

Article 3 of the Agreement provided that the specific duties of the Superior Council would be the preparation of the legislation necessary for each of the joint administrations, the supervision of the joint administrations, the delineation of the power and jurisdiction of each of these administrations in order to prevent conflicts, the appointment of the employees of the administrations, and the preparation of drafts of international trade and economic agreements to be submitted to the two governments for their approval.

Article 6 of the Agreement made it clear that the Superior Council was not to be a supranational body. It provided that "the Superior Council will prepare drafts, in the nature of legislation, and submit them to the Council of Ministers in Syria and Lebanon, and if and when the countries issue their agreed decisions, then the Superior Council will publish and implement them."

Regarding the distribution of the duty and tax proceeds to be collected by the joint administrations, it was provided that after deductions had been made to pay their expenses, the proceeds would be divided between the two countries in the proportions that the people of Syria and Lebanon participated in the paying of the duties and taxes making up the resources of the administrations. A provisional distribution was agreed on whereby 40 percent of the net income was to go to each country and the remaining 20 percent was to be distributed according to a decision of the Superior Council to be issued within one year on the basis of the aforementioned principle.[6]

The Agreement was to remain in effect for a period of two years and was to be renewed by force of law for similar periods unless one of the parties expressed its desire to terminate the Agreement by giving six months notice.[7]

On December 22, 1943, an agreement was signed in Damascus between General Catroux, on behalf of the Free French Government, and representatives of Syria and Lebanon, which provided for the transfer of the functions of the joint administrations to the two countries on January 1, 1944. Decrees were subsequently issued in both countries to implement the provisions of the Agreement of October 1, 1943.[8]

While control of the functions of the joint administrations was being transferred and the organization of the customs union was being established, Syria and Lebanon proceeded to conclude with

France and with each other various monetary agreements involving their respective currencies and the organization for the control of foreign exchange in the two countries.

On January 25, 1944, both countries concluded a financial agreement with France in which the value of the Syrian and Lebanese pounds was fixed with regard to the French franc and the British pound sterling.[9] On April 18, 1944, a convention between the two countries, the French General Delegation, and the Banque de Syrie et du Liban (BSL) was signed in which it was stated that the foreign exchange holdings of the Syrian and Lebanese Office of Exchange were transferred to the BSL on April 15, 1944, and in which it was provided that from April 15 on, the Office of Exchange would turn over the foreign exchange that it acquired to the BSL and would receive from the BSL the foreign exchange that it needed.[10] The Office of Exchange in turn was transferred to Syria and Lebanon by a protocol, dated April 19, 1944, which was annexed to the April 18 convention.[11] Decrees were issued subsequently in 1944, specifying the nature of the Office of Exchange and defining its functions.[12]

Another protocol, dated April 19, 1944, which was also annexed to the April 18 convention, provided that the Syrian-Lebanese Exchange Control would be an autonomous organization constituted by a Committee composed of representatives from France, Syria, and Lebanon.[13] This Committee (known as the Supervisory Committee) was to prepare the necessary details regarding the exchange organization in the two countries, which details would then be issued by the respective governments in the form of decrees. In addition, the Committee was to act as a supervisory body and was authorized to designate a French inspector and Syrian and Lebanese inspectors to assist it in ensuring that exchange controls would be respected by the Office of Exchange and by the residents of the two countries. Decisions of the Committee were to be made by unanimous vote.

With the transfer of the Office of Exchange,[14] the customs administration, and the other joint administrations from the French to Syria and Lebanon, the two countries were ready to commence an undertaking that was destined to end in failure six years later. As a result of the type of transition being effected, the recently acquired independence of the two countries, and, as will be seen, the dissimilar objectives sought by the two countries and the dissimilar trade policies favored by them with regard to third countries, the 1943 Agreement was almost devoid of any substantive provisions. The two countries merely continued some of the measures that had been applicable when they were under French Mandate. There were no provisions dealing specifically with the common tariff or with excise taxes, nor was anything said regarding quantitative restrictions such as quotas or prohibitions. The distribution of the income of the joint administrations was agreed to on a provisional basis only. Nothing specific was said regarding the power of payment of the Syrian and Lebanese currencies that circulated throughout the customs union, and the organization and structure of the customs administration and other joint administrations (which under the French Mandate had been heavily staffed with Lebanese) were set forth in the briefest terms.

All of these matters were to become the subject of future negotiations. But whereas under the French Mandate the High Commissioner made the ultimate decisions, following the termination of the Mandate the agreement of both Syria and Lebanon was needed for all major decisions; and, as will be seen, the two countries were often unable to reach agreement.

EARLY ATTEMPTS AT COOPERATION AND COORDINATION

Following World War II, Syria and Lebanon continued to retain the framework of an economic union even though their economic relationship was defined in terms of a customs union. Both the Syrian and Lebanese pounds circulated freely, at par, in the two countries; there was the free movement of capital, goods, and persons between the two states; there was a common external tariff; and although some difficulties had arisen regarding the unification or equalization of the excise taxes of the two countries and the coordination of their economic and financial policies, there were periodic meetings during 1946 and 1947 at which these matters were discussed.[15]

Since the early postwar period was a period of continued inflation and a shortage of hard currency, the discussions at these meetings emphasized the necessity of curbing inflation, of limiting imports in order to conserve scarce foreign exchange, and of allocating this exchange in accordance with the policies of the two countries. In addition, Syria stressed the need to protect and help its industrial and agricultural establishments. In particular, it was interested in having wheat and various other cereals, cereal flours, and cereal starches subjected to high rates of duty, as they had been before the war,[16] and in having higher duties imposed on the importation of commodities which its industries produced and lower duties imposed on raw materials and equipment which those industries needed.

Representatives of the two countries also discussed the distribution of the foreign exchange expended in Syria and Lebanon by the Trans-Arabian Pipeline Company; commitments by Lebanon to buy so much wheat and other cereals from Syria at certain prices and by Syria, through the wheat agency called MIRA, to deliver so much wheat and other cereals to Lebanon; [17] the granting of export and import licenses; the proposed prohibition of the importation or exportation of certain articles; the various matters which arose from time to time regarding the railroads that served both countries; and the tariff negotiations in progress with other countries that resulted in the General Agreement on Tariffs and Trade (GATT).[18]

The most significant thing about these meetings was the stress put on the need for the "achieving of unity in economic policy made necessary by the customs union between the two countries" [19] and on the need to resolve the prevailing difficulties in order to make "harmonious the economic policies." [20] Both Syria and Lebanon realized that if their customs union were to succeed, the trade, financial, monetary, and economic policies of the two countries would have to be coordinated to some extent. On the other hand, the parties were unable to agree as to what the joint policies should be. As a result, most of the changes sought during 1946 and 1947 by each of the two countries, especially Syria, in the common external tariff were not put into effect;[21] the excise taxes in the two countries were different with regard to various products; [22] the exchange control system remained virtually unchanged; and the granting of import and export licenses was in many cases in accordance with no uniform established policy for both countries.[23]

This early postwar period could best be described as the lull before the storm—a period during which relatively few substantive changes were made since the parties were unable to agree on the type of economic relationship that they wanted. However, as is usually the case when two parties become dissatisfied with the relationship that exists between them, either changes are effected—bilaterally or unilaterally—or the relationship is dissolved. In the Syrian-Lebanese Customs Union, the changes were to be made unilaterally and were to lead to the dissolution of the customs union.

FRENCH-LEBANESE MONETARY AGREEMENT

On January 26, 1948, France devalued its franc for the second time since the end of World War II. Prior to that date, Syria and Lebanon had been negotiating with France with regard to the guarantee of the sterling value of the French francs possessed by the two countries, which guarantee Syria and Lebanon alleged was implicit in their Agreement of January 25, 1944, with France.[24] France had informed Syria and Lebanon on December 10, 1946, that the obligation that it had undertaken to maintain the sterling value of the two countries' franc assets had been fulfilled when the franc was devalued in 1945 and therefore was no longer in force. Syria and Lebanon had refused to accept France's interpretation of the 1944 commitments, and on August 30, 1947, France had invited representatives of the Syrian and Lebanese Governments to negotiate with regard to all outstanding problems. These negotiations had failed to result in an agreement between the three countries prior to the devaluation of the franc. Shortly thereafter, however, Lebanon proceeded to sign a new agreement with France, whereas Syria, which was dissatisfied with some of the provisions of the proposed agreement, did not.[25]

The monetary agreement between Lebanon and France, which was initialled by Lebanon on January 31, 1948, and signed in its final form by the two countries on February 6, 1948, was dated January 24, 1948, so that its guarantee provisions would be applicable to the franc devaluation. The agreement provided for the maintenance, for ten years, of the guarantee by France of the sterling value of the franc assets held by the Lebanese issue department of the BSL as a cover for the Lebanese pound.[26] These francs could not be used to pay for imports from the French franc area or to transfer capital to countries within that area until 1953, and then only at a specified annual rate. The remainder of Lebanon's franc assets, which amounted to about 4,084 million francs, carried no sterling guarantee. They could, however, be used to pay for imports from the French franc area and to purchase, up to a certain amount, European currencies from the Bank of France at official rates. The agreement also provided that payments for imports into Lebanon from the French franc area and capital transfers from Lebanon to the French franc area, as well as payments for invisibles, were not to be subjected to exchange restrictions if effected through authorized dealers. [27]

BEGINNING OF THE DISSOLUTION
OF THE CUSTOMS UNION

With the signing of the agreement, demand decreased for the Syrian pound and increased for the Lebanese pound. In the absence of an agreement with Syria, France refused to accept Syria's franc holdings in payment for imports from France or for the purchase of other European currencies. Moreover, these assets had depreciated in value by about 44 percent, in terms of sterling, as a result of the franc devaluation of January 26, 1948. Since Syria's other exchange reserves were insufficient to meet demand, Syrian pounds began to be exchanged for Lebanese pounds, which in turn were exchanged for French francs or other currencies to pay for imports from the French franc area or other countries or to transfer capital overseas. This reduced the value of the Syrian pound vis-à-vis the Lebanese. Lebanon thereupon cancelled the power of payment of the Syrian pound in Lebanon and gave the persons who possessed Syrian currency a short period of time in which to exchange their Syrian currency for Lebanese before taking into consideration the drop in the value of the Syrian pound. Syria responded by requesting Lebanon to withdraw from circulation the approximately 44 million Syrian pounds in Lebanon and by prohibiting the exportation to and importation from Lebanon of certain articles. The beginning of the end was in sight for the customs union.

During the first half of 1948, the Premiers of Syria and Lebanon held a series of meetings at which they agreed to submit the transfer of Syrian or Lebanese currency between the two countries, exceeding 200 Syrian or Lebanese pounds per person, to a license from the Finance Minister of the country from which the money was to be transferred; to temporarily permit, with certain exceptions, the free movement of goods between the two countries; to temporarily continue the acceptance of either currency without distinction for the payment of customs duties in Syria or Lebanon, provided that each of the respective currencies did not exceed one-half of the customs receipts of the other country; and to temporarily continue the joint administrations and the powers of the Superior Council connected with the administration of customs. In addition, the parties agreed to permit the Syrian branch of the BSL to transfer to the Lebanese branch the Lebanese pounds held by it and the Lebanese branch to transfer to the Syrian branch the Syrian pounds which it possessed. Syria also promised to furnish Lebanon with enough wheat to satisfy Lebanon's consumption needs until the season of 1949.[28]

While these meetings were being held, the Syrian representative on the Supervisory Committee of the Exchange Control stopped participating in the affairs of that Committee, and in August 1948, a free exchange market was officially recognized in Syria. Exporters were obliged to cede only part of their receipts, and imports continued to be licensed but were paid for mainly by foreign exchange obtained in the free market.[29] In November 1948, a free market was legalized in Lebanon; 10 percent of certain foreign currency remittances was to be sold to the Lebanese Government at official rates,[30] and the balance was to be permitted to be sold in the free market.[31] Import licenses continued to be required for the importation of all goods, with importers obtaining their foreign currencies in the free market.[32]

By the end of 1948, Syria and Lebanon each had its own exchange system; the Lebanese pound was worth more than the Syrian pound; certain restrictions were in effect on commerce between the two countries; the joint customs administration was retained on a temporary basis only; the excise taxes in Syria and Lebanon continued to be different;[33] and the power of payment of the Syrian currency in Lebanon and the Lebanese currency in Syria was limited to the payment of customs duties.

FRENCH-SYRIAN MONETARY AGREEMENT

In February 1949, Syria withdrew from the franc area. An agreement was concluded with France during the same month with regard to the Syrian franc reserves held by the BSL.[34] The francs held as a cover for the Syrian pound were guaranteed in terms of sterling by France for a period of ten years from

January 24, 1948.[35] Provision was made for the release of these francs in fourteen equal semiannual installments by 1955. An account was to be established to be debited and credited with the value of Syria's current transactions with the French franc area, and any deficit for Syria in this account could be settled with the use of the amounts released from the guaranteed franc reserves. The balance of Syria's holdings, consisting of about 3,189 million francs, was not guaranteed in terms of any other currency. After deduction of French claims on Syria, these holdings could be used for the purchase from the Bank of France of European currencies at the French official rates.[36]

Unlike the Lebanese agreement with France, the Syrian agreement did not provide for the free movement of capital from Syria to the French franc area.[37] Since Syria continued to subject such capital transfers to exchange restrictions, one of the basic reasons for the disparity in the values of the Syrian and Lebanese pounds continued to exist. Hence, notwithstanding the conclusion of the French-Syrian agreement, many of the problems regarding the two currencies that had arisen when Lebanon signed its agreement with France in 1948 were still present.

ATTEMPTS TO SALVAGE THE CUSTOMS UNION

On June 5, 1949, the Syrian Minister of Finance and National Economy sent the following letter to the Lebanese Ministry of National Economy:

... It is known that the basic causes of disagreement concern the wish of Syria to limit imports within the framework of unity in order to achieve a true equilibrium in the balance of payments, to protect the industrial and agricultural production of the two countries, and to preserve their wealth, as opposed to Lebanon's policy of free importation (as far as finished products are concerned) in order to widen the trade horizon in Lebanon, and of continuing to have a free market in Syria for the same purpose.

The result of these differences became more serious as the local industries expanded and agricultural production increased. Moreover, after Lebanon signed the monetary agreement, it cancelled the purchasing power of the Syrian currency in Lebanon without any negotiations with Syria. This ended the period of unity of the two currencies, which was basic for the exchange of goods between the two countries and for economic unity. Differences have widened between Syria and Lebanon, and the difference between the currencies has varied between 3 and 7 percent. As a result, Syrians have suffered big losses of about 10 million Syrian pounds. Syria had to take measures to avoid further injury.

Syria realizes that in view of all of the trials and tribulations of the last 15 months it is necessary to adopt final measures this month.

Syria has considered all possibilities and is prepared to accept one of the following three solutions:
1. Economic unity on the basis of the enclosed plan.
2. Organization of free exchange between the two countries on the following basis:
   a. Unified external tariff.
   b. Exchange of local produce between the two countries free of customs duties.
   c. Subjecting foreign goods exchanged between the two countries to the normal tariff which the exporting country will pay to the importing country.
   It is implicit that the choice of an organization such as this means freedom for each country in its economic and monetary policies and in its affairs other than those mentioned.
3. Improvement of the present organization by making the adjustments necessary within the limits of the accompanying enclosure, including especially the creation of a joint council to supervise imports and exports, the restriction of imports for the protection of local production, and the equalization of the currencies of the two states.[38]

The enclosed plan of economic unity referred to in Item 1 of the letter called for the establishment of a joint economic council which was to prepare and submit to the Councils of Ministers in the two countries, for their approval, drafts of trade agreements and legislative drafts relating to customs duties, exports, imports, and the supervision of the joint railroads and the administration of the tobacco monopoly. After adoption of these drafts by the Councils of Ministers, the joint economic council was to issue the legislation and agreements and administer the aforementioned affairs accordingly. The plan also provided that the participation of Syria and Lebanon in the customs duties would be on a proportional basis and authorized the joint economic council to unite the organizations of currency and exchange in the two countries, to determine the indirect taxes to be applicable in both countries to the consumption of articles exchanged between Syria and Lebanon, and to specify the rules to be followed in rejecting or collecting them. In addition, the joint economic council was to prepare the necessary legislation leading to similar financial, economic, and social policies in the two countries relating to such matters as the monetary organizations, direct taxes, and employment.[39]

The enclosed plan referred to in Item 3 of the letter did not call for the degree of unification set forth in the aforementioned plan. It provided for the formation of a joint economic council which was to suggest to and prepare for the respective governments the measures needed to unify the economic legislation of the two countries with regard to exports and imports and which was to administer exports and imports for the two countries in accordance with certain provisions set forth in the plan. These provisions specified that imports and exports (with certain exceptions) would be licensed; that some of the foreign exchange derived from exports would be handed over to the Office of Exchange; that the joint economic council would set the export prices for the most important articles; that there would be freedom of transit trade; and that Syria would receive 78 percent and Lebanon 22 percent of the foreign exchange derived from exports, with the exception of the foreign exchange derived from the sale of grains and their by-products (which would go to Syria) and silk thread and fruits (which would go to Lebanon). The plan also provided that the Lebanese and Syrian currencies would be accepted on an equal basis in government circles and by the joint administrations of the two countries and that the acceptance of the two currencies on an equal basis would be permitted in the money markets in Syria and Lebanon. In addition, separate accounts for the two countries would be set up by both the Syrian and Lebanese branches of the BSL to handle the receipts and expenditures arising in part from government operations, the joint administrations, and certain other establishments in the two countries, with the added stipulation that when the over-all balance with regard to either Syria's or Lebanon's account reached 20 million pounds, the parties would reconsider the agreement. Finally, provision was made in the plan for the free exchange of goods, with certain exceptions, between the countries.[40]

Following Syria's letter of June 5, the two countries, on July 8, 1949, entered into an agreement covering certain matters which the parties stated had to be resolved with speed. The agreement provided for the cancellation of the resolution which suspended the import duties on wheat, barley, and their derivatives during World War II, and for the application of a 50 percent rate of duty to those articles. Provision was made for the exemption from duty of such articles if imported by the Lebanese Government for its account in order to feed its people during a period of poor harvests or rising prices in the two countries. Syria promised not to impose any restrictions on the shipment of these products to Lebanon, and Lebanon promised to prevent their reexport. The agreement also provided for the imposition of a 11 percent rate of duty on rice,[41] the application of increased duties to various cotton textiles and artificial silk textiles, and the exemption from duty of various artificial silk threads and yarns. In addition, the Superior Council of Common Interests was directed to study the changes in the prevailing tariff needed to abolish or lower the duties on raw materials which were not produced in the two countries and which were necessary for the local industries and the changes needed to protect the domestic industries— especially the spinning, weaving, olive oil, leather, soap, glass, and sugar industries.[42] The remainder of the agreement provided for the continuation of the joint administration for the railroads and the joint administration of tobacco; the setting up of a committee to study the organizations of exchange in force in the two states and to suggest measures for unifying them; the compilation by each country of a schedule of its internal taxes in order to reach an agreement regarding the unification of these taxes in accordance with the rules followed in each country; and the adoption by the two countries of joint measures necessary to remove the difference between their currencies. With regard to the latter, experts were to be appointed to make a study and to submit their recommendations.[43]

The appointed Syrian and Lebanese economic experts met on August 30 and 31 and September 1, 1949, and submitted shortly thereafter a report to the two governments. In their report, they pointed out that the elimination of the difference between the two currencies should be accomplished as soon as possible in order to bring maximum benefits to both countries within the framework of the customs union, and that the longer this difference persisted the more difficult it would be to remove. They analyzed five possible solutions and urged the two governments to adopt the measures necessary to effect equilibrium in the balance of payments between the two countries.[44]

Very little, however, was accomplished by the report or the agreement of July 8, 1949. Each party accused the other of failing to carry out the recommendations of the experts and of failing to implement the provisions of the agreement which dealt with the unification of the internal taxes of the two countries, the equalization of the values of their currencies, the unification of their exchange organizations, the coordination of their economic and financial policies, and the shipment and reexport of wheat.

DISSOLUTION OF THE CUSTOMS UNION

In December 1949, the Syrian Government prohibited the exportation of wheat and its derivatives to Lebanon. In a letter of December 10, 1949, the Lebanese Government charged the Syrian Government with acting contrary to the agreement of July 8, 1949, and asked if the Syrian Government intended to abide by that agreement.[45] Syria responded in a note of January 14, 1950, in which it accused Lebanon of increasing the differences between the internal taxes of the two countries rather than attempting to equalize them as required by the July 8 agreement. It stated that Lebanon had failed to respond to the suggestions made by the experts of the two countries in their report and the suggestions submitted by Syria at a meeting held on November 4, 1949. And it concluded by stating that Lebanese nationals still held most of the jobs in the joint administrations and that Syrian nationals should have a larger proportion of the jobs, which proportion should be commensurate with the share of Syria in the imports of the customs union.[46]

Finally, Syria, in a note dated March 7, 1950, after stating that there had not been any definite policy covering the economic relations between the two countries, asked Lebanon if it was willing to accept the principle of complete economic unity between the two countries, including the unification of the customs and monetary systems, the unification of the economic policies concerning exports and imports in a way which would lead to mutual benefits, and the administration of the joint administrations on an equal footing. It asked Lebanon to answer by not later than March 20, 1950, and stated that if Lebanon was willing to accept this principle, then the two countries could enter into negotiations leading to complete economic unity; but if it was not willing to accept this principle, then Syria would consider the customs union to be at an end and would be compelled to take whatever steps were necessary.[47]

Lebanon answered Syria's note in a note dated March 10, 1950, in which it stated that there would be no advantage in establishing a common currency for the two countries and that it was incumbent upon Syria to bring the value of its currency up to Lebanon's by whatever means it decides. In addition, it stated that it could not accept Syria's proposal for complete economic unity between the two countries since it could not go beyond its position of following a policy preserving to each country its speciality. It indicated that it hoped that Syria would change its position, but that if it did not, then Lebanon would follow a policy consistent with its interests. [48]

In an announcement of March 13, 1950, Syria withdrew from the customs union and stated that the following measures would become effective on March 14, 1950: (1) Persons entering and leaving Syria would be permitted to bring in and take out only 50 Syrian pounds each; (2) the importation of merchandise from Lebanon into Syria would be prohibited with the exception of goods in transit, goods exempt from duty, and certain other articles; (3) customs' and inspectors' offices would be strengthened to prevent smuggling; and (4) the travel of Syrians to Lebanon would be prohibited except by permit to be given only in cases of necessity. [49]

In an announcement of March 14, 1950, Lebanon took cognizance of Syria's withdrawal and stated that as of that date the customs union did not exist. In his announcement the Lebanese Prime Minister made the following statement:

> We have been asked, "Why do you not accept complete economic and monetary unity?" To this inquiry we answer that Syria and Lebanon are complementary to each other in economic affairs by natural and existing law, and on these bases the countries have sought to coordinate their economic policies in a manner to preserve to each its nature and speciality. The continuance of the customs union, which had existed during the French period, involving the free movement of goods and the joint administrations has been good for both governments. But economic coordination is one thing while economic unity is another. The forming of complete economic unity will harm us without benefiting the Syrians.[50]

The dissolution of the customs union resulted in a substantial loss of trade for both countries. After prolonged negotiations and several interim modifications of the initial measures applicable to trade between the two countries, Syria and Lebanon signed a temporary agreement in November 1950, which provided for the removal of the prohibitions on the importation of agricultural products and of industrial products containing domestic raw materials that constituted at least 50 percent of the value of such products. These agricultural and industrial products, however, were to be subject to the normal customs duties and, like other foreign products, were to be subject to the applicable Syrian or Lebanese licensing requirements.[51]

The normal duties that Syria initially applied to many Lebanese products were those which had been in the common external tariff and which, in various cases, had been rather high in order to protect Lebanon's and Syria's industrial and agricultural establishments. In addition, Syria proceeded to increase many of these duties during 1950 and 1951.[52] Lebanon, on the other hand, proceeded during those years to apply its liberal trade policy, and as a result its duties on many articles were removed or reduced.[53]

By the end of 1951, there was little semblance of any economic unity between Syria and Lebanon. The transition had been completed; the two countries were going their separate ways.[54]

CONCLUSIONS

As is apparent from the contents of this chapter, the failure of the Syrian-Lebanese Customs Union reflected the lack of cooperation and coordination by the two countries in the many matters heretofore mentioned. This in turn reflected the different economies of the two countries and the desire of each country to favor economic measures that conformed to the prevailing interests in its own economy − agricultural and industrial production in Syria and trade and services in Lebanon. In other words, there was no meeting of minds as to what type of binational economy within a world framework should exist between the two countries. As a result, there was no coordination or unification of excise taxes; the granting of import and export licenses was in many cases in accordance with no uniform established policy for both countries; the two countries were often unable to agree on changes in the common tariff proposed by each other; the exchange controls imposed by two countries were different; and the

two countries did not adopt any measures to remove the dif-
ference in the values of their two currencies which occurred when
Lebanon signed without Syria the monetary agreement with
France in 1948.

Under such circumstances, the need for a strong institutional
organization operating within the framework of an agreement
under which it would have had a great deal of authority to deal
with these matters was obvious. But, as has been indicated, the
Superior Council of Common Interests, which was the main organ
provided for in the 1943 customs union agreement, possessed very
little authority to act independently of the governments of the
two countries. The Syrian note of June 1949 stated that Syria was
in favor of creating an organ with greater authority than that
possessed by the Superior Council so as to coordinate some of the
policies of the two countries, but the Lebanese note of March 10,
1950, made it quite clear that Lebanon preferred to follow a
live-and-let-live policy. Syria's termination of the customs union
indicated to Lebanon that it could follow any policy it wanted but
not within a so-called customs union in which there was the free
movement of persons, goods, and capital.

In essence, the weakness of the Syrian-Lebanese Customs Union
lay in the fact that the framework of the economic union that had
existed between the two countries under the French Mandate was
retained following independence without the strong institutional
machinery and without any joint sense of direction. Moreover,
neither of the countries was powerful enough to impose its will on
the other. Many of the difficulties that plagued the Syrian-
Lebanese Customs Union were not peculiar to that union. Some of
the very same difficulties, including the form of the common
tariff, the division of the customs revenues, and the unification of
the internal taxes, had been encountered by other customs unions.
Some of these customs unions had failed; others, notwithstanding
these differences, had succeeded and had served as stepping stones
to closer economic or political unity.[55] However, in neither the
customs unions that failed nor in those that succeeded had the
parties involved decided upon a lesser degree of economic unity by
establishing in name and modus operandi a customs union while
retaining in fact the framework of an economic union. The
Syrian-Lebanese Customs Union was unique to that extent, and
inherent in that uniqueness was the destined failure of the union.

4 REGIONALISM IN REVERSE: EARLY POSTWAR PERIOD (1946-51)

The deterioration in trade relations between Syria and Lebanon was paralleled during the early postwar period by a further deterioration in inter-Arab trade relations in general. The hostilities that developed over Palestine and the aftermath of these hostilities, including the complete embargo on trade and economic relations between the Arab countries and Israel, constituted—along with the breakup of the Syrian-Lebanese Customs Union—the biggest blow to inter-Arab trade during this period.

As indicated, Palestine had been an integral part of the economic life of the Near East, accounting for the bulk of inter-Arab trade both before and during World War II. There had existed a preferential trade area comprised of Palestine, Syria, Lebanon, and Transjordan; the Palestinian pound had been the unit of currency in Transjordan; Palestine, along with some of the other Arab countries, had been in the sterling area; and Egypt's sole overland route to the Fertile Crescent had been through Palestine. Moreover, a large portion of the industrialization in the Near East during World War II took place in Palestine. As a result, Palestine became the supplier of many manufactured articles to the other Arab countries and consumed in return substantial amounts of their raw materials and foodstuffs, as well as their manufactured products. What semblance there was of functional economic integration in the region during World War II involved Palestine, for the most part. Hence, the loss of Palestine constituted not only a political setback for the Arab countries but also a significant economic setback.

As a result of the hostilities over Palestine, the difficulties in inter-Arab political relations, postwar economic difficulties, international commitments, economic and political nationalism, and various other factors, the Arab countries did very little during the early postwar period to effect, or maintain, close trade relations with each other. In fact, the trend was in the opposite direction as tariffs and quantitative restrictions were utilized by many of these countries within virtually a nonpreferential framework for inter-Arab trade to increase governmental revenue, protect domestic agricultural and industrial establishments, facilitate the development of domestic seaports and tertiary trades, ensure the availability of domestic production for domestic needs, and control and channel limited supplies of foreign exchange.

QUANTITATIVE RESTRICTIONS AND INCREASED TARIFFS

Iraq

In Iraq, as in most of the Arab countries, the quantitative controls that had been introduced on November 24, 1941, were relaxed considerably following the termination of World War II. In September 1948, however, the Iraqi Government required special licenses for the importation of practically all commodities in an endeavor to prevent the drain on the country's sterling balances accumulated during the war.[1] Further major revisions were made in 1950 to strengthen these quantitative controls[2] and import duties were increased substantially on a number of products,[3] so that by the end of 1951 restrictions on trade were rather formidable. Mainly as a protective device, many articles were prohibited from being imported into Iraq,[4] and practically all other imports required licenses and were generally subject to fixed annual quotas. Exchange was usually granted with the import license, but licenses for certain goods were issued with the understanding that the importer would provide his own exchange. Certain exports were prohibited, and exports of scarce essential goods required licenses. The exchange proceeds of all exports to outside the sterling area had to be received in acceptable foreign exchange, in sterling from an account appropriate to the country of destination, or, in the case of a limited number of nonsterling area countries, in Iraqi currency from a nonresident account. Foreign exchange proceeds in other than sterling area currencies were required to be surrendered.[5]

Jordan

In Jordan, the quantitative controls on trade that had been introduced in September 1939 were likewise relaxed to a large extent following the termination of World War II, but, as in Iraq, they were subsequently reimposed, and additional controls were adopted which were aimed directly at commercial relations between Jordan and some of the other Arab countries. When Palestine withdrew from the sterling area on February 22, 1948, Jordan found it technically impossible to remain in the area since the Jordanian unit of currency was the Palestinian pound. It informed Great Britain at that time that it intended to embark on such currency and control arrangements as would enable it to return to the sterling area. Following its withdrawal, Jordan imposed strict import licensing and exchange controls, and in April 1950, it imposed additional restrictions which were aimed at the middlemen in Lebanon and Syria. Foreign goods were not to be purchased from intermediaries in Lebanon and Syria, and Jordanian importers were required to make a direct approach to exporters in the countries of origin rather than through a third party medium in a foreign country.[7]

On July 1, 1950, Jordan began to issue its own currency, the Jordanian dinar, and reentered the sterling area. It thereupon proceeded to further strengthen its quantitative trade controls, as well as to raise its tariffs on a large number of products in order to increase its customs revenue.[8] By the end of 1951, all imports into Jordan, with the exception of domestic products of Syria and Lebanon imported from those countries, required an import license and an exchange permit.[9] Imports could be made only by registered importers, who received foreign exchange allocations in hard or soft currencies on the basis of the government's import program for each commodity group. The Director of Imports and Exports issued licenses for individual imports on the basis of these allocations. Exports were not to be shipped unless the exporter had satisfied the Controller of Currency as to the manner in which payment for the goods would be received, and exporters were normally required to repatriate their export proceeds within six months of exportation.[10]

Syria and Lebanon

The system of quantitative controls that was in effect in Syria and Lebanon prior to the termination of their customs union was discussed in the preceding chapter. Following the termination of the customs union, Syria strengthened its controls. Various articles were prohibited from being imported, and practically all other imports required licenses. In addition, Syria's most important exports to countries other than Bahrain, Iraq, Jordan, Kuwait, and Saudi Arabia[11] had to be paid for in specified currencies and the proceeds repatriated and registered with an accepted bank as exportation exchange. Commodities subject to the exportation exchange arrangement constituted about 80 percent of the value of Syria's total exports.[12] Export proceeds subject to repatriation had to be repatriated within eight days of their receipt by the exporter. Once repatriated and registered as exportation exchange with an accepted bank operating in Syria, they could either be retained by the exporter or sold to an accepted bank at the current exportation exchange rate. Their transfer abroad, however, was restricted to paying for licensed imports and for other transactions authorized by the Exchange Office. Moreover, unless specifically authorized by the Exchange Office, exportation exchange could not be used to pay for imports from those neighboring countries the earnings from exports to which were not subject to repatriation. Such imports were to be financed through the free exchange market in Syria.[13]

In addition to the foregoing controls and the rather high tariffs that Syria was imposing on a number of products,[14] certain articles considered essential to the domestic economy were prohibited from being exported, and licenses for exports to other than neighboring countries of certain other articles (notably cotton) were granted only if such articles were shipped through the Syrian port of Latakia.[15] Likewise, certain articles were permitted to be imported through that port only.[16] Syria, like Jordan, was endeavoring to cut out the middlemen in Lebanon, and, in addition, was attempting to develop its own port at Latakia by diverting its trade from Beirut to that port.

Lebanon, unlike Syria, relaxed its quantitative controls on trade following the breakup of the customs union. Only a few exports required licenses. All imports continued to be licensed, but such licensing was restrictively applied—to protect certain domestic producers—to a limited number of articles. Some tariff increases were also made during 1951 for the same purpose.[17] Foreign exchange to pay for imports was generally obtained in the free market.[18]

Egypt

In Egypt, the wartime quantitative controls on trade were substantially lessened following the termination of the war. But on

July 14, 1947, Egypt withdrew from the sterling area, and the following day it extended its licensing requirements to cover imports from whatever origin. It subsequently found, however, that very little of the sterling that was released in accordance with the British-Egyptian Financial Agreement of June 30, 1947, was being utilized, and it, therefore, relaxed to a large extent its soft currency controls in March 1948.[19] Bilateral payments agreements were subsequently concluded with France and certain other countries which led to a further relaxation of these controls. As of the end of 1951, imports from the sterling area, the French franc area, those countries to which the United Kingdom transferable account arrangements applied, and certain other countries to which transfers in sterling could be made did not require licenses. Imports of only a few articles, such as cotton and cottonseed, were prohibited, and appropriate exchange was automatically granted for authorized imports. Various exports, however, were prohibited or required licenses; and export proceeds, which were required to be surrendered, had to be received in appropriate foreign exchange, in sterling eligible for credit to an Egyptian transferable account in the United Kingdom, or in Egyptian pounds from a nonresident account appropriate to the country of destination or, for certain countries, from a nonresident export account.[20]

Although Egypt liberalized its quantitative import controls during the early postwar period, it increased its import duties on a wide range of products. In 1946, the additional customs duty—which was imposed on the c.i.f. value of all imported goods—was increased to 7 percent ad valorem,[21] and during 1949 and 1950 a supplementary duty of 10 to 20 percent ad valorem—that is, supplementary to the 7 percent ad valorem duty—was imposed on various articles.[22] A number of base duties were also increased substantially, including very large increases in the duties on various cotton yarns and fabrics.[23] However, during 1950 and 1951, in an attempt to slow down the rise in the domestic price level, Egypt proceeded to exempt from the base duties many agricultural products, including wheat, barley, maize, apples, pears, quinces, cheese, bananas, melons, oranges, lemons, and cottonseed and sesame seed oil.[24] In addition, various agricultural products were exempted from the 7 percent ad valorem duty, and others were subjected to a reduced ad valorem rate of 1 percent.[25] By the end of 1951, it appeared that Egypt was embarking on free trade in agricultural products while maintaining protective tariffs on many of the articles produced by its industries—a policy that reflected its increasing emphasis on industrialization.

Sudan and Arabian Peninsula Countries

The quantitative controls and tariffs imposed by the Sudan and the Arabian Peninsula countries during the early postwar period were generally less restrictive than those imposed by the afore-mentioned Arab countries. The Sudan left the sterling area when Egypt did because its unit of currency was the Egyptian pound. It, like Egypt, tightened its import controls at that time and then later relaxed them considerably. [26] The rate of duty that it imposed on most imports during most of the postwar period was 15 percent ad valorem. [27] Kuwait imposed very few quantitative controls and an import duty of only 6.5 percent ad valorem; [28] and Yemen had few specified quantitative controls and applied low duties to most products. [29] Saudi Arabia, on the other hand, licensed imports and imposed rather high duties on various products; however, import licenses were freely granted for most products. [30]

INTER-ARAB TRADE AND PAYMENTS AGREEMENTS

As during the 1930's, there were no significant attempts by the Arab countries during the early postwar period to effect closer inter-Arab trade relations by extending preferential treatment within the prevailing quantitative and tariff frameworks. Only a few bilateral trade and payments agreements were concluded by the Arab countries with each other during this period, and most of these agreements were rather limited in scope—providing primarily for most-favored-nation treatment and for the authorization by the respective governments of the importation and exportation of a limited number of named commodities.

Egypt was a party to most of the inter-Arab agreements concluded during the early postwar period. After it withdrew from the sterling area in 1947, it entered into a series of bilateral agreements with various countries, including some of the Arab countries, in an attempt to increase its trade and to approach equilibrium in its balance of payments. Egypt, like most countries, experienced a shortage of hard foreign currencies during the early postwar period. It received only limited allocations of dollars and other hard currencies under its financial agreements with Great Britain, and it earned only limited amounts of such currencies from its exports of cotton and a few other commodities and from the Suez Canal revenues. Moreover, although its allocations and earnings of sterling were apparently sufficient to pay for the products that it wanted and could obtain from the sterling area, sterling was not a convertible currency, except for a brief period during the summer of 1947, nor was it completely transferable. Hence, due in part to the shortage of hard currencies and to the difficulties that it and the nonsterling area countries were encountering in utilizing sterling to finance their trade with each other, Egypt decided to conclude a number of trade and payments agreements providing for the authorization by the contracting parties of specified imports from each other and for the utilization of the Egyptian pound or the currency of the other country, or of both, as the unit to finance such bilateral trade. Among the agreements concluded were trade and payments agreements with Saudi Arabia in 1949 and Lebanon in 1951 and trade agreements with Syria in 1950 and Jordan in 1951.

Egypt-Saudi Arabia Agreement

The trade and payments agreement between Egypt and Saudi Arabia, which was signed in Cairo on May 31, 1949,[31] contained two lists of commodities that Egypt promised to authorize to be exported to Saudi Arabia and that Saudi Arabia promised to authorize to be imported. Payment by Saudi Arabia for imports of the commodities contained on one list was to be effected by debiting an account in Egyptian pounds that was to be opened in the National Bank of Egypt for Saudi Arabia.[32] Credits to this account for Saudi Arabia were to consist of the repatriated amounts of Egyptian pounds permitted to be taken to Saudi Arabia by pilgrims and other travelers.[33] Payment by Saudi Arabia for the Egyptian commodities contained on the other list was to be effected in accordance with the stipulations in the export licenses.[34] With regard to Saudi Arabia's exports to Egypt, the agreement simply provided that Saudi Arabia would authorize the exportation of those items that Egypt might need and that Egypt would permit the importation of such commodities. In an exchange of letters annexed to the agreement, the two countries agreed to extend most-favored-nation treatment to each other's products, except for preferential treatment accorded to products of adjacent countries. The agreement, which was for one year's duration, expired on May 30, 1950. It was, however, renewed in 1951 with a few modifications.

The trade and payments agreement reflected mainly an attempt, on the one hand, to continue the practice of permitting Egyptian pilgrims and other Egyptian travelers to Saudi Arabia to use Egyptian pounds as a means of payment in that country, and, on the other hand, to utilize such Egyptian currency for the purchase of products from Egypt. Saudi Arabia, for its part, agreed to authorize the importation of such articles, with the understanding that any credit balance in the account in its name in the National Bank of Egypt would be converted to pounds sterling when the agreement terminated. With regard to the Egyptian articles for which payment was required in specified currencies, they were products that were either in short supply or could be sold for hard currencies in other countries. Hence, Egypt was not willing to permit their exportation to Saudi Arabia for payment in Egyptian pounds. The provision relating to Saudi Arabia's exports to Egypt was of limited significance since Saudi Arabia had little to export to Egypt with the exception of camels and petroleum products, and the latter were usually sold for hard currencies.

Egypt-Syria, Egypt-Jordan, and Egypt-Lebanon Agreements

The agreements that Egypt negotiated with Syria in 1950 and Jordan and Lebanon in 1951 were very similar in content.[35] Each consisted of eleven provisions and two attached lists of domestic products whose exportation and importation the contracting parties agreed to authorize. One list in each agreement consisted of Egyptian products, and the other list consisted of products of the other contracting party.[36]

The contracting parties promised in each agreement that they would "extend every facility to develop to the greatest possible extent the trade relations between themselves, within the economic regulations applicable in each country."[37] Most-favored-nation treatment was granted by the countries to each other with respect to customs duties, regulations, and formalities, with the exception of the advantages granted or to be granted by them to contiguous countries.[38] The parties agreed not to authorize the reexport to a third country of the products exchanged between themselves under the provisions of the agreements.[39] Most-favored-nation treatment was also extended to transit and re-export trade, and national treatment was provided for with regard to internal taxation. The trade agreements with Syria and Jordan provided that all payments resulting from the agreements, as well as other current payments specified in a list annexed to each agree-ment,[40] would be made in accordance with the currency control regulations in force in the respective countries.[41] In the agreement with Lebanon it was provided that a nonresident account in Egyptian pounds would be opened in the National Bank of Egypt for authorized Lebanese banks, which would be credited with cur-rent payments due by Egypt to Lebanon and debited with current payments due by Lebanon to Egypt.[42] Payments relating to the execution of this agreement were to be made in accordance with the rules and regulations governing foreign exchange operations in force in Egypt.[43] There was no mention in the agreement of any swing credit. Each of these agreements was to be valid for one year from the date of signature and was to be subject annually to automatic renewal unless one of the parties advised the other party, two months before the end of the yearly expiration period, of its desire to modify or terminate the agreement.

The lists attached to these agreements setting forth the products that Egypt would authorize to be imported and Syria, Lebanon, or Jordan would authorize to be exported were rather comprehen-sive.[44] They contained most of the agricultural commodities pro-duced in the latter three countries and a substantial number of their manufactured products. Jordan's list of exports was not as long as Syria's and Lebanon's since Jordan did not have as many industries. There were a few notable exceptions, such as cotton textiles, from these lists, but, generally speaking, they reflected the Egyptian Government's rather liberal quantitative import control policy with regard to trade in soft currencies.

Since Egypt's controls over imports were relatively liberal, all three agreements contained language to the effect that Egypt would authorize the importation of the products on the attached lists "if any or all of them are subject at present or become subject in the future to the requirement of import licensing."[45] Egypt was quite willing, while maintaining high tariffs to protect its industries, to allow these countries to attempt to earn Egyptian pounds or pounds sterling. Quantitative restrictions were generally not relied upon by the Egyptian Government as a means of protection.

The attached lists that set forth the products that Syria, Lebanon, or Jordan would authorize to be imported and Egypt would authorize to be exported contained mainly manufactured articles.[46] For various reasons, few of Egypt's agricultural commodities were on these lists. Certain of these excluded agricultural products were licensed for export for payment mainly in hard currencies; certain others were in short supply in Egypt; and still others were produced in Syria, Lebanon, and/or Jordan, and those countries were apparently not willing to commit themselves to authorize the importation of such competitive products.

The list of authorized Egyptian products attached to the Syrian agreement also contained only a few Egyptian manufactured articles, including electric light bulbs, tarbooshes, buttons, books, films, records, essential and aromatic oils, flax yarn and other flax products, carpets and rugs, and certain cotton yarns. Excluded from the list were most of the products of Egypt's textile, leather, glassware, confectionery, beverage, food processing, and furniture industries. Syria employed quantitative restrictions and rather high tariffs to protect many of its industries, which in most cases produced articles similar to those produced in Egypt. It apparently did not want to take the chance of exposing such industries to Egyptian competition nor did it wish to risk the creation of a large adverse balance of payments with Egypt and the resultant loss of scarce foreign currencies.

The lists of authorized Egyptian products attached to the Jordanian and Lebanese agreements contained more manufactured articles than did the list attached to the Syrian agreement, and, in addition, contained certain agricultural commodities that were not on the latter list. These lists included most of the products specified in the list to the Syrian agreement plus shoes, cotton cloth, wines, chocolate, pharmaceutical products, glassware, rice starch, onions, potatoes, and a few other commodities. However, even these lists were rather limited and many Egyptian industrial products were excluded therefrom. Although Jordan had few industries to protect, it was very short of foreign currencies, and its export potential was limited. Consequently, it was not in a position to enlarge an already large adverse trade balance with Egypt. Moreover, notwithstanding that Jordan promised to authorize the importation of the Egyptian products on the list attached to the agreement, it did so with the understanding that all payments to Egypt resulting from the agreement would be made in accordance with the currency control regulations in force in Jordan. And, as has been indicated, foreign exchange allocations in Jordan were made on the basis of the Jordanian Government's import program for each commodity group. Lebanon, on the other hand, although it pursued a relatively liberal trade and exchange policy with regard to most products, did restrict the importation of various manufactured products to protect domestic producers, and, as a result, most of these commodities were not on the list of Egyptian products attached to the Egyptian-Lebanese agreement. Various other Egyptian manufactured products not on this list were in short supply in Egypt or were licensed for export for payment mainly in hard currencies.

All three of the aforementioned agreements constituted a rather limited attempt by the contracting parties to increase their trade with each other. Under the terms of these agreements, Lebanese, Syrian, and Jordanian products were to continue to receive only most-favored-nation tariff treatment when imported into Egypt, and Egyptian products were to be accorded the same treatment when imported into those countries.[47] Moreover, in view of the limited scope of the lists of Egyptian products attached to these agreements, it becomes apparent that the quantitative restrictions being imposed by Syria, Jordan, and—to a lesser extent—Lebanon were still applicable to many Egyptian products, as were the export restrictions being imposed by Egypt. In addition, even with regard to the Egyptian, Jordanian, Lebanese, and Syrian articles on the attached lists, the contracting parties to these agreements committed themselves only to authorize the exportation or importation of such articles. They did not commit themselves to free such articles from licensing requirements, and they specifically provided that all payments resulting from the agreements were to be made in accordance with the currency control regulations in force in the contracting countries.

Lebanon-Iraq Agreement

A trade and payments agreement was also concluded between Lebanon and Iraq in 1951.[48] The two countries promised to coordinate and develop their economic and commercial relations and, taking into account the laws and regulations in effect in each of the countries, to facilitate commercial exchanges by granting import and export licenses.[49] Most-favored-nation treatment was provided for with regard to customs duties, transit trade, and the issuance of import and export licenses, and national treatment was provided for with regard to internal taxes.[50] Iraq promised to grant Lebanon space in the proposed free trade zone in Basra, and Lebanon promised to grant Iraq space in the free trade zone in Beirut and in the proposed free trade zone in Tripoli.[51] In addition to the foregoing provisions, Iraq agreed to admit free of duty Lebanese potatoes, dried kidney beans, bananas, apples, medlars, cherries, peaches, fruit juice, certain cardboard, books and magazines, and certain silk thread and silk yarn.[52] Lebanon agreed to admit free of duty Iraqi livestock, lentils, dates, rice, sesame, gum tragacanth, date molasses, raw hides and skins, books and magazines, raw wool and certain other animal hair and the yarn or thread of such products, and woolen blankets.[53]

The methods of payment set forth in an appendix to the agreement provided for the establishment in Iraq of Lebanese nonresident accounts in Iraqi dinars, which were to be credited with the proceeds of visible and invisible imports into Iraq from Lebanon and debited with the proceeds of visible and invisible imports into Lebanon from Iraq. It was agreed that if at the end of each six-month period the nonresident account to be opened in the name of the Lebanese branch of the Banque de Syrie et du Liban showed a credit balance exceeding I.D. 100,000, then the Iraqi Government would authorize the conversion into pounds sterling of the excess amount.

The trade and payments agreement, which was concluded on February 20, 1951, did not go into effect until the early part of 1952.[54] The agreement was for one year subject to automatic renewal from year to year unless one of the countries expressed three months in advance its desire to terminate or change it.[55]

Although the Lebanese-Iraqi agreement constituted a step in the direction of increasing trade between the two countries, it was a rather small step. The attached lists did not contain many articles, and very few of the products of Lebanon's industries were included among the articles that were to be admitted into Iraq free of duty.

The agreement did not reflect any substantial departure by Iraq from its nonpreferential tariff policy, nor did it reflect any change in its quantitative trade control policy. There were no provisions exempting Lebanese products from the prohibitions or restrictive import licensing that Iraq was applying to many products. The agreement provided simply that the contracting parties undertake to grant import and export licenses, taking into account the laws and regulations in effect in each of the two countries. The small number of Iraqi products that were to be accorded duty-free treatment and the fact that some of these products, whatever their origin, were not subject to duty by Lebanon also indicated a reluctance by Lebanon to extend preferential tariff treatment on a broad scale to Iraqi products in the absence of a reciprocal undertaking by Iraq. In essence, the agreement constituted an attempt by Lebanon to increase its trade with Iraq by getting Iraq to remove its duties on a limited number of Lebanese agricultural products, by utilizing the Iraqi dinar as the unit of currency to finance such trade, and by allowing Iraq a swing credit of 100,000 dinars. At the time of the conclusion of the agreement, Iraq was very short of foreign currencies.

Other Trade Agreements

The aforementioned trade and payments agreements, plus the provisional agreement heretofore mentioned between Syria and Lebanon, were the most significant agreements that the Arab countries concluded with each other during the early postwar period. Provisional most-favored-nation agreements were also concluded by Egypt with Yemen in 1945[56] and Jordan in 1947,[57] and a trade agreement was concluded in 1950 by Syria with Saudi Arabia in conjunction with a $6 million loan that Saudi Arabia (whose oil revenues had increased substantially) made to Syria.[58] The latter provided for most-favored-nation treatment and for the authorization by each country of exports to and imports from the other country within the framework of the export and import regulations in force in each of the countries. The $6 million loan was to be repaid in the form of exports to Saudi Arabia of various Syrian products. As for prior trade agreements or arrangements between the Arab countries, the Transjordanian agreement of 1923 with Syria and Lebanon[59] and the free trade arrangements between Egypt and the Sudan remained in force during the early postwar period. However, the Transjordanian agreement was in the process of being revised and was to be replaced by less favorable agreements concluded with Lebanon and Syria in 1952 and 1953. Other than the preceding agreements and the agreements heretofore mentioned, there were few attempts to increase on a bilateral basis trade between the Arab countries.

INTER-ARAB TRADE

As a result of the embargo on trade with Palestine, the breakup of the Syrian-Lebanese Customs Union, the quantitative controls and tariff increases within the region, and the virtual absence of a preferential framework for inter-Arab trade, what semblance there was of Arab economic integration during World War II had all but disappeared by the end of 1951. The value of intraregional trade in the Fertile Crescent and between it and Egypt had decreased in absolute and proportional terms from the high levels that had been attained during World War II. The loss of Palestine as an economic part of the Near East and the breakup of the Syrian-Lebanese Customs Union were mainly responsible for the absolute decrease, whereas the substantial increase in trade with countries outside the region was mainly responsible for the sharp proportional decrease.

Although bilateral trade between some of the Arab countries increased in terms of value from the end of the war to 1951,[60] most of these increases consisted of a greater exchange of a few agricultural commodities and did not entail any significant changes in the patterns of trade between the Arab countries involved. Notwithstanding the increases in industrialization in Egypt and in some of the Fertile Crescent countries during the early postwar period,[61] there were for the most part few manufactured products entering into inter-Arab trade. For example, Egypt's imports from Syria and Lebanon increased from approximately L.E. 650,000 in 1945 to about L.E. 3,050,000 in 1951 (L.E. 1,070,000 from Syria and L.E. 1,980,000 from Lebanon). However, almost 50 percent of its imports from Lebanon in 1951 consisted of one commodity—fresh apples (apple production had increased substantially in Lebanon)—and most of the remainder consisted of date paste, cattle, sesame, plums, and a few other fruits. Likewise, about 70 percent of its imports from Syria in 1951 consisted of just five products—cattle, sheep, apricot paste, maize, and sesame—and practically all of the remainder consisted of a few other agricultural products. As for Egypt's exports to Syria and Lebanon, as well as to Jordan, they continued to consist mainly of one product— rice.

Iraq's exports (excluding petroleum and petroleum products) showed a similar pattern. Its exports to Lebanon and Jordan were substantial in 1951, but about 80 percent of the value of its exports to Lebanon consisted of wheat flour, raw wool, and raw cotton,[62] and about 75 percent of the value of its exports to Jordan consisted of wheat and dates. The poor wheat harvests in Syria, Jordan, and Lebanon accounted for the large quantities of wheat and wheat flour shipped to Jordan and Lebanon, and the high prices engendered by the Korean War for raw cotton and raw wool were responsible in part for the large exports to Lebanon of those commodities; substantial amounts of this raw cotton and wool were subsequently reexported by Lebanon to Europe and the United States. Iraq's exports to Syria and Egypt also consisted for the most part of just a few commodities; over 80 percent of the value of its exports to Syria and Egypt in 1951 consisted of livestock and dates.[63]

Iraq's imports from Arab countries other than Syria were likewise quite small in composition, as well as in size. Most of its imports from Egypt in 1951, for example, consisted of motion picture films and printed matter, and most of its imports from Lebanon during that year consisted of envelopes, cotton cloth, and small amounts of a few other textiles.

Trade between Syria, Lebanon, and Jordan, and exports from Syria to Iraq consisted of a greater variety of products, but not to the extent that would appear at first blush from the statistics of those countries. Syria's and Lebanon's export statistics contained a large number of reexports, and, in addition, the statistics of the importing Arab country listed many of these reexports as imports from Syria or Lebanon. However, Syria did export substantial amounts of its soap and textiles to Iraq and its textiles and agricultural products[64] to Jordan. Jordan, in turn, where relatively little industrialization took place during the early postwar period, exported rather large quantities of its fruits and vegetables, hides and skins, olive oil, and wool to Syria. Trade between Syria and Jordan, which was still being conducted within essentially a free trade framework, increased substantially during the early postwar period as a result of the loss of the Palestinian market for Jordan's agricultural producers and the loss of Palestine as a source of supply for Jordan of various manufactured products. Trade between Lebanon and Jordan, which was also being conducted within such a framework, likewise increased but to a much lesser extent than did trade between Syria and Jordan.

Although trade between Syria and Lebanon appears from the statistics to have remained rather substantial notwithstanding the restrictions that each country (especially Syria) was imposing in 1951 and notwithstanding the absence of preferential treatment for each other's products, this trade consisted for the most part of agricultural commodities. There were few manufactured products being traded between the two countries. Moreover, Syria's statistics reflect substantial amounts of petroleum products that were shipped from the refinery at Tripoli in Lebanon to Syria. Almost 60 percent of Syria's imports of approximately L.S. 34 million from Lebanon in 1951 consisted of these petroleum products,[65] and another 10 percent consisted of oranges and bananas. Approximately 75 percent of Syria's exports of about L.S. 59 million to Lebanon during the same year consisted of cattle, sheep, butter, cottonseed, raw cotton, and raw wool; and substantial quantities of the latter two commodities were destined for reexport by Lebanon.

As for the trade of the Sudan and the Arabian Peninsula countries, the Sudan, except for its trade with Egypt (which continued to be substantial within their free trade framework), obtained only a small amount of its imports from other Arab countries and sent only a small amount of its exports to those countries; Kuwait's inter-Arab trade was also small, except for its imports from Iraq; and Yemen carried on very little inter-Arab trade. Saudi Arabia, on the other hand, obtained a rather substantial amount of its imports from Egypt, Syria, and Lebanon, including various manufactured products.[66]

THE ARAB LEAGUE

As is apparent from what has been presented, the attempts that were made during the early postwar period to increase inter-Arab trade were made within a bilateral framework. Hardly any significant measures were adopted or implemented by the Arab countries to increase multilateral trade within the region. The Arab League, which was established in 1945[67] and which was to have effected "the close cooperation of the member states [in] economic and financial matters, including trade, customs, currency, agriculture and industry,"[68] accomplished very little in its endeavors to facilitate and increase inter-Arab trade or to integrate the economies of the member states. Recommendations in the form of resolutions were made by the League regarding the unification of the members' currencies; the establishment of a preferential trading area among the member states; and the strengthening and coordination of land, sea, and air transportation and communication between the Arab countries. But little action was taken by the member states with regard to these resolutions.[69]

On June 17, 1950, however, some of the Arab League states, in an endeavor to provide for a collective security system and to consolidate and coordinate their armed forces, signed a Treaty of Joint Defense and Economic Cooperation.[70] Although the treaty was primarily a military defense pact, it contained an undertaking in general terms by the contracting parties to cooperate in the development of their economies, to coordinate their economic activities, and to facilitate trade among themselves.[71] In addition, it provided for the formation of an Economic Council to be composed of the Ministers in charge of economic affairs in the member states.[72] The Council was authorized to submit recommendations for the fulfillment of the undertaking and could, in the performance of its duties, seek the cooperation of the Arab League Committee for Financial and Economic Affairs which had been established pursuant to Article 4 of the Arab League Pact.

As will be seen in the following chapter, the Economic Council was to become the principal organ for multilateral Arab trade negotiations. But the multilateral measures that were to be subsequently approved by the Economic Council and adopted by some of the Arab countries were to be rather limited in scope, as were to be the effects that such measures were to have on inter-Arab trade.

SUMMARY

By the end of 1951, the Arab countries for practically all intents and purposes were functioning and developing as separate political and economic entities vis-à-vis each other. There was a virtual absence of preferential treatment for Arab products within the restrictive quantitative control and tariff frameworks that were being utilized by many of these countries to control and channel their scarce supplies of foreign exchange, protect their domestic industrial and agricultural establishments, and finance their governmental operations. The only significant preferential trade ties that remained in the Arab world were the free trade relations between Egypt and the Sudan within the framework of the Anglo-Egyptian condominium and between Jordan and Syria and Lebanon. The latter were in the process of being modified, and modification of the former was to await Sudanese independence.

Arab economic disintegration, however, had still to run its course. As will be seen in the following chapter, the Arab countries as independent states had still to fully utilize quantitative controls as tools for national economic development and as political weapons.

CHAPTER **5** SALVAGE AND RECONSTRUCTION:
1952-63

In an apparent endeavor to effect closer trade relations with each other, the Fertile Crescent countries, Egypt, and Saudi Arabia negotiated during the 1950's and early 1960's a number of bilateral and multilateral agreements. However, although the network of trade and payments agreements that evolved during this period resulted in the creation of a tariff-free area for most of the agricultural products of these countries, it had in most instances a very limited effect in lessening, or preventing the imposition of, quantitative controls on trade in such products or in creating a regional market for Arab industrial products. As will be seen, the multilateral Arab League trade and payments conventions that were concluded in 1953 were not aimed at removing, lessening, or preventing the imposition of quantitative trade restrictions, nor did they provide in most cases for any significant reduction in the import duties imposed on manufactured products, or commit the contracting parties not to increase their rates of duty on such products. Some of the bilateral agreements that were concluded during the 1950's also failed to provide for any inroads into the quantitative control systems of the Arab countries involved, while others contained rather limited and circumscribed concessions with regard to industrial products. Moreover, the strained political relations that developed between some of the Arab countries and the continually changing alignments within the region resulted at various times in the nonapplication of or failure to implement in a positive manner some of the agreements that were concluded.

Many attempts were made to create a framework within which a sustained undertaking could be pursued, but these attempts did not reach fruition due to political and economic developments within the region. The political unions in 1958 of Egypt and Syria (United Arab Republic), the U.A.R. and Yemen (United Arab

States), and Jordan and Iraq were unsuccessful; the U.A.R.'s attempts to integrate economically the Egyptian and Syrian Regions failed; and the Arab Development Bank and Arab Economic Unity agreements which were drafted and signed during the late 1950's and early 1960's had not been implemented by the end of 1963.

Although the Maghreb countries and the Sudan became independent during this period and members of the Arab League, they continued to be economically detached from the other Arab countries. No preferential trade ties were established by these countries with the other Arab countries, and the Sudan terminated its monetary union and free trade area with Egypt.

In considering in the following pages the trade control systems that evolved during this period in the Arab countries, the provisions of the trade and payments agreements that were concluded, and the amount and composition of inter-Arab trade, it will become apparent that these countries during the period under consideration were pursuing for the most part a course of economic nationalism toward each other while making periodic contributions to closer inter-Arab trade ties. Notwithstanding the semblance of regionalism created by a network of inter-Arab agreements, the over-all trend was one of further economic disintegration rather than Arab economic integration.

TRADE CONTROL SYSTEMS

Quantitative Restrictions

The trade control systems of most of the Arab countries became more comprehensive and restrictive during the 1950's and early 1960's as many of these countries continued to experience balance-of-payments difficulties and to furnish protection to domestic industry and agriculture.[1] Rather broad economic development programs, with emphasis on industrialization, were undertaken by some of these countries,[2] and quantitative restrictions came to be regarded as an essential part of such programs. Moreover, Arab socialism had become or was becoming an additional impediment to trade.

United Arab Republic (Egypt)

Egypt, which had a relatively liberal system of quantitative controls in 1951, tightened considerably its trade controls following the revolution in 1952, as the very sharp decrease in its cotton exports during the second half of 1951 and the first half of 1952 coupled with its increased imports, particularly of wheat, resulted in the exhaustion of its free sterling balances.[3] Practically all imports became subject to individual licensing, and the issuance of a license was dependent on the currency and method of settlement and the category of the goods to be imported. This tight trade control framework was maintained as Egypt began to gradually transform its economy into a socialist economy during the latter part of the 1950's and the early 1960's. By the end of the period under consideration, the U.A.R. (Egypt) had incorporated both the import and export sectors into its rapidly developing socialist economy. Virtually all imports had to be made by either governmental departments, certain governmental general organizations which were authorized to make imports directly for firms or projects in the sectors of the economy under their supervision, industrial firms affiliated with general organizations in the industrial sector, or state trading companies. Import licenses were granted within the limits of the foreign exchange allocations made under the annual foreign exchange budget. Where local production was adequate, the importation of similar articles was prohibited or restricted to protect domestic establishments and conserve foreign exchange. Imports of luxury and nonessential commodities were also prohibited or restricted. Prescription of currency and repatriation requirements were applied to exports, and the exportation of a number of products was subjected to restrictive licensing.

Syria

Syria during the first part of the 1950's loosened somewhat its quantitative controls on trade. However, after it united with Egypt in 1958 to form the United Arab Republic, it gradually tightened and extended its trade controls, and, in 1961, following the abolition of its free exchange market in February of that year, imposed a comprehensive system of exchange controls. But after its withdrawal from the U.A.R. in September 1961, Syria proceeded to rescind many of the exchange controls and to reestablish the free market for specified transactions. Then, in 1963, following the revolution in March of that year, Syria once again abolished the free exchange market and reimposed many of the exchange controls that it had previously terminated. During the three years from 1961 through 1963 while it was abolishing, reestablishing, and abolishing its free exchange market, Syria continued to license most imports and exports and to impose prescription of currency and repatriation requirements on most of its major exports. The import licensing system, which reflected the exchange control variations during the aforementioned three years, was very restrictive prior to Syria's withdrawal from the U.A.R., was liberalized considerably during the latter part of 1961 and during 1962, and then was tightened once again in 1963.

As of January 1964, imports into Syria were divided into three main categories: (1) imports prohibited by decree and specified in a prohibited list, which comprised 65 tariff items (mostly commodities that were produced domestically, including various textiles); (2) imports on a restrictive list, which comprised 201 tariff items covering commodities that were temporarily not permitted to be imported for either balance-of-payments or protective reasons; and (3) imports not included in the first two lists, which were authorized. Imports included in the third category required individual licenses, except various commodities exempted from licensing in accordance with bilateral agreements with some of the Arab countries. In certain instances of domestic need, commodities included in the restrictive list were to be permitted to be imported under special individual license.

Iraq

Iraq liberalized its quantitative trade controls during the first part of the 1950's, especially in trade with soft currency countries. But shortly after the revolution in July 1958, it applied a system of restrictive licensing to virtually all imports. Trade controls tended to become more restrictive during the following years until the overthrow of the Kassem regime in February 1963. In April 1963, licensing controls on many products were abolished. Then, in September of that year, they were reimposed. As of the end of 1963, Iraq prohibited the importation of over 65 items, and virtually all other imports were subjected to individual licensing and quotas. The exportation of various commodities was also subjected to quantitative restrictions, and proceeds from exports were required to be repatriated.

Jordan

Jordan, which continued to rely heavily on foreign grants and aid to sustain its weak economy, maintained throughout the period under consideration a rather comprehensive system of trade controls involving licensing and prescription of currency and re-patriation requirements. The restrictiveness of the import licensing system varied, depending on the merchandise to be imported, the source of the importation, the means of payment, and the availability of the foreign exchange sought. A free exchange market in Arab League currencies (mostly Syrian and Lebanese pounds) was legally recognized in Jordan in January 1955 for the purpose of financing imports from other Arab League states.[4] However, the scope of the free market was reduced substantially during 1959 and 1960, and in 1961 the Jordanian Government provided that proceeds of exports to and invisibles received from Syria and Lebanon had to be surrendered in sterling or Jordanian dinars from a nonresident external account, or in any specified currency, and that payments for goods originating in and imported from those two countries could be made in sterling at the official rate. Prior to 1961, such proceeds were permitted to be received in any Arab League currency and to be sold in the free market.

Maghreb Countries and Sudan

Most of the North African Arab countries (other than the U.A.R.) also maintained comprehensive systems of trade controls during the 1950's and early 1960's. Following their independence Morocco and Tunisia (which became independent in March 1956) and Algeria (which became independent in July 1962) applied trade controls involving licensing, global and bilateral quotas, and prescription of currency and repatriation requirements. All three countries, however, continued to maintain their close trade ties with France within the framework of the French franc area and imposed fewer or less stringent controls on imports of French products.

Libya (which had become independent on December 24, 1951) and the Sudan (which became independent on January 1, 1956) for a period of time following their independence imposed rather liberal controls on imports from soft currency countries. However, Libya tightened its controls considerably in 1956, and the Sudan did likewise in 1958. But in 1959 both countries once again liberalized these controls. By the end of 1963, the import controls being applied by Libya and the Sudan were much less stringent than those being applied by the aforementioned Arab countries. Although virtually all imports were licensed, a large number of products were permitted to be imported under an open general license. Exports, on the other hand, were subject to individual licensing so as to ensure the repatriation of export proceeds.

Other Arab Countries

The remaining Arab countries—Lebanon, Saudi Arabia, Kuwait, and Yemen—imposed very few quantitative trade controls during most of the period under consideration. On January 1, 1955, Lebanon lifted its import licensing requirements for all but a limited number of products. Imports continued to be financed through the free exchange market; there were virtually no prescription of currency or repatriation requirements; and exports of only a few commodities were licensed. Saudi Arabia, whose oil revenues were rising rapidly, lifted its import licensing requirements for most products during the early 1950's and imposed thereafter very few quantitative trade controls until the latter part of 1956. Beginning in November of that year, it proceeded to license practically all imports and exports and to require an exchange permit for the obtaining of foreign exchange at the official rate from official sources. However, in 1958 it substantially liberalized its controls, and in January 1960 it terminated practically all of its trade controls. Kuwait (which became independent on June 19, 1961, and which received large oil revenues) applied very few licensing requirements, exchange controls, or quantitative restrictions either before or after it achieved independence, and Yemen apparently did likewise.

Tariffs

In addition to the aforementioned trade controls, many of the Arab countries during the 1950's and early 1960's also imposed high tariffs on numerous industrial and various agricultural products. Many rates of duty were substantially increased to protect domestic producers, to curb the importation of luxury items, or to increase or maintain the revenues derived from customs duties. Low rates of duty or exemptions, on the other hand, were applied to most machinery, primary metal products, chemical products, and raw materials for domestic industrial and agricultural establishments. And like the aforementioned quantitative controls, the use of high tariffs, and the purposes for which they were used, varied from country to country.

United Arab Republic (Egypt)

The U.A.R. during the 1950's and early 1960's imposed high duties on many industrial and agricultural products, which reflected the increases in the base duties and the imposition of or increases in various additional duties during that period. On January 1, 1962, the U.A.R. revised its tariff schedules by consolidating its base duties and various supplementary duties.[5] Although the revisions that became effective in 1962 did not increase total duties on most imported products, they did make more apparent, by virtue of the consolidations, the high duties that the U.A.R. had been and was imposing on many products.

For example, the consolidated import duties that were imposed on most textile fabrics were 100 percent ad valorem or more; the import duties on most textile wearing apparel ranged from 120 to 160 percent; the duty on most footwear and furniture was 100 percent; the duty on table glassware was 125 percent; the duty on matches, carpets, most headwear, luggage, handbags, most gloves, and most other leather or composition leather wearing apparel was 100 percent; the duty on candy was 150 percent; and the import duties on alcoholic beverages, which were also subject to high excise duties, ranged from 100 to 300 percent. Many agricultural products, as well as other industrial products, were likewise subject to high import duties. The duty on fresh citrus fruits, peaches, watermelons, grapes, and various other fresh fruits and on pistachio and pine nuts was 50 percent; on white cheese, 40 percent; on rice, 40 percent; on rice flour, 50 percent; on other cereal flours, 35 percent; on various prepared or preserved meats, 50 percent; on tomato puree, 120 percent; on various fruit pastes, jams, jellies, and juices, 100 percent; and on various other prepared or preserved fruits or vegetables, 75 percent.[6]

However, although the U.A.R. imposed high rates of duty on many products, the role that the tariff played in the U.A.R. economy had undergone a fundamental change. Customs duties still constituted a principal source of revenue for the government, but their protective function had declined in importance since the U.A.R.'s import trade was concentrated largely in state-owned importing agencies and was designed to conform to the government's comprehensive economic development plan.

Fertile Crescent Countries

In the Fertile Crescent, high import duties—although generally not as high as the U.A.R.'s—were imposed by Syria and Iraq on a number of products, including duties ranging from 30 to 100 percent or more on many of the aforementioned products.[7] Lebanon also had rather high rates of duty specified in its tariff act for a wide range of industrial and agricultural products, but the actual duties that were imposed on many of these products were much less than was apparent from the rates specified in the tariff schedules. A number of products were subject to an ad valorem rate of duty of 40 or 50 percent (very few products were subject to an ad valorem rate higher than 50 percent), but these rates were imposed on the domestic currency value of imports computed at the official rate of exchange for the Lebanese pound, which was roughly 30 percent higher than the free market rate. Since virtually all transactions took place at the free market rate, the Lebanese Government was in effect undervaluing such products by 30 percent.[8] However, Lebanon also subjected a number of products to rather high specific rates of duty with a specified ad valorem minimum of 40 or 50 percent.[9]

Jordan had a relatively low tariff during the 1950's, notwithstanding the increases made in many of its import duties to enlarge its customs revenues. But during the early 1960's, it proceeded to undertake a program of economic development and reform, and its duties were increased substantially on various products to protect domestic industries.[10] For most products, however, the duties remained relatively low compared to those imposed by the aforementioned Arab countries.[11] Jordan had just begun to industrialize on any noticeable scale; hence, the protective function of its tariff had just begun to assume some significance.

Other Arab Countries

As for the other Arab countries, the Sudan and Morocco imposed high import duties ranging from 50 to 100 percent or more on a large number of products,[12] whereas Tunisia, Algeria, Libya, Saudi Arabia, and Yemen imposed relatively low import duties on most products, and Kuwait imposed a very low import duty on practically all products. Only a small number of articles were subject under the Tunisian, Algerian, and Libyan tariffs to rates of duty higher than 30 percent ad valorem;[13] Kuwait reduced its general import duty from 6.5 percent ad valorem to 4 percent during the period under consideration;[14] and Saudi Arabia reduced or eliminated its import duties on a wide range of articles during the second half of the 1950's and the early part of the 1960's.[15]

Yemen revised its tariff schedule in 1963, and although increases were made in the rates on various articles, most products continued to be subject to rather low rates of duty, ranging between 5 and 25 percent ad valorem. [16]

INTER-ARAB TRADE AND PAYMENTS AGREEMENTS

The trade and payments agreements framework for inter-Arab trade which evolved during this period within the aforementioned Arab quantitative control and tariff systems consisted for the most part of bilateral agreements between the Fertile Crescent countries, between those countries and Egypt and Saudi Arabia, between the latter two countries, and between Egypt and the other North African Arab countries, and of multilateral agreements involving the Fertile Crescent countries, Egypt, and Saudi Arabia. [17] Some of these agreements reflected more the deterioration in trade relations between the countries involved than an attempt to effect closer trade relations; some were concluded as a concomitant of and implemented in accordance with the political changes and changes in alignments within the region; and some constituted in effect mere gestures toward effecting closer trade relations. Consequently, as will be seen, the conclusion of these agreements did not lead in most cases to any significant sustained increases in inter-Arab trade during this period.

Trade relations between Lebanon, Syria, Jordan, Iraq, Egypt, and Saudi Arabia were governed during most or a part of the period under consideration by bilateral agreements that the Fertile Crescent countries concluded with each other during 1952 and 1953, by the Arab League trade and payments conventions of 1953, and by bilateral agreements that Egypt and Saudi Arabia concluded with the Fertile Crescent countries and with each other during the second half of the 1950's and the early part of the 1960's.

Agreements Between Fertile Crescent Countries

The bilateral agreements between the Fertile Crescent countries—which consisted of the Syrian-Lebanese trade agreements of 1952[18] and 1953,[19] the Jordanian-Lebanese and Jordanian-Syrian trade agreements of 1952 [20] and 1953,[21] respectively, and the

Jordanian-Iraqi trade agreement of 1953[22]–provided for the exemption from customs duties and import and export licenses of most of the agricultural and animal products of the contracting parties.[23] Various industrial products were also exempted from duty or subjected to preferential rates and, in addition, were exempted under some of these agreements from import and export licensing and/or the imposition of quantitative restrictions.

The 1952 Syrian-Lebanese agreement contained two lists of industrial products. The products of local origin (Syrian or Lebanese) contained in one of the lists were to be admitted free of customs duties by the importing country,[24] and the products of local origin contained in the other list were to be assessed at reduced rates of duty amounting to two-thirds of the normal rates in effect in the importing country.[25] Each of the products on the lists was to be considered of local origin if the cost of the raw materials of local origin and the cost of the local labor were not less than 50 percent of the cost of the manufacture of the product. Industrial products of local origin other than those contained in the lists and industrial products made in Syria or Lebanon of which the local cost was less than 50 percent of the cost of manufacture were to be subject to the normal customs duties.[26]

The two lists containing industrial products were not very comprehensive, and the agreement did not specifically provide for the exemption of such products from import licensing or the imposition of quantitative restrictions.[27] Among the articles produced in Syria and Lebanon that were excluded from the lists were various oils of animal or vegetable origin; matches; various manufactures of leather, paper, or cardboard; footwear; and various silk, artificial silk, wool, or cotton fabrics and articles, including most wearing apparel.

The 1953 Syrian-Lebanese agreement, which replaced the 1952 agreement, was very similar to the latter and constituted in effect an extension, with some modifications, of it. Certain silk yarns and perfumery articles were added to the industrial products contained in the duty-free list in the 1952 agreement; industrial products which were subject to reduced customs duties equal to two-thirds of the normal duties under the 1952 agreement became subject to reduced customs duties equal to one-half of the normal customs duties;[28] and various items were added to the latter list of products.[29]

The 1953 agreement contained, in addition to the afore-mentioned two lists, another list of industrial products of Syrian or Lebanese origin whose exchange the two countries agreed to authorize, but it was provided that these products would be subject to the ordinary or normal customs duties in the country of importation.[30] Syria had prohibited the importation of many articles during 1952, including some of the articles named in this list. The agreement contained, however, a reservation which permitted either contracting party to prohibit or restrict the importation or exportation of industrial products from or to the territory of the other if such prohibitions or restrictions were made applicable to all other countries.[31] It was provided that this reservation would not be applicable to any of the industrial products named in the duty-free or reduced-duty list.

The Jordanian agreements with Syria and Lebanon, which replaced the 1923 agreement with those countries, followed with regard to industrial products a format somewhat similar to that of the Syrian-Lebanese agreements. Products of local origin contained in certain of the lists annexed to the agreements were to be exempt from customs duties and import licenses;[32] local products contained in other lists were to be exempt from import licenses but subject to reduced customs duties equal to one-third or two-thirds of the normal rates in effect in the importing country;[33] and products of local origin contained in still other lists were to be subject to the normal duties and to import licenses.[34] The latter lists contained a rather substantial number of Syrian and Lebanese industrial products, including cement and cement products, olive oil, soap, shoes, furniture, macaroni and similar products, and various textiles.

Industrial products of Syrian or Lebanese origin which were not contained in the duty-free, reduced-duty (one-third of the normal rates), or full-duty lists were to be exempt from import licenses and subject to reduced duties equal to one-third of the normal rates when imported directly into Jordan. Industrial products of Jordanian origin which were not contained in the duty-free list or in the full-duty list in the trade agreement between Jordan and Lebanon were to be exempt from import licenses and subject to a similar reduction in the rates of duty when imported directly into Lebanon. There was no reduced-duty list of Jordanian products attached to the Jordanian-Lebanese agreement. Industrial products of domestic origin imported directly into Syria from Jordan which were not contained in the duty-free list or in the reduced-duty list (two-thirds of the normal rates) in the trade agreement between those countries could be added within a period not exceeding one month to either of those lists. There was no full-duty list of Jordanian products attached to the Jordanian-Syrian agreement.

Within the terms of the agreements, products were to be considered of local origin if the raw materials of local origin and the cost of local labor amounted to at least 50 percent of the cost of manufacture of the product. However, both agreements provided that the products contained in the duty-free and reduced-duty lists which were imported directly from the territory of a contracting party would be considered of local origin and no proof of composition would be required.

Like the 1953 Syrian-Lebanese agreement, each of the agreements contained a reservation which permitted either of the contracting parties to prohibit or restrict the importation of industrial products from the territory of the other if such prohibitions or restrictions were made applicable to all other countries. [35]

The Jordanian-Iraqi agreement of 1953 contained lists of Jordanian and Iraqi industrial products that were to be exempt from customs duties and import licenses but, unlike the aforementioned agreements, did not contain any reduced-duty lists. The duty-free lists attached to the agreement were rather small,[36] and the agreement contained a reservation similar to the reservations in the aforementioned agreements. [37]

Of the preceding agreements, the Syrian-Lebanese agreements and the Jordanian agreements with Syria and Lebanon were essentially attempts by the contracting parties to salvage what they could from their former free trade relations. Although the parties were successful in maintaining or reinstituting a free trade area for most of their agricultural products, most of their industrial products became or continued to be, in accordance with the provisions of the agreements, subject to import duties and, in many cases, to quantitative restrictions. Moreover, Syria subsequently made rather liberal use of the reservations in its agreements with Lebanon and Jordan by prohibiting or subjecting to restrictive licensing the importation of a wide range of industrial products. Jordan, on the other hand, made during the early 1960's substantial increases in its import duties on various industrial products which in effect nullified the benefits of the tariff preferences accorded to Lebanon and Syria on such products. As will be seen, trade between these countries, with the exception of Syrian textile exports to Jordan, tended to be generally confined to the exchange of agricultural products. Such agricultural trade, however, continued to be quite substantial, notwithstanding that it too became subject to a number of import and export controls, especially by Syria.

Whereas the agreements between Syria, Lebanon, and Jordan represented essentially salvage attempts, the agreement between Jordan and Iraq constituted the first substantial departure by Iraq from the nonpreferential trade policy that it had been following since the end of World War I. However, although the concessions in the agreement regarding agricultural products were rather comprehensive in scope and those regarding industrial products covered a substantial portion of the small industrial production of the two countries, the agreement had a very limited effect on their trade with each other. Iraq prohibited or restricted the exportation and importation of a wide range of agricultural and industrial products during the Kassem regime, and Jordan reciprocated by tightening its controls. Iraqi exports to Jordan dropped precipitously during the period under consideration, and although Jordanian exports to Iraq registered a sizable increase during a part of this period, they consisted of larger quantities of only a few agricultural commodities.

Arab League Agreements

The bilateral framework for trade between the Fertile Crescent countries was supplemented and preferential tariff relations were established between those countries and Egypt and Saudi Arabia by the conclusion in 1953 of multilateral trade and payments conventions. These conventions, which were drafted by the Ministers of Finance and Economics of the Arab League States in an attempt to facilitate multilateral trade among the Arab countries, entered into force in December of that year for Lebanon, Jordan, and Egypt; in 1954 for Saudi Arabia and Syria; and in January 1955 for Iraq.[38]

The trade convention[39] provided for the exemption from import duties of most of the contracting parties' agricultural and animal products, as well as salt, sulphur, calcium, gypsum, talc, mica, marble, and various other minerals.[40] Most of the industrial commodities produced by these states were to be subject to reduced rates amounting to 75 percent of the import duties in effect in the importing country. [41] The contracting parties also promised to grant most-favored-nation treatment to each other with regard to import and export licenses, and promised that agricultural, animal, and industrial commodities produced in the territory of any of the parties and imported into the territory of another would not be subject to excise duties exceeding those imposed by the importing country on similar domestic products or on their component raw materials. In addition, the countries pledged to facilitate transit trade across their territories.

It was specifically provided that the convention's provisions would not be applicable to articles subject to government monopoly and that any goods which were prohibited from importation would be liable to confiscation if imported unless a transit permit was obtained prior to importation. The parties also promised to confiscate goods imported into their territories whose exportation was prohibited by a contracting party.

The payments convention provided that the contracting parties would—to the limit of their power, and in accordance with existing regulations regarding the transfer of foreign currency and imports—grant to each other most-favored-nation treatment and facilitate the transfer of the payments of current transactions set forth in a list attached to the convention.[42] The convention also provided that if a contracting party imposed restrictions on the transfer of payments of current transactions to the other parties, and if the balance of payments of the contracting party did not make it possible for it to effect current payment in foreign currencies acceptable to the other parties, then it was to grant to residents of the other contracting parties at least the following facilities:

    a. The right of utilizing their credit accounts for the settlement of current transactions, payment of which falls due in the territory of the debtor's country, as well as for the payment for all goods imported into the territory of the creditor's country from the territory of the debtor's country which allows export of such goods to all countries.

    b. The right of transferring to residents of any of the contracting parties, or to another country, a portion or the whole of their credit accounts.

    c. The right of utilizing their credit accounts to pay for goods purchased in the territory of the debtor's country for the purpose of exporting them to the territory of any of the other contracting parties, or to another country, provided their export is allowed by the debtor's country.

d. If the procedure followed by the debtor's country imposed the settlement of part of the payment for specified items in a specified foreign currency, then the owner of the credit account was to be entitled, in the cases provided for by the preceding subparagraphs (a) and (c), to settle in foreign currency only a part of the value (within the limits of the best rates allowed by the debtor's country in similar cases), and to settle the remaining part through his account.

The contracting parties also agreed to permit the transfer of capital to enable their subjects and residents to participate in any constructive enterprises agreed upon by the interested parties. It was provided that the transfer of capital would be permitted within the limits of the regulations laid down by each party for safeguarding its capital or the capital which was transferred to it. Capital being transferred from the territory of one contracting party to the territory of another was not to be subject to any duty or excise tax imposed to preclude transfers of capital, and the contracting parties agreed to the free repatriation of such transferred capital.

It was provided in the convention that its provisions would not be applicable where there existed a bilateral payments agreement between any of the contracting parties.

On December 15, 1954, the Arab League Economic Council approved certain amendments to the trade convention, which provided for the addition of a few articles to the convention's free list, for the addition of various articles to the convention's list of industrial products benefiting from a 25 percent reduction in import duties, and for the addition of a new list of industrial products which were to benefit from a 50 percent reduction in import duties. [43] Most of the important industrial articles produced by the aforementioned Arab countries remained, however, on the 25 percent list. In addition to the tariff changes, the transit provisions in the trade convention were modified, and the provision in the payments convention concerning the transferability of credit accounts was changed so as to restrict the transfer of such credit accounts to residents of the contracting parties. Moreover, the provision dealing with the transfer of capital was amended to make clear that the constructive enterprises in which the contracting countries were to permit their nationals to participate were to be for "economic development." [44]

Further amendments were approved by the Economic Council on January 25, 1956, and May 29, 1957, which provided for the addition of a few articles to the trade convention's 25 percent and 50 percent lists.[45] The 1956 amendments also provided for a 20 percent reduction in customs duties for products assembled in the contracting countries if the cost of domestic labor or Arab raw materials, or both, comprised not less than 20 percent of the total cost of the product.[46]

The Arab League trade convention and the bilateral trade agreements that had been and were to be concluded during the 1950's and early 1960's between the contracting parties to the multilateral convention complemented each other in some respects. The reduction of 25 percent provided for in the trade convention was applicable to various industrial products that were not accorded under some of the bilateral trade agreements any reduced-duty or duty-free treatment. In addition, various agricultural products that were dutiable under the 1952 and 1953 Jordanian agreements with Lebanon and Syria were exempted under the convention. The trade convention also constituted, during the period or part of it, the only commitment that some of the contracting parties had to each other to accord duty-free or reduced-duty treatment. On the other hand, the reductions or exemptions provided for in some of the bilateral agreements were greater for various industrial products than the reductions provided for in the Arab League convention, and various products (such as cheese, butter, fruit juice, and flour) which were regarded as agricultural or animal products and exempted from duty under certain bilateral agreements were regarded as industrial products in the trade convention and subject to a 25 percent or 50 percent reduction in duty. Moreover, some of the bilateral agreements provided that import licenses would not be required for the importation of most agricultural commodities and various industrial products and/or that the importation of such products would not be subjected to quantitative restrictions, whereas the Arab League convention did not exempt any product from import licensing, and it specifically provided that prohibited articles would be liable to confiscation if imported. In effect, the trade convention was not aimed at removing or lessening quantitative restrictions on inter-Arab trade in industrial or agricultural products, nor did it provide for sizable tariff preferences for most of the important Arab industrial products or commit the contracting parties not to increase their duties on industrial products. Although it extended the scope of the tariff-free area in agricultural products and the preferential tariff area in industrial products between Syria, Lebanon, and Jordan to include Egypt, Iraq, and Saudi Arabia, the contributions that it was to make toward increasing inter-Arab trade were, in the absence of inroads into the Arab quantitative control systems, to be quite limited.

The payments convention constituted a limited attempt by the contracting parties to facilitate the transfer of capital between themselves and to increase their trade and other current transactions with each other by unblocking to a certain extent various accounts in some of the Arab countries. In addition, by providing for the transferability of credit accounts, the contracting parties attempted to facilitate and increase multilateral trade through the use of such accounts as a medium of exchange. However, no attempt was made in the convention to provide for alterations in the prescription of currency requirements or in the import and export quantitative restrictions being applied by most of the Arab countries, nor was any attempt made to provide for preferential licensing treatment in the allocation of scarce currencies or to establish any general payments mechanism to facilitate inter-Arab trade. Moreover, the provisions of the payments convention were not applicable where there existed a bilateral payments agreement between any of the contracting parties, and, as will be seen, a number of such agreements were concluded during the period under consideration.

Egyptian Agreements with Fertile Crescent Countries

During the second half of the 1950's, Egypt sought, outside the framework of the multilateral conventions, closer trade relations with some of the Fertile Crescent countries through bilateral trade and payments agreements. However, these agreements—with Syria in 1956 and 1957, Lebanon in 1956, and Iraq in 1958—were essentially concomitants of attempts to establish closer political relations and did not significantly affect trade relations with these countries. The agreements with Iraq were virtually suspended during most of this period; trade between Lebanon and Egypt was almost at a standstill; and although trade increased substantially between Syria and Egypt following their political merger, this increase was due primarily to various measures adopted after the union rather than to the pre-union agreements.

Egypt-Syria Agreements

The lists of concessions in the Egyptian-Syrian agreement of 1956 were practically carbon copies of the concession lists annexed to the Arab League trade convention, as amended.[47] The agreement constituted in effect a mere formalization on a bilateral basis of the obligations and pending obligations of the two countries toward each other under that convention. In addition to the trade agreement, the two countries concluded a payments agreement which provided for the establishment in the National Bank of Egypt of an account in Egyptian pounds for authorized Syrian banks, with a swing credit of L.E. 300,000.[48]

On November 13, 1957, as a prelude to their political unification, the two countries signed agreements providing for an increase in the swing credit to L.E. 600,000, for the exemption from import duty of various articles which were formerly dutiable,[49] and for the reduction of import duties on various other articles.[50] Then, during the latter part of 1958, shortly after the merger, trade between the two regions of the U.A.R. was exempt, with some exceptions, from customs duties and licensing,[51] and a new payments agreement providing for a bilateral account denominated in Egyptian pounds was put into effect.[52] In addition, other steps concerning payments for goods exported from the Egyptian Region to the Syrian Region were taken to increase, on the one hand, Egyptian exports to Syria and to protect, on the other hand, certain Syrian industries.[53]

During 1959, the U.A.R. Government proceeded to adopt various measures and to make preparations for greater governmental participation in and regulation of the two regions. Arab socialism, which was to become an important factor in future Arab economic negotiations and in relations between the two regions, had begun to assume greater significance in the Egyptian Region,[54] and plans were being made for its application to the Syrian Region. In addition, the U.A.R. Government was preparing for both regions a comprehensive five-year economic development plan.

In 1960 the U.A.R. put into effect its economic plan, and about one year later, on July 20, 1961, it nationalized all of the banks and insurance companies and a number of other companies in both regions of the U.A.R.[55] However, in September of that year, Syria terminated its political and economic ties with Egypt, and trade between the two countries, which had increased substantially during the period of their political merger, virtually ceased. As of the end of 1963, there was no bilateral trade or payments agreement in effect between Egypt and Syria.

Egypt-Lebanon Agreements

The concession lists in the Egyptian-Lebanese trade agreement of 1956,[56] like the lists in the 1956 Egyptian-Syrian agreement, followed closely the format of the lists attached to the Arab League trade convention[57] and had for the most part little effect on trade relations between the two countries. The duty-free list in the agreement included some articles which were subject to reduced duties under the trade convention;[58] the 50 percent list included various articles which were subject to a 25 percent reduction or to no reduction under that convention;[59] and the 25 percent list included some products which were not included in any of the lists attached to the convention.[60] However, most of the important Egyptian and Lebanese industrial products were accorded the same preference (25 percent) that they received under the Arab League trade convention, and the bilateral agreement did not provide for the exemption of any industrial or agricultural product from licensing or quantitative restrictions.

The provisions in the payments agreement signed by Egypt and Lebanon were very similar to those contained in the 1951 agreement between the two countries. The 1956 agreement provided that a nonresident account in Egyptian pounds would be opened in the National Bank of Egypt for authorized Lebanese banks, which would be credited with current payments due by Egypt to Lebanon and debited with current payments due by Lebanon to Egypt. As in 1951, there was no mention of any swing credit.

U.A.R.-Iraq Agreements

The trade and payments agreements between the U.A.R., on behalf of both its regions, and Iraq were concluded by the two countries shortly after the Iraqi revolution of July 14, 1958, as part of an endeavor to effect closer cooperation in the military, political, economic, and educational fields.[61] The payments agreement provided for the establishment in the Central Bank of Iraq of accounts in Iraqi dinars for the two regions of the U.A.R. to be used in the settlement of current payments between them and Iraq. Each account could show a debit or credit balance of I.D. 500,000, and any amounts in excess were to be settled either by a transfer from one regional account to the other or in a transferable third currency agreed to by both contracting parties.

The trade agreement was patterned after the Arab League trade convention. It provided that exchanges would take place within the limits of the economic possibilities of each country and in accordance with the prevailing systems of exportation and importation. Three lists of domestic products were annexed to the agreement. The products contained in the first list were to be exempt from duty;[62] those in the second were to be subject to rates of duty equal to 25 percent of the rates of duty prevailing in the importing country;[63] and those in the third list were to be subject to rates of duty equal to 50 percent.[64] All products not mentioned in the three lists which were exempt from duty or subject to reduced duties under the Arab League trade convention were to be subject to the customs treatment provided for in that convention.[65]

Although the annexed lists contained a substantial number of industrial products that were to benefit from greater reductions, either in the form of duty-free or reduced-duty treatment, than they did under the Arab League convention, no provisions were contained in the trade agreement for alterations in the systems of quantitative restrictions applied by the contracting parties. Moreover, notwithstanding the negotiation of the trade and payments agreements, early in 1959 the U.A.R. and Iraq began to move further apart rather than closer together. The agreements came into force but were in a virtual state of suspension during the Kassem regime in Iraq. It was not until March 8, 1963, that Iraq announced the formal reapplication of the provisions of the trade agreement to its trade with the U.A.R.[66]

Saudi Arabian Agreements with Fertile Crescent Countries and Egypt

Saudi Arabia also concluded during the second half of the 1950's and the early 1960's bilateral trade agreements with the Fertile Crescent countries, as well as a bilateral trade agreement with Egypt. Agreements were concluded with Syria in 1955 and 1961,[67] Iraq and Lebanon in 1957,[68] Egypt in 1958,[69] and Jordan in 1963.[70] These agreements provided for the exemption from customs duties of agricultural and animal products, as well as certain industrial products, including various textiles,[71] and for the application to various other industrial products of reduced duties amounting to one-third of the normal rates imposed by the importing country.[72] In addition, such products were to be exempt from import and export licenses and/or quantitative restrictions.[73] The duty-free lists of industrial products in the 1961 and 1963 agreements with Syria and Jordan contained a larger number of articles than did the duty-free lists in the earlier agreements that Saudi Arabia concluded with Syria and the other Arab countries. The latter lists contained mainly textiles.

In addition to the above trade agreements, Saudi Arabia also concluded a number of loan and payments agreements with some of these countries. In 1955 it signed a payments agreement with Egypt that was broader in scope than the one concluded in 1949.[74] The 1955 agreement provided for the establishment in the National Bank of Egypt of an account in Egyptian pounds for the Saudi Arabian Monetary Agency, with a swing credit of L.E. 500,000. This was to be credited and debited with specified current payments involving commodity trade, pilgrimage expenditures, and various other transactions. For the use of Egyptian pilgrims, the Saudi Arabian Monetary Agency was to issue checks in Saudi riyals, at the rate of 10 Saudi riyals for 1 Egyptian pound, which could be unconditionally exchanged for cash in all parts of Saudi Arabia.[75]

On October 13, 1956, the two countries signed a protocol to the payments agreement, which provided for the sale by Egypt to Saudi Arabia of L.E. 5 million for an equivalent amount in United States dollars at the rate of 37.5 Egyptian piasters for $1. The Egyptian pounds were to be entered in a special nonresident Saudi Arabian account (in the name of the Saudi Arabian Monetary Agency) in the National Bank of Egypt, and Saudi Arabia was to transfer to Switzerland for the account of the National Bank of Egypt the equivalent in United States dollars.[76] Saudi Arabia's nonresident account could be debited to make the current payments specified in the payments agreement, as well as to make payments connected with services and investments in Egypt and with transfers to Egypt of profits and revenues of Egyptians in Saudi Arabia. Any balance, or part thereof, in Saudi Arabia's account could, with Egypt's consent, be transferred to a third Arab country or to any other country with which Egypt maintained a favorable balance in its payments agreement account.

The swing credit provided for in the 1955 agreement was subsequently increased to L.E. 1 million, and payments under the 1958 trade agreement between the two countries were, with one exception, to be effected pursuant to the 1955 agreement, as amended. The one exception was crude petroleum exports from Saudi Arabia to Egypt.[77]

Syria and Saudi Arabia concluded a loan agreement in 1955 at the time of the signing of their trade agreement, which provided for a $10 million loan, without interest, by Saudi Arabia to Syria. The loan was to be made in three installments during the latter part of 1955 and the first month of 1956. In addition, the repayment of the loan of $6 million that Saudi Arabia had made to Syria in 1950 and that became due in part in 1955 was postponed. The two loans, both without interest, were combined, and Syria was not required to begin repayments until 1961. The combined loan was to be repaid in ten equal installments beginning in 1961 and ending in 1970. Repayment was to be in the form of Syrian industrial and agricultural products, particularly those set forth in the attached lists to the trade agreement, and Saudi Arabia was authorized to reexport such products if it wished to do so. Subsequently, in 1961, Saudi Arabia, in conjunction with the trade agreement that it concluded with Syria during the latter part of that year, postponed until December 1963 the due date for the commencement of repayment of the $16 million loan.[78]

Payments agreements were also concluded by Saudi Arabia with Iraq and Lebanon at the time of the conclusion of the aforementioned trade agreements with those countries.[79] The agreement with Iraq provided for the establishment of a Saudi account in Iraqi dinars, with a swing credit of I.D. 250,000, which could be increased to I.D. 500,000;[80] and the agreement with Lebanon provided for the establishment of a Saudi account in Lebanese pounds, with a swing credit of L.L. 6 million, which could be increased to L.L. 10 million.

Notwithstanding the large number of bilateral trade and payments agreements concluded by Saudi Arabia during the second half of the 1950's and the early part of the 1960's, most of them had a very limited, if any, effect on Saudi Arabia's inter-Arab trade relations. The trade and payments agreements with Lebanon were apparently not implemented by the two countries, and although the trade and payments agreements with Iraq were put into effect, they were in all probability virtually inoperative during most of the remainder of the period under consideration. The trade agreement with Jordan was concluded in 1963, after Saudi Arabia had terminated its system of quantitative controls and reduced or eliminated its duties on a wide range of products. And the concessions that Saudi Arabia received under the bilateral agreements were of little consequence since Saudi Arabia produced very few industrial and agricultural commodities. The trade, loan, and payments agreements with Egypt and Syria, on the other hand, did facilitate during a part of the period under consideration the rather substantial increase in imports of Syrian and Egyptian textiles. Moreover, there was a sizable increase during the 1950's and early 1960's in imports of agricultural products into Saudi Arabia from Egypt and Syria, as well as from the other Fertile Crescent countries, which resulted in large part from Saudi Arabia's increasing oil revenues and free exchange and general free trade policies regarding agricultural imports. There were also, however, a number of wide fluctuations in Saudi Arabia's trade with some of the aforementioned Arab countries during this period due principally to political developments within the region. Egyptian exports to Saudi Arabia, for example, decreased substantially during 1963, reflecting the strained political relations between the two countries due to the revolution in Yemen.

Egyptian Agreements with Maghreb Countries and Sudan

In addition to the agreements that it concluded with the Fertile Crescent countries and Saudi Arabia, Egypt also concluded a number of trade and payments agreements with the Maghreb countries and the Sudan during the period under consideration. Agreements were concluded with Libya in 1953, 1956, and 1960;[81] Tunisia in 1957 and 1962;[82] Morocco in 1958 and 1959;[83] the Sudan in 1957 and 1959;[84] and Algeria in 1963.[85] There were also a number of protocols to these agreements. Although these countries became members of the Arab League following their independence, they did not adhere to the multilateral Arab League trade and payments conventions.

With the exception of the Egyptian-Sudanese agreements, these bilateral trade and payments agreements provided primarily for the authorization by the contracting parties, within the limits of their laws and regulations, of the importation from and exportation to each other of various products[86] and for the establishment of mutual clearing accounts with swing credits.[87] These agreements led to some periodic increases in Egypt's trade with the

Maghreb countries, but for the most part such trade continued to be rather small.

The agreements with the Sudan were much more significant since they marked the end of the free trade area and monetary union that had existed between the two countries for over 50 years. On April 8, 1957, a little over a year after independence, the Sudanese Government put into circulation Sudanese bank notes to replace the Egyptian bank notes, which ceased on that day to be legal tender in the Sudan.[88] On the previous day, the two countries had signed a currency agreement providing for the exchange for British Government securities of the Egyptian bank notes and coins that were to be taken out of circulation in the Sudan. On April 7 the Sudan had also imposed exchange controls on all financial transactions with Egypt and had concluded a payments agreement under which various current payments between the two countries were to be made.

The payments agreement provided for the establishment of a Sudanese account in Egyptian pounds with the National Bank of Egypt, which, at the exchange rate of one Egyptian pound for one Sudanese pound, was to be credited with specified current payments made by Egypt to the Sudan and debited with such payments made by the Sudan to Egypt. A swing credit of L.E. 500,000 was provided for in the agreement, and any deficit outstanding upon the termination of the agreement was to be settled within six months by commodity exports or other current transactions or thereafter in a third currency to be agreed upon by the two countries. Reexports by either country of products imported from the other country were prohibited without the prior consent of the other country. Transfers could be made from the Sudanese account to the account of a third country with which Egypt or the Sudan had a payments agreement provided all three countries consented.

Following the signing of the payments agreement, Egypt proceeded to supplement and tighten the exchange controls that it had been imposing on financial transactions with the Sudan since 1953. All commodities imported from the Sudan became subject to import licensing restrictions and, in addition, to an import tax of 7 percent.

In 1958, the restrictions being imposed by the two countries were applied in such a manner that their trade with each other decreased substantially. In an attempt to arrest the deterioration, the Egyptian Region of the U.A.R. and the Sudan concluded in January 1959 new payments arrangements to supplement those of 1957. The 1959 arrangements provided for the establishment of two new Sudanese accounts in Egyptian pounds. The first account was for L.E. 1 million, and all commercial transactions relating to trade in certain commodities were to be channeled through this account.[89] Import licenses were to be issued for these commodities by the two countries free of any conditions, and the final liquidation of the account was to be effected by commodity exports rather than by payment in a third currency. The second account was for L.E. 250,000 and was established for the purpose of bartering certain commodities.[90] Both of these accounts were to terminate on April 30, 1959. Commodity trade other than in the aforementioned products and other current transactions between the two countries were to continue to be carried out under the 1957 payments agreement.

On November 8, 1959, the Egyptian Region and the Sudan in a further attempt to increase trade between themselves concluded a new trade and payments agreement and a sugar agreement. In addition, however, the U.A.R. Government on behalf of both its regions concluded on the same day a customs agreement with the Sudan that marked the end of the period during which Egypt and the Sudan had accorded duty-free treatment to practically all of each other's products. In the trade and payments agreement,[91] the Egyptian Region promised to undertake to import certain commodities from the Sudan, totaling in value not less than L.E. 5 million, within one year from the effective date of the agreement, and the Sudan promised to undertake to import within the same period certain commodities from the Egyptian Region totaling not less than approximately L.E. 6 million. The difference of approximately L.E. 1 million was to offset the contemplated favorable balance for the Sudan in invisible payments. The commodities and amount of each commodity that the countries undertook to import were set forth in an annex to the agreement. Among the Egyptian commodities that the Sudan promised to undertake to import were rice, oranges and other fruits, tires and tubes, wrapping paper and cardboard, textiles, footwear, cement, metal products, glassware, films, books, laundry blue, leather and leather products, and asphalt; and among the Sudanese commodities that the Egyptian Region promised to undertake to import were camels, cattle, chickpeas, certain beans, hides and skins, cottonseed, ground nuts, cottonseed oil, millet, maize, sesame, and gum. Of the aforementioned Egyptian commodities, the Sudan promised to undertake to import not less than L.E. 3.5 million in Egyptian textiles. The two countries promised to issue the necessary import and export licenses with regard to the commodities on the attached lists and to permit and facilitate trade in commodities not on the lists.

Payments for commodities exchanged between the two countries, as well as for other current transactions specified in an appendix, were to be effected through two new Sudanese accounts to be established with the National Bank of Egypt in Egyptian pounds. One account was to be credited with the payments for commodities exported by the Sudan to the Egyptian Region and debited with payments for commodities exported by the Egyptian Region to the Sudan. The other was to be credited and debited with the specified current payments other than those relating to commodity trade.[92] On June 30 of each year, any outstanding deficit balance for the Egyptian Region was to be paid in a third currency acceptable to the Sudan, and any deficit balance for the Sudan was to be paid by debiting the special account that had been established for the Sudan under the 1957 currency agreement to cover the amount over and above L.E. 20 million due the Sudan from the withdrawal of Egyptian currency. However, if the minimum amounts of the products specified in the agreement had not been purchased by the creditor country, such payments could be deferred by the debtor country until the specified amounts were purchased. Upon signature of the 1959 trade and payments agreement, the Sudanese account established under the 1957 payments agreement was to be closed, as were to be the accounts established under the payments arrangements concluded in January 1959. The duration of the latter accounts, which were to have terminated on April 30, 1959, had apparently been extended. The Sudanese credit balance of about L.E. 500,000 in the 1957 account was to be paid within six months in a third currency acceptable to the Sudan.

Under the sugar agreement, Egypt promised to sell to the Sudan 40,000 tons of certain Egyptian sugar for which payment was to be made by debiting the special account established for the Sudan under the 1957 currency agreement. Under Article IV of the latter agreement, Egypt had promised to export annually to the Sudan the aforementioned amount; however, it had defaulted in meeting this obligation. The sugar agreement constituted in effect a reaffirmation of this undertaking by Egypt.

The customs agreement which the U.A.R. signed with the Sudan on behalf of both its regions contained very few provisions.[93] It simply provided certain preferential tariff treatment for the products of U.A.R. or Sudanese origin specified in a list annexed to the agreement and for duty-free transit trade, except with regard to passage through the Suez Canal. The annexed list was not very comprehensive, and only a relatively small number of the articles on the list were to be accorded duty-free treatment.[94] Most of the other products on the list were to receive only 25 percent preferences (reductions).[95] Excluded from the list were many of Egypt's most important manufactured products, including wearing apparel (other than footwear), confectionery, macaroni and similar products, matches, nonalcoholic or alcoholic beverages, cement, and soap. Moreover, practically all Egyptian and Sudanese fresh fruits and vegetables were excluded from the list. Products not on the list were to be subject to full Egyptian or Sudanese import duties, which in many cases were quite high.

With the termination of the Egyptian-Sudanese free trade area, the last relic of Arab economic unity had disappeared, and notwithstanding the commitments contained in the 1959 trade and payments agreement, trade between the two countries during 1959 and 1960 was substantially below the amounts specified. As will be seen, the aforementioned alterations in Egyptian-Sudanese trade relations led during the period under consideration to a very sharp decrease in Egyptian exports to the Sudan and, except in 1963, in Sudanese exports to Egypt.

INTER-ARAB TRADE

Inter-Arab trade during the 1950's and early 1960's reflected the aforementioned political and economic factors. There were very wide fluctuations in trade between some of the Arab countries, due in part to the difficulties that they were encountering in their political and economic relations with each other. Moreover, in the absence of any sustained undertaking to effect closer trade relations, inter-Arab trade by the end of 1963 showed, with the notable exception of trade in petroleum and petroleum products and exports of agricultural products from the Fertile Crescent countries to Saudi Arabia and Kuwait, few significant increases when compared with such trade during the last year (1951) of the early postwar period.[96]

The fluctuations in Egypt's trade with some of the other Arab countries were especially noticeable. Exports from Egypt to Syria increased from a little over L.E. 500,000 in 1951 to almost L.E. 7,200,000 during the first nine months of 1961 and then decreased following the breakup of the union to about L.E. 400,000 in 1962. Likewise, imports into Egypt from Syria increased from a little over L.E. 1,000,000 in 1951 to over L.E. 7,000,000 in each of the years 1959 and 1960. During the first nine months of 1961 such imports amounted to about L.E. 5,300,000, then decreased in 1962 to about L.E. 800,000 and in 1963 to about L.E. 200,000.

Egypt's trade with the Sudan showed similar fluctuations. Exports from Egypt to the Sudan increased from about L.E. 4,250,000 in 1951 to a little over L.E. 9,000,000 in 1956 and then decreased to less than L.E. 3,000,000 in 1963. Imports into Egypt from the Sudan increased from about L.E. 3,000,000 in 1951 to almost L.E. 5,000,000 in 1957, fell to less than L.E. 2,000,000 in 1959, and then rose to a little over L.E. 6,000,000 in 1963.

Like its imports from Syria, Egypt's imports during 1963 from most other Arab countries were less than they were in 1951, and its exports showed few significant increases. Its inter-Arab trade (including reexports to the other Arab countries) accounted for about 7 percent of the total value of its trade in 1963, and the composition of such trade consisted for the most part of a rather small number of products. Crude petroleum and petroleum products from Saudi Arabia and Kuwait accounted for about 70 percent of the value of Egypt's total imports from all of the Arab countries during that year, and a small number of products also accounted for most of the total value of Egypt's exports to those countries.[97]

Iraq, like Egypt, obtained during the period under consideration only a small proportion—about 5 percent in 1963—of the total value of its imports from the other Arab countries, and such imports, except for those from Syria and Lebanon, generally consisted of a small number of products. For example, during 1963 about 90 percent of the total value of Iraq's imports from Jordan consisted of only two products—tomatoes and bananas; virtually

all of its imports from the Sudan consisted of shelled and unshelled ground nuts; and over 80 percent of the total value of its
imports from Egypt consisted of potatoes, film, printed matter,
cement, and cotton yarn and fabrics. Although Iraq imported during 1963 a greater variety of agricultural and industrial products
from Syria and Lebanon, including various textile products, its
imports from Syria had been subject to wide fluctuations during
the Kassem regime. Restrictions were imposed on imports of
Syrian textiles, fruits and vegetables, and other products, and as a
result imports into Iraq from Syria decreased from about I.D.
2,500,000 in 1957 to about I.D. 110,000 in 1960. Following the
breakup of the union of Syria and Egypt and the establishment of
closer economic ties between Syria and Iraq, imports increased to
a little over I.D. 2,500,000 in 1963.

Iraq's exports to other Arab countries during this period accounted for a sizable percentage of the value of its total exports
(excluding petroleum and petroleum products) but were in many
cases less by the end of the period than in 1951 and were generally
quite limited in composition.[98] Iraq's agricultural production and
total exports decreased substantially during the second half of the
1950's and the early part of the 1960's, due mainly to unfavorable
weather conditions. What was especially noticeable with regard to
Iraq's export trade were the sharp fluctuations in its exports to
Kuwait, which reflected the dispute between the two countries
following Kuwait's independence in 1961. Exports dropped from
a high of about I.D. 1,500,000 in 1953 and 1957 to a low of
about I.D. 10,000 in 1962 and then increased to about I.D.
1,300,000 in 1963, of which about two-thirds consisted of cement
and barley.

Inter-Arab trade accounted for a larger portion of the total
value of the trade of Syria, Lebanon, and Jordan. During 1963, for
example, about 15 percent of Syria's imports and about 28 percent of its exports came from and went to the other Arab countries, while about 22 percent of Jordan's imports and about 73
percent of its exports came from and went to other Arab countries. The comparable approximate percentages for Lebanon were
20 percent of imports and 48 percent of exports. However, a
substantial part of the imports of these countries during the period
under consideration consisted of imports of petroleum and petroleum products from Kuwait, Saudi Arabia, and Iraq.[99] In addition,
Syria's and Lebanon's exports included commodity reexports, as

well as exports or reexports of gold, gold products, bank notes, coin, stocks, bonds, and other financial paper. For example, most of the large total value of exports from Lebanon to Kuwait and Saudi Arabia in 1960 and 1961 consisted of the aforementioned items. In its commodity trade statistics for 1962 and 1963, Lebanon did not include bank notes, stocks, bonds, and other financial paper, but it did include gold, gold products, and coin, and these items, as well as its reexports of other products, constituted a large portion of its exports to Saudi Arabia and Kuwait in those years. The inclusion of the aforementioned items in Lebanon's trade statistics for 1960 and 1961 also resulted in inflated figures for Lebanon's total imports from Egypt during those years.

Syria, Lebanon, and Jordan did, however, sell substantially increased amounts of their agricultural commodities to Saudi Arabia and Kuwait, and these exports constituted virtually the only significant sustained increases in the inter-Arab trade of these Fertile Crescent countries during this period. On the other hand, with the exception of Saudi Arabian imports of Syrian textiles, Saudi Arabia and Kuwait purchased relatively little of their manufactured products from these countries.[100]

Although trade between Syria, Lebanon, and Jordan continued to constitute a substantial portion of their total trade, the composition of such trade, except for Syrian textile exports to Jordan, was generally limited to agricultural products, and the periodic increases in this trade reflected more an improvement in crop conditions than trade relations.[101] Syria's exports to Lebanon showed great variations during the 1950's and early 1960's, due in large part to the fluctuations in Syria's cereal harvests. Similarly, Jordanian imports from Syria more than doubled in value from 1962 to 1963, due mainly to the very large imports of wheat and other cereals.[102]

The inter-Arab trade of the North African countries other than Egypt constituted, with the exception of the Sudan's trade with Egypt, an insignificant part of their total trade during the period under consideration. Libya during 1963, for example, purchased less than 3 percent of the total value of its imports from and sold about 1 percent of the total value of its exports (including petroleum) to other Arab countries. During the same year, inter-Arab trade accounted for less than 3 percent of Morocco's imports and less than 4 percent of its exports. Tunisia during 1963 carried on with other Arab countries about 1 percent of its import trade and about 6 percent of its export trade; the Sudan, notwithstanding its fairly substantial trade with Egypt, carried on with all Arab countries during the same year less than 6 percent of the total value of its trade; and Algeria during 1961 carried on with other Arab countries only about 2 percent of its trade.[103]

In essence, inter-Arab trade during the 1950's and early 1960's was characterized by the following features: A very large portion of such trade consisted of trade in petroleum and agricultural products and involved to a large extent only a limited number of agricultural products. Trade in industrial products was, with a few exceptions, insignificant, notwithstanding the gains in industrialization made by some of the Arab countries during this period. In addition, trade between some of the Arab countries was subject to wide fluctuations due in part to the many factors heretofore mentioned, and there were few significant increases in inter-Arab trade that developed and were sustained.

There were during this period practically no alterations effected by inter-Arab trade in the international patterns of trade of the Arab countries. The international trade of these countries continued to be oriented toward non-Arab, industrialized countries and involved for the most part exports of a few primary products,[104] predominantly oil,[105] and substantially increased imports of capital goods, foodstuffs, and, in many cases, manufactured consumer products.

SUMMARY

By the end of 1963, there was virtually no significant improvement in inter-Arab trade relations, notwithstanding the large number of trade and payments agreements concluded during the period. In fact, the trend in many instances was in the opposite direction. The free trade areas between Jordan and Syria and Lebanon and between the Sudan and the U.A.R. were terminated; trade between Syria and Lebanon was subjected to many restrictions; there was virtually an embargo on trade between Syria and the U.A.R. for a period of time following the dissolution of their political union and attempted economic union; during the Kassem regime, Iraq placed an embargo on trade with Kuwait and severely restricted trade with other Arab countries; the U.A.R.'s exports to Saudi Arabia decreased substantially in 1963 due to the strained political relations between the two countries resulting from the revolution in Yemen; Arab socialism had become an additional impediment to trade with the U.A.R. and was in the process of becoming an impediment to trade with Syria and Iraq; the quantitative control and tariff systems of most of the Arab countries had become more comprehensive and restrictive; and what inroads had been made into these systems by the inter-Arab trade and payments agreements were limited and circumscribed and in many cases of short duration. Without question, the over-all effect during this period was one of further political and economic disintegration, which, as will be seen, placed the Arab countries in a position of being for the most part neither politically nor economically oriented toward each other for a common market undertaking.[106]

CHAPTER **6** ARAB COMMON MARKET
AGREEMENTS: 1964-67

Although proposals to form an Arab common market had been considered by the Arab League Economic Council at a number of meetings during the 1950's, it was not until March 1960 that the Arab countries approved in principle the establishment of a common market and set up a special committee to determine the steps to be taken to effect its formation.[1] In June 1961, the Council met to consider the plans for economic integration that had been prepared. Discussions at the meeting centered around three proposals for economic integration. The U.A.R., with a developing planned economy, advocated full economic union under an Economic Unity Council in Cairo, which would have full power to decide the economic, fiscal, industrial, trade, and agricultural policies of the Arab countries.[2] Most of the other states were either lukewarm or completely opposed to the U.A.R.'s proposal. Iraq countered with a proposal for a "complementary and coordinated economy for the Arab states." It advocated the gradual achieving of free trade and economic cooperation and proposed Baghdad as the institutional headquarters. Lebanon, with essentially a free enterprise economy, asked that the Arab states first abolish legislation discriminating against the business activities of each other's nationals and then provide for the free flow of capital, labor, and goods, as the first steps toward full economic integration. Lebanon would have backed the Iraqi proposal, but it refrained from doing so because the U.A.R. indicated that it would not support that proposal. The result of the meeting was that no agreement was reached, and the subject of economic integration was again postponed to a later date.[3]

In the spring of 1962, the Economic Council met in Cairo. The meeting was attended by delegates from the U.A.R., Morocco, Jordan, Saudi Arabia, Syria, Kuwait, Yemen, and Lebanon, and by

107

observers from Tunisia, Libya, Algeria, and the Sudan. Iraq, which had proceeded to boycott Arab League meetings after the admission of Kuwait, was not represented. The main item on the Economic Council's agenda was a modified version of the U.A.R.'s proposed agreement for the establishment of an economic union. After about a week of discussion, representatives of the U.A.R., Morocco, Kuwait, Syria, and Jordan signed the Economic Unity Agreement between the States of the Arab League on June 6, 1962.[4] Lebanon did not sign, nor did Saudi Arabia and Yemen. And, as indicated, Iraq did not send a delegate or observer to the meeting.

ECONOMIC UNITY AGREEMENT

The Economic Unity Agreement, which went into effect in 1964 (as will be seen), constituted essentially a statement of the goal of the contracting parties and a commitment by them to undertake certain general measures at an unspecified future date in order to achieve that goal. The parties stated in the agreement that their goal or aim was to establish among themselves complete economic unity that would ensure for them and their citizens on an equal basis the freedom of movement of persons, capital, and goods; the freedom of residence, employment, and economic activity; the freedom of transport and transit; and the right to own, bequeath, and inherit. To achieve this goal of complete economic unity, they promised to make their countries a single customs entity with a unified external tariff and unified customs laws and regulations; to unify their export and import policies and regulations and their transport and transit regulations; to coordinate their agricultural, industrial, commercial, and economic policies, their labor and social security legislation, and their taxes, so as to ensure uniform opportunity for their citizens; to coordinate their monetary and financial policies and regulations as a prelude to the unification of their currencies; and to conclude jointly trade and payments agreements with foreign countries.

To determine the measures necessary for the implementation in stages of the foregoing, the contracting parties provided in the agreement for the establishment in Cairo of an Arab Economic Unity Council. The Council was to be composed of one or more delegates from each of the contracting states and was to adopt its resolutions by a two-thirds majority of the votes of the contracting states, with each state having one vote. Provision was also made for subordinate committees to assist the Council in carrying out its functions. In accordance with the provisions of Articles 12 and 14 of the agreement and the provisions of an annex to the agreement, the Council was to make the necessary studies and determinations regarding the abovementioned matters within five years and submit its determinations to the contracting parties for implementation in accordance with their constitutional procedures. However, the Council could recommend to the member states, if necessary, that the preparatory period be extended for another five years. If two or more member states were to decide to bypass the preparatory period or any of the implementing stages and to move directly to complete economic unity, they were to be permitted to do so.

Following the signing of the Economic Unity Agreement, certain political developments in Yemen and Iraq—namely, the overthrow of the Imam of Yemen in 1962 and of the Kassem and Baath regimes in Iraq in 1963—led to an increase in the number of signatories to the Economic Unity Agreement and to its coming into force. The agreement was signed by Iraq on December 9, 1963, and by Yemen on December 17, 1963. On January 30, 1964, Iraq brought the agreement into force, as of April 30, 1964, by becoming the third country to deposit its instrument of ratification. Kuwait and the U.A.R. had deposited their instruments on September 9, 1962, and May 25, 1963, respectively. Instruments of ratification were subsequently deposited by Syria on February 24, 1964, and Jordan on June 1, 1964. Morocco and Yemen, the other signatories to the agreement, did not deposit instruments of ratification.

ARAB COMMON MARKET RESOLUTION

On August 13, 1964, the Economic Unity Council took the first substantive step toward the creation of a common market. It adopted a resolution that provided—pending the drafting of schedules containing more favorable treatment—for the removal by January 1, 1974, of customs duties and other restrictions on trade in domestic products between the countries that had ratified the Economic Unity Agreement.[5] Agricultural, animal, and mineral products contained in the amended schedule of such products annexed to the Arab League trade convention were to be or continue to be exempt from import duties and taxes.[6] The duties and taxes on such products not contained in that schedule were to be reduced annually by 20 percent of the initial rates, with the first reduction taking effect on January 1, 1965. Likewise, the export and import quantitative restrictions imposed on agricultural, animal, and mineral products were to be removed in five annual stages, with the first stage taking effect as of the foregoing date. Two months prior to each stage, each of the member states was to furnish the Economic Unity Council with a list of the products, representing 20 percent of the agricultural, animal, and mineral products subject to quantitative restrictions, which were to be exempt from such restrictions.

With regard to industrial products, such products contained in the amended Arab League trade convention schedule of commodities subject to a 25 percent reduction in import duties were to be subject to seven annual 10 percentage point increases in the reduction, with the first increase commencing on January 1, 1965.[7] The final 5 percentage point increase in the reduction was to take effect on July 1, 1971. Industrial products contained in the amended trade convention schedule of commodities subject to a 50 percent reduction in import duties were to be subject to five annual 10 percentage point increases in the reduction, with the first increase also on January 1, 1965.[8] Import duties and taxes on industrial products not contained in the aforementioned schedules were to be reduced annually, as of the preceding date, by 10 percent of the initial rates. Likewise, the quantitative restrictions imposed on industrial products were to be removed in ten annual stages, with the first stage also taking effect as of that date. Two months prior to each stage, each of the member states was to furnish the Economic Unity Council with a list of the products, representing 10 percent of the industrial products subject to quantitative restrictions, which were to be exempt from such restrictions.

The resolution also provided for the exemption from export duties of domestic products traded between the member countries. In addition, it provided that the quantitative restrictions and various duties and taxes on importation and exportation "presently in force" in the member countries were fixed for the purpose of preventing any member state from imposing new restrictions, duties, or taxes, or increasing those already in existence, on the exchange of products with the other member states.[9]

Article 8 of the resolution prohibited a member state from subsidizing exports of its domestic products to another member state if such products were produced in the importing state, and Article 9 provided that existing concessions and monopolies in the member states were not to be altered so as to interfere with the implementation of the provisions of the Arab common market. Article 14, on the other hand, reserved to each member state the right to request of the Economic Unity Council that certain products be excepted from the exemptions from and reductions in duties and taxes and from the removal of quantitative restrictions. The Council was empowered to approve such exceptions for a period not to exceed that of the implementing stages.

The resolution further provided that, pending the institution of an Arab Payments Union and an Arab Monetary Fund to enable the member states to make their currencies convertible between themselves, the payments for commodities and services exchanged between the member states would be made under the bilateral payments agreements in force between such states. If no bilateral agreement existed, the payments were to be made in United States dollars, pounds sterling, or in any other convertible currency agreed upon by the two countries involved, and each of the countries was committed to permit without delay the transfer of all amounts due to the exporting country.

In compliance with Article 12 of the Economic Unity Agreement, the resolution was to be implemented by the member states in accordance with their constitutional procedures. Since the resolution involved only the member states of the Economic Unity Council, the other Arab countries in order to become eligible to participate in the common market had to ratify or adhere to the Economic Unity Agreement so as to become members of the Council.

IMPLEMENTATION OF COMMON MARKET AGREEMENTS

On or as of January 1, 1965, the initial tariff reductions and the exemptions from quantitative restrictions provided for in the resolution were placed into effect by the five member countries of the

Economic Unity Council. However, only four of these countries—
Syria, Iraq, Jordan, and the U.A.R.—had ratified the resolution,
and they reserved a rather substantial number of industrial products from the specified tariff reductions and/or the removal of
quantitative restrictions.

In accordance with Article 14 of the common market resolution, during the latter part of 1964 the five member countries of
the Economic Unity Council had submitted lists of the items—
which consisted chiefly of industrial products—that they wanted
excepted from the tariff reductions and/or the removal of quantitative restrictions specified in the resolution.[10] Although there was
only one item on the Kuwaiti list, there were reportedly 88 on the
Jordanian list, 71 on the Syrian list, 52 on the U.A.R. list, and 35
on the Iraqi list.[11] Moreover, whereas Kuwait requested that its
exception be for only one year, the other Arab countries requested that their exceptions be for the entire period of the implementing stages. The reasons advanced consisted for the most part
of the need to protect domestic industries, to maintain the customs revenues, and to prevent interference with certain domestic
monopolies.

Although the Economic Unity Council expressed its concern
over the sizable number of requested exceptions in relation to the
limited production of industrial articles within the region, it nevertheless approved the lists for 1965 without alteration. A special
committee was established, however, to consider the lists and to
make recommendations regarding their revision. In March 1966,
following the implementation by the four participating countries
(Kuwait had not ratified the resolution) of the second stage of
reductions and exemptions, the special committee recommended
that the Iraqi, Syrian, and U.A.R. lists of exceptions be terminated
and that the Jordanian list be reduced in scope and subsequently
reconsidered.[12] In accordance with these recommendations, it was
expected that the lists would be terminated or substantially revised.

The expected termination or revision of such lists appeared to
be significant though only with respect to the lowering of tariffs.
The common market resolution did not call for an across-the-
board reduction in quantitative restrictions; it required the exemption from quantitative restrictions of a specified annual percentage
of the products subject to such restrictions. Since most industrial
products and a large number of agricultural products were subject

to some form of restriction by the participating countries, these countries were in a position during the early stages to exercise a great deal of discretion in selecting the items making up the percentage requirements. This discretion was exercised in such a way by them in 1965 and 1966 that these items consisted for the most part of products that had been subject to perfunctory licensing or that bore little significance with respect to inter-Arab trade.[13]

Although the manner of implementation of the common market resolution was cause for concern during 1965 and 1966, the economic transformations taking place within the region were much more significant, tending to minimize the importance of the resolution itself. The international trade of the U.A.R. and Syria and, to a lesser extent, Iraq had become a function of the state, and planned trade had replaced or was gradually replacing tariffs and specified quantitative restrictions as the regulator of access to and of exports from such countries. Hence, there was some question as to what effect the gradual elimination of duties and specified quantitative restrictions would have in facilitating multilateral trade between the common market participants, especially in view of the strained political relations that existed between most of them and the absence of such requisites for economic integration as a multilateral payments and credit mechanism.

Trade between the common market participants during 1965 and 1966 reflected the aforementioned political and economic factors, as well as various other factors.[14] Trade between Syria and Iraq, for example, dropped precipitously, as the political and economic ties that had been established between the two countries after the breakup of the political union between Syria and Egypt were dissolved following the overthrow of the Baath regime in Iraq in 1963. Although exports from Syria to Iraq remained substantial during 1964, amounting to about L.S. 26 million, they decreased during 1965 and 1966 to about L.S. 5 million and L.S. 7.5 million, respectively.[15] Over 50 percent of the total value of Syria's exports (including reexports) to Iraq during 1966 consisted of tomatoes, seeds for sowing, and apricot and raisin paste, and most of the remainder consisted of substantially reduced amounts of Syrian textiles. Imports into Syria from Iraq were likewise exceedingly limited, except for imports of crude petroleum and gas oil. Virtually all of Syria's imports from Iraq in 1966 consisted of those two products plus dates.

Trade between Syria and the U.A.R. and between the U.A.R. and Jordan was also very small in size and composition during 1965 and 1966. Over 90 percent of the value of Syria's imports from the U.A.R. in 1966 consisted of potatoes, rice, and salt; a like percentage of the value of its exports to the U.A.R. consisted of lentils and cottonseed oil; about 75 percent of the value of Jordan's imports from the U.A.R. consisted of rice; and Jordanian exports to the U.A.R. continued to be practically nonexistent, amounting to less than J.D. 1,000 in 1966.

Trade between Jordan and Syria, on the other hand, remained rather substantial during 1965 and 1966. There was, however, no significant change in its composition. During 1966, it consisted predominantly of Syrian imports of tomatoes, eggplants, bananas, watermelons, beans, and certain other fruits and vegetables, and Syrian exports of various agricultural products [16] and textiles, cement, glassware, and wooden boxes. Likewise, there was no significant change in Jordan's trade with Iraq, even though it showed a rather large increase in value in 1966. It continued to be very limited in composition, consisting for the most part of larger exports of Jordanian tomatoes and bananas and imports of Iraqi wheat and barley. During 1966, these commodities accounted for about 70 percent of the value of Jordanian exports to Iraq and about 85 percent of the value of Jordanian imports from Iraq.

The one significant development in common market trade that occurred during 1965 and 1966 was in the trade between the U.A.R. and Iraq, but the substantial increase in this trade reflected the establishment of closer political and economic ties between the two countries on a bilateral basis rather than the common market undertaking. [17] U.A.R. imports from Iraq increased from about L.E. 200,000 in 1963 to about L.E. 4,000,000 in 1966, and U.A.R. exports to Iraq increased from about L.E. 500,000 to about L.E. 2,000,000. [18] These sizable increases involved mainly Iraqi exports of crude petroleum, wool, cement, dates, and wheat and U.A.R. exports of textiles.

Notwithstanding the implementation on January 1, 1967, and January 1, 1968, of the third and fourth stages of reductions and exemptions under the common market resolution, the establishment of an Arab common market appeared, as of the beginning of 1968, to be very far removed. With the exception of political relations between Iraq and the U.A.R., there was a virtual absence of political rapport between the four participating countries; three of these countries were pursuing a policy of Arab socialism, with apparently few inroads having been made into their trade control systems; and the economies of Jordan and the U.A.R. had suffered serious dislocations as a result of the hostilities with Israel. The specifics with regard to the formation of a common tariff and common export and import policies and regulations; the coordination of agricultural, industrial, fiscal, and monetary policies; the establishment of a multilateral payments mechanism and development bank; and the many other matters mentioned in the Economic Unity Agreement still had to be drafted and agreed to—not to mention implemented. And the ultimate scope of an Arab common market was a matter of uncertainty. Kuwait still had not ratified the common market resolution, [19] and most of the remainder of the Arab League countries [20] who, in accordance with the terms of the common market resolution, had to ratify or adhere to the Economic Unity Agreement to become eligible to participate in the common market undertaking showed a reluctance to do so. [21]

7 ARAB ECONOMIC INTEGRATION: AN EVALUATION

In the preceding chapters, an attempt was made to place Arab economic integration in its proper perspective by considering the developments in inter-Arab trade relations, including the recent common market agreements. In this chapter, an attempt will be made to weigh in general economic terms the significance of Arab economic integration by considering some of the economic factors that have constituted and could continue to constitute impediments and deterrents to such integration and some of the economic factors contingent on the integration process that could present opportunities for economic gains.

DIFFICULTIES

Different Economic Systems

One of the primary difficulties involved in Arab economic integration stems from the existence of different economic systems in the Arab world, which range from the socialist economy of the U.A.R. to the virtual laissez-faire economy in Lebanon. Four of the Arab countries—Algeria, Iraq, Syria, and the U.A.R.—have been pursuing a policy of socialism involving state ownership, control, or regulation of various sectors of the domestic economy. In the U.A.R., which began to convert its economy to a socialist economy during the second half of the 1950's, virtually all industries are owned or controlled by the government; public transportation is almost entirely government-owned and -operated; foreign trade is under the control of the government; the financial sector of the U.A.R. economy has been taken over by the government through the nationalization of the banks and insurance companies; a sub-

116

stantial portion of the U.A.R.'s agricultural sector is under the direct control and supervision of the government; and the prices of various products for domestic consumption and export are set or controlled by the government. In addition, the government has taken over most of the wholesale trade and is participating in the retail trade through government-controlled retail cooperatives and government-owned department stores.[1] In Syria and, to a lesser extent, in Iraq and Algeria similar conversions have taken place in the domestic economies.[2]

The economies of the remainder of the Arab countries are essentially private or free enterprise economies with varying amounts of state participation. There is little participation by the state in the Lebanese economy, whereas there is a substantial amount in the Moroccan economy. Within the economic admixture in the Arab world, the Lebanese economy is about as far removed from state socialism as one could expect.

With the presence of Arab socialism, the difficulties involved in economic integration become quite apparent. Since planned trade through state agencies acting within the framework of an over-all economic plan has replaced, or is gradually replacing, tariffs and specified quantitative restrictions as the regulator of access to and of exports from the socialist countries, reductions in or the removal of such artificial restrictions by these countries have had and could have a very limited effect on facilitating access to their markets. Moreover, restrictions on the use of foreign capital in these countries and governmental ownership and control at the production, wholesale, and retail levels have constituted and could constitute further inhibitions, as could the price structures gradually evolving within these countries that reflect to a large extent fixed prices.

On the other hand, unlimited access to and egress from the markets of the socialist countries, as advocated by the private enterprise countries, would be incompatible with the economic planning involved in pursuing a policy of socialism. For the socialist countries to permit private companies to establish agencies in the socialist countries and to freely import and sell their products would be tantamount to discarding over-all economic planning.

In effect, what the U.A.R. proposed at the Arab League Economic Council meeting in 1961 and what is apparently sought by the Arab Economic Unity Agreement is to translate national planning into regional planning. Under the Economic Unity Agreement, the Arab Economic Unity Council has been assigned the tasks of preparing the external framework for an Arab common market; coordinating the economic development programs of the participating Arab countries; preparing programs for the realization of joint Arab development projects; and coordinating the agricultural, industrial, and trade policies of the member countries. However, the Council is also supposed to prepare legislation to effect the free movement of capital, labor, and goods between the participating countries and the free exercise of economic activity and the right to own property in such countries. If all of the objectives and tasks set forth in the Economic Unity Agreement were to be achieved, then there would perforce be alterations in the economic policies of the socialist countries, as well as those of the nonsocialist countries that are or might become participants in the common market undertaking. But it does not appear likely that the U.A.R. and Syria, and possibly Iraq, would be willing to compromise Arab socialism for Arab economic unity, nor does it appear that the nonsocialist countries, such as Kuwait and Lebanon, would be willing to compromise the nature of their economies.

The U.A.R. made its position quite clear in December 1961 when it dissolved its political union with Yemen—the United Arab States. In his announcement of the termination of the loose confederation, Abdel Kader Hatem, the U.A.R.'s Minister of State, stated:

> The United Arab Republic finds it necessary to define its attitude toward unity . . . which cannot be based on correct principles while there is no accord between the two sides as to the solution of problems inherent in the social revolution. The United Arab Republic believes that socialism is the correct solution to the Arab reality . . . and in making the decision to form the union believed it would become an instrument in the service of the Yemeni people. However, the experience of the past years has shown beyond any doubt that the people of Yemen have not benefitted from this experiment.[3]

Lebanon's position was stated unequivocally at the time of the dissolution of its customs union with Syria. Likewise, at the meeting of the Arab League Economic Council in 1961, Lebanon called upon the Arab countries to abolish legislation discriminating against the business activities of each other's nationals and to provide for the free flow of capital, labor, and goods before considering the adoption of whatever other measures might be necessary for Arab economic integration.

In view of the foregoing divergent positions regarding Arab economic integration, it is not surprising that the Arab common market undertaking has been so limited in membership. What is equally apparent is that, due to the presence of Arab socialism, the very nature of Arab economic integration has undergone a significant change. For unless the socialist countries are willing to transform their economies within a common market framework, Arab economic integration will become more a matter of how much planned trade can be effected within the region than of how much trade can be effected by the removal of tariffs and other specified restrictions and by the establishment of common external controls. Even though the removal of such restrictions and the establishment of such controls could create a semblance of a common market for Arab products, such a market, in the absence of an undertaking by the Arab countries to cast economic planning in regional terms, would in effect consist of a number of separate markets: The markets of the nonsocialist Arab countries would constitute one market, and the remainder of the so-called common market would be composed of the individual markets of the socialist countries. Although any constructive approach to economic integration involving underdeveloped countries would entail a great deal of economic planning and cooperation irrespective of the divergences in the economic systems of the countries involved, the additional factor that Arab socialism introduces is the transforming of economic planning on a regional scale from being a complement to the creation of an Arab common market to being a prime determinant of what market or markets shall exist for regional products.[4]

Different Levels of Industrial Development

Another principal difficulty involved in economic integration stems from the different levels of industrial development in the Arab world. The U.A.R. has a much broader industrial base than have the other countries; Syria and Lebanon have much broader industrial bases than have Jordan and Iraq; and the latter two countries, in turn, have much broader industrial bases than have Yemen, Saudi Arabia, Kuwait, and Libya. Of the countries in North Africa, Morocco has a broader industrial base than have

Algeria, Tunisia, Libya, and the Sudan, but a smaller base than has the U.A.R.[5]

It is difficult to say whether these disparities emanating from the production by some of these countries of a wider range and a larger output of articles reflect, in addition, differences in economic efficiency. Apparently few studies, if any, have been made regarding the comparative efficiency of similar industries in the Arab countries. In any case, the existence in some of the Arab countries of older, larger, and more numerous industrial establishments has acted as a deterrent to economic integration. Some of the very industries in which the more-industrialized countries are best able to expand production are those that have been or are being established in the less-industrialized countries—namely, industries that depend on domestic raw materials. Since the less-industrialized countries have established or are establishing such industries to provide employment for their nationals, to increase their rates of economic growth, and to conserve their foreign exchange for further economic development, there has been a reluctance on their part to expose their existing industries to competitive imports or to permit imports to interfere with their industrialization programs.

Due in part to the uneven rate of industrialization in the Arab countries and in part to the apparent insistence by these countries on reciprocity in their trade agreement negotiations, a large portion of Arab industrial or contemplated industrial production was effectively sheltered from the provisions of the trade agreements concluded during the 1950's and early 1960's. This was done either by specifically providing that imports of such products would be subject to full duties and licensing, by a failure to include such products in the lists that were to be subject to reduced duties and exemptions from licensing, by a failure to provide for any inroads into the quantitative control systems, or by reserving the right to impose quantitative restrictions on industrial products. Likewise, there were numerous reservations to or withholdings from the removal of quantitative restrictions under the Arab common market resolution, reflecting a continued reluctance on the part of the member countries to facilitate trade creation within their multilateral framework. Moreover, the element of state trading in three of the four member countries provided an additional safeguard.

In essence, the difficulties in economic integration that emanate from the existence of different levels of industrial development tend to revolve around the relative importance attached to industrialization and diversification within national boundaries, as compared to regional industrialization and specialization. Although each Arab country would like to have a broader market for the products of its existing and contemplated industrial establishments, most of these countries appear to be reluctant to undertake the necessary measures to establish a broader market for each other's products. And one of the factors underlying the reluctance of the less-industrialized countries is the fear that the creation of such a market might lead to the concentration of industrialization in the more-advanced Arab countries. Although such a concentration conceivably could have the desirable effect for the region as a whole of a faster rate of regional economic growth, it could, on the other hand, increase the inequality existing within the region, in terms of national economic entities, unless it were to have significant spilling-over or trickling-down effects. But with the similarity in agricultural production in the Arab countries and the difficulties involved in such production, such effects might not be felt for some time. As a result, some of the less-advanced Arab countries could be faced with much the same difficulties within a regional framework—including balance-of-payments problems—that they have encountered within an international framework and that they have sought to rectify through industrialization.

Measures could be taken, however, within a regional framework, as within a national framework, to achieve balanced growth both in geographic and economic terms, with the degree and pace of integration depending on the measures taken and the resources available. Hence, in one sense, fear of industrial concentration constitutes a deterrent for the less-advanced Arab countries insofar as they are unwilling to rely on regional economic planning to effect an allocation and integration of industry within the region. But, as indicated in the preceding section, with the existence of socialist economies in the Arab world, economic planning on a regional scale—including planned industrial integration involving, among other things, vertical and horizontal specialization— becomes virtually a sine qua non for Arab economic integration. Without such planned industrial integration with regard both to existing and to contemplated light and heavy industry, the opportunities for economic gains from an Arab common market undertaking could be quite limited indeed.

Shortages of Convertible Currencies

An additional factor underlying the reluctance of most Arab countries to dismantle their controls on inter-Arab trade in industrial and agricultural products has been the shortage of convertible foreign exchange. The only Arab states that appear to have ample supplies of convertible currencies within their present social, political, and economic frameworks are Kuwait, Saudi Arabia, and Libya, which have been receiving increasingly large amounts of oil revenues, and Lebanon. Both the Kuwaiti and Saudi Arabian currencies, in accordance with Article VIII of the Articles of Agreement of the International Monetary Fund, are convertible currencies for purposes of current transactions. Iraq and, to a lesser extent, Algeria also have been receiving substantial oil revenues but nevertheless have been unable to make their currencies convertible or to lessen their quantitative controls on international trade. The earnings of foreign exchange of the remaining countries have been inadequate for their needs, and they, as well as Algeria, have had to rely on grants and loans to supplement their foreign exchange earnings.

The shortage of convertible currencies in most of the Arab countries has tended to impede economic integration in a number of ways. In order to increase their supplies of such currencies, most of these countries have applied prescription of currency requirements to their most important exports, as well as to products in short supply domestically, necessitating payment in a convertible currency. Conversely, in order to conserve and allocate these foreign exchange earnings, most of these countries have applied rather comprehensive systems of quantitative controls to imports and other current transactions, as well as to capital movements. For balance-of-payments purposes, many articles have been prohibited from importation or have been subject to restrictive quotas or licensing. Due in part to these import and export controls, the Arab countries have found it exceedingly difficult to increase their trade with each other. On the one hand, they either have lacked convertible currencies or have been unwilling to allocate such currencies for imports of consumer products from each other; and, on the other hand, they have been unwilling to permit many of their products to be sold for other than convertible currencies. Moreover, this shortage of convertible currencies has constituted an impediment to economic integration not only in the financing of inter-Arab trade but also in the expansion of Arab industrial production, which is dependent on imports of capital goods and, in many cases, of raw materials and intermediate products from outside the region.

Although there have been a number of bilateral payments agreements concluded by the Arab countries with each other in an apparent endeavor to provide an alternative method of financing their trade, these agreements, as well as the multilateral Arab League payments convention, have had very little effect on increasing inter-Arab trade. The Arab League payments convention contained no provisions for the establishment of a multilateral payments mechanism; many of the bilateral payments arrangements were of short duration; and the payments arrangements between the Maghreb countries and the U.A.R. provided for rather small swing credits and were intended to finance trade between the contracting countries within a nonpreferential tariff framework. In addition, the difficulties in balancing inter-Arab bilateral trade have led to a reluctance on the part of certain of the Arab countries to conclude any bilateral payments arrangements or to channel their trade through the bilateral accounts that have been established.

As indicated in the preceding chapter, the Arab common market resolution contemplates the establishment of an Arab Payments Union and an Arab Monetary Fund. But, as of 1967, such matters still were under consideration by the Arab Economic Unity Council, including a proposal submitted to the Council by the Central Bank of Iraq. The basic features of the Iraqi proposal involved the operation of a clearing system on a multilateral basis, with settlements to be made at regular intervals (in national currencies, unless otherwise required by the Arab Payments Union), and the creation of a common fund, formed with contributions from the members consisting initially of 20 percent in foreign reserves and 80 percent in national currencies. The compensation mechanism was to operate basically on the principle of mandatory clearings, and the common fund's credit facilities of an automatic nature were to be linked to the intraregional balance of payments of the members. The Arab Payments Union was to be a legal entity with authority to borrow from member and other countries

and international institutions to supplement its resources of
foreign and national currencies. Such authority was to be used to
enable the Union to extend loans to member countries, on discretionary terms, to meet over-all, temporary balance-of-payments
needs.[6]

Although the Iraqi proposal addressed itself to the need for a
clearing and credit mechanism to alleviate balance-of-payments
difficulties that could arise within the framework of an Arab
common market both with regard to inter-Arab trade and trade
with countries outside the region, it did not contain any details
concerning the credit ceilings to be assigned to the member countries or concerning the terms of repayment. Without doubt, the
extent and pace of Arab economic integration would depend in
large part on the size of such credits. Most of the Arab countries
are not in a position to undertake to import substantial quantities
of consumer products, nor do they have the foreign exchange
necessary to effect a large-scale expansion of their industrial production.[7] Hence, until some of the less-industrialized Arab countries have established some semblance of an industrial base or have
substantially increased agricultural production to enable themselves to balance their regional exchanges, and until the more-
industrialized Arab countries, as well as some of the less-
industrialized Arab countries, are able to earn enough foreign exchange to purchase the necessary raw materials, intermediate products, and capital goods, they would require sizable credits for a
sufficiently long period of time.

In this connection, it is noted once again that the similarity in
Arab agricultural production and the large stretches of desert,
periodic unfavorable climatic conditions, and inadequate irrigation
systems in the Arab world would tend to minimize trade in agricultural products—at least in the short run—as a factor that could
enable the less-industrialized Arab countries to achieve some
semblance of a balance in their regional exchanges. The bulk of
inter-Arab trade in agricultural commodities has consisted of
exports from most of the Arab countries to the desert states of
Kuwait and Saudi Arabia, of trade between the Fertile Crescent
countries, of trade between the U.A.R. and the Sudan, and of
trade between Morocco and Algeria and Tunisia and Algeria.
Although trade in agricultural commodities has been significant
between the Fertile Crescent countries and between the U.A.R.
and the Sudan, it has been a two-way trade, and in many instances

the more-industrialized Arab countries—the U.A.R., Syria, and Lebanon—have exported more agricultural products in terms of value to the Sudan and Jordan and Iraq than they have imported from those countries. Both Jordan and Iraq have had unfavorable balances in their commodity trade with Lebanon and Syria (excluding trade in petroleum and petroleum products), and the Sudan has generally had an unfavorable balance in its commodity trade with the U.A.R.

Not all of the less-industrialized Arab countries, however, are short of foreign exchange. It is therefore further noted in considering the Iraqi proposal that the provision therein for automatic credits to finance net regional deficits could in some instances lead to rather anomalous results. Kuwait, for example, has exported substantial amounts of petroleum to the other Arab countries, but petroleum has been virtually its only significant export. Hence, it would be quite possible for Kuwait, pending the diversification of its economy, to be a net deficit country with regard to intra-regional trade and to be a recipient of credit within the proposed Arab Payments Union. However, Kuwait has in the past extended rather sizable grants and loans to other Arab countries, notwithstanding any imbalance it may have had in its intraregional trade. Consequently, it would appear to be incongruous for it to be extended credits when it is the Arab country in the best position to finance inter-Arab trade with convertible currencies, which in turn could be used by the recipient countries to finance their purchases from outside the region. It would appear that the position of the underdeveloped countries in the world with regard to trade versus aid would be equally applicable within the framework of an Arab common market. In effect, the automaticity approach keyed to net regional balances could short-circuit the beneficial effects that could result from regional economic integration. The discretionary factor is needed with regard not only to the granting of credits to finance extraregional trade but also to the granting of credits to finance intraregional trade. A country's over-all balance-of-payments position and its supplies of convertible currencies should be considered in determining whether credit should be extended to finance intraregional trade.

The Iraqi proposal, however, does serve to point up the vital interrelationship in the integration process between balanced growth in geographic and economic terms and the operation of a payments and credit mechanism. Without the former, the latter in all probability would eventually be placed in jeopardy, and without the latter, the former might well be beyond attainment. To make regional demand and supply effective, sizable credits of sufficient duration would be needed; and to prevent regional imbalances and imbalances with countries outside the region from becoming or remaining chronic, some semblance of balanced growth would have to be achieved.

Tariffs As a Source of Revenue

The importance of customs duties as a source of revenue for most of the Arab countries has also constituted an impediment to Arab economic integration. Whereas in many of the industrialized countries, direct taxes constitute the main budgetary source of revenue, in most of the Arab countries, indirect taxes are the principal source of revenue of the ordinary budgets (as distinct from the development budgets). Indirect taxes, mainly in the form of excise taxes and customs duties, constituted about 40 to 60 percent of the revenues of the ordinary budgets of most of the Arab countries during the early 1960's, whereas direct taxes constituted about 10 to 20 percent. Customs duties in many cases were the most important single source of revenue, accounting for approximately 20 to 40 percent of the total revenues of the ordinary budgets.[8]

In view of the heavy reliance placed by most of the Arab countries on customs revenue to finance governmental operations and programs, there has been a noticeable reluctance on their part either to negotiate comprehensive and substantial tariff reductions with each other on manufactured consumer products or to commit themselves, with regard to products on which they have extended preferences, not to increase the rates of duty. There has been no such commitment in any of the inter-Arab bilateral trade agreements or in the Arab League trade convention, and, as has been indicated, most of the Arab countries substantially increased their tariffs on a wide range of consumer products during the 1950's and early 1960's.

Although the Arab common market resolution does contain a commitment on the part of member countries not to increase their duties or taxes on the exchange of products with each other, there were, as indicated, a number of products reserved in part for customs revenue purposes by these countries from the staged reductions specified in the resolution. Moreover, Jordan requested at the time of the adoption of the Arab common market resolution that the other participating Arab countries indemnify it for any losses in total customs revenue that might arise from the implementation of the provisions of the resolution. Despite the fact that such losses would constitute essentially an internal transfer matter, the Jordanian Government's insistence on indemnification pointed up the importance attached to such revenue and the apparent reluctance to attempt to alter the internal taxation structure to compensate for such losses. Fiscal reform involving the imposition or modification and the collection of personal and corporate income taxes and other direct taxes has been a perennial problem for the underdeveloped countries with their low per capita incomes, dearth of industries, and scarcity of capital. In contrast, indirect taxes (such as customs duties, excise taxes, and various fees) have constituted less of a problem, both in collecting and adjusting.

The possibility of losses in customs revenue from economic integration tends to take on added significance for some of the less-industrialized Arab countries when considered in conjunction with some of the other factors mentioned in the preceding sections of this chapter. If the purpose of Arab economic integration is to accelerate the rate of regional industrial growth, then it would appear to necessitate a significant amount of trade diversion, and the Arab countries that would appear most likely initially to sustain losses in customs revenue from such trade diversion would be the less-industrialized countries since the more-industrialized countries would probably be in a better position to increase their exports of manufactured products. But, as indicated, the former countries might reap little in the way of benefits from any trend toward industrial concentration within the region and could encounter balance-of-payments difficulties. Moreover, trade diversion for the less-industrialized countries in many instances might entail the purchase of higher-priced regional products.

In view of the inequalities that might arise from economic integration among underdeveloped countries, it has been suggested that some kind of machinery—such as a common fund along the lines of the Solidarity Fund of the Central African Customs and Economic Union—should be established to transfer resources from the more-industrialized to the less-industrialized countries. Part of the revenue collected by participating governments could be

pooled in such a fund and could be redistributed among the participating countries with a view toward ensuring an equitable allocation.[9]

It has also been suggested that losses in customs revenue might
be avoided if underdeveloped countries undertaking regional
integration were prepared to replace their import duties on manufactured products that account for a substantial part of their
customs revenue with excise taxes that would be applicable to
domestic, regional, and extraregional products.[10] However, such
taxes on products not being manufactured in the importing
country would constitute merely a replacement in the form of
taxation, without effecting any substantive change in the form of
trade relations. Moreover, if such taxes were to apply equally to
regional and extraregional products, then the trade-diversion
effects dependent on tariff preferences would be impeded. In addition, where tariffs are used as both a source of revenue and a
means of protection, such a substitution could result in a loss of
protection for the domestic industries involved without effecting
any trade creation or trade diversion within the region.

As in the case of the other difficulties heretofore mentioned in
considering Arab economic integration, the difficulties relating to
customs revenue do not lend themselves to any easy solution. It
might well be that substantial losses in customs revenue would not
result from Arab economic integration. This would depend on the
pace, extent, and manner of regional economic development; the
height of a common tariff; the possibility of increased imports of
complementary products from outside the region due to possible
increases in the production and sales of products within the
region; and on a number of other factors. However, the fact that
customs duties are such an important source of revenue for most
of the Arab countries and that Arab economic integration might
result in a decrease in such revenue for some of the less-
industrialized countries points to the need for some compensation
mechanism or possible alterations in the taxation structures of the
countries involved as a part of the integration process.

Variations in Trade and Exchange Controls and Economic Relations with Third Countries

In addition to the aforementioned difficulties, there are also a
number of difficulties involved in Arab economic integration that

stem from the external trade and economic policies and relations of the individual Arab countries. As indicated in Chapter 5, there are variations in the trade and exchange controls of these countries, in their economic relations with third countries, and in their international patterns of trade—reflecting a number of economic factors that have conditioned to a large extent their attitudes toward Arab economic integration.

Kuwait, Saudi Arabia, and Libya (with large annual supplies of foreign exchange in the form of oil royalties but with a virtual absence of an industrial base) have shied away from participation in an Arab common market undertaking that in all probability would have eventually entailed the imposition by them of a comprehensive system of trade and exchange controls, with consequent restrictions on their capital movements as well as alterations in their patterns of trade. As in most underdeveloped countries, there is a preference in these countries for many of the consumer products of the industrialized countries, and the prospect of the utilization of their oil revenues and of uneconomic trade diversion within the framework of a common market to aid industrialization in the more-advanced Arab countries has apparently found little support in these oil states. Although a wider market could facilitate and accelerate industrial development in the oil states, these states appear to have strong reservations as to whether participation in an Arab common market involving socialist and more industrially advanced countries would in fact be to their benefit.

Lebanon, like the above oil states, has maintained an economic posture that tends to favor an outward-looking rather than inward-looking policy toward international trade and commerce. The dominant position of trade and other services in the Lebanese economy and its dependence on the inward flow of capital underly its laissez-faire character and the virtual absence of quantitative trade and exchange controls.[11] Industrial development for a long time has occupied a position of secondary importance to that of services in the Lebanese economy. Consequently, whereas Lebanon has pronounced itself in favor of free inter-Arab trade and the free movement of capital and labor, it has avoided becoming a participant in any regional undertaking that might necessitate substantial alterations in the Lebanese economy for the sake of industrial and economic development within the region.

Algeria, Morocco, and Tunisia also find themselves in an international position that militates against their participation in an

Arab common market. Although the very close economic ties that these countries had with France prior to their independence have been gradually loosened, their trade and economies are still oriented toward France, in particular, and the European Economic Community (EEC), in general. Most of their trade is carried on with France and the other EEC countries; they are still members of the French franc area; most of their foreign exchange supplies are in French francs; all, especially Algeria, have received from France sizable grants and loans, a substantial portion of which has consisted of tied grants and loans; French investments in the exploration and production of petroleum in Algeria have been very large; most of the petroleum that has been produced in Algeria has been shipped to France; Algeria, due to its former status as a part of the French policy, has been receiving from the EEC provisional duty-free treatment for its products and is seeking the continuation of such treatment; Morocco and Tunisia have been conducting negotiations with the EEC for the purpose of obtaining similar tariff treatment for their products; all three countries have applied preferential licensing and quota treatment to French products; and Algeria has been applying preferential tariffs to imports from France, as well as smaller preferences to imports from the other EEC countries.

Under such circumstances and in view of their long economic estrangement from the other Arab countries, these countries have not shown much interest in participating in a common market undertaking involving an Arab Economic Unity Council with authority to prepare a common external tariff and common quantitative controls, to approve or disapprove of the conclusion of trade and payments agreements with foreign countries, to coordinate the financial and monetary policies and the economic development programs of the member states, and to prepare programs for the realization of joint development projects. Participation in such a comprehensive undertaking under an Economic Unity Council headquartered in Cairo could easily jeopardize the present economic relations of these countries with France and the preferential position that they have or are seeking in the European Common Market. Maghreb economic unity, which apparently would create less economic complications within the broader international framework in which these countries are seeking to evolve, appears to be their more immediate goal.

The remainder of the Arab countries, except for the Sudan and Yemen, are the countries that have been participating in the Arab common market. All of the participating countries have been imposing high tariffs and comprehensive systems of quantitative trade and exchange controls that reflect a number of similar underlying economic factors—including a shortage of foreign exchange (except possibly in Iraq), the implementation of economic development programs with emphasis on industrialization, and a dependence on tariffs as an important source of revenue. Consequently, the establishment of a common external trade and exchange framework for these countries would not appear to involve as many economic ramifications as for the Arab countries heretofore mentioned in this section. This is not to say, however, that there would not be difficulties involved in the coordinating of the foreign trade policies of these countries for the purpose, to quote from the Arab Economic Unity Agreement, of ensuring the harmonization of a regional economy with the world economy.[12] It remains to be seen how far these countries, especially the socialist countries, will be willing to alter their patterns of trade with regard both to imports and to exports. This might well depend in large part on the terms of trade and the products sought to be exchanged within the region, the extent to which such terms would involve uneconomic trade diversion, the extent to which the diversion of exports to countries within the region and the importation of complementary products from countries outside the region would affect convertible currency supplies, and the extent to and manner in which convertible currencies and credits would be made available through regional institutions. The Comecon countries have encountered many difficulties in attempting to coordinate their foreign trade policies for the purpose of effecting regional economic integration, and it is not expected that under present circumstances the socialist Arab countries would find this task any less difficult.

Other Economic Factors

There are, of course, numerous other economic factors that constitute impediments to economic integration and to the creation of a viable regional entity; these arise from the underdeveloped state of the Arab economies and from the functioning of the Arab countries as separate economic entities. Inadequate transportation facilities and insufficient skilled labor and technical knowledge are but a few of the many impediments that the Arab countries have encountered in pursuing economic development within a national framework and that could limit the significance that the removal of tariffs and quantitative restrictions could have in creating a common market. As in other underdeveloped parts of the world, in the Near East the creation of a regional infrastructure, the development of human resources, and the acquisition of foreign technology are prime requisites for economic integration.

The impediments that arise from the functioning of the Arab countries as separate economic entities likewise are quite numerous. There are, for example, a number of Arab countries, besides the Arab countries with socialist economies, that have industrial laws that discriminate in favor of domestic capital and labor. Kuwait, for instance, requires that at least 51 percent of the capital of a company in Kuwait, except the petroleum companies, be owned by Kuwaiti nationals and that foreign firms doing business in Kuwait be represented by agents who are citizens of Kuwait or by companies meeting the foregoing requirement. [13] Such laws—which have their counterpart in most other Arab countries—have been obstacles in the path of the free flow of capital and labor between these countries and of the development of markets for their products.

Transportation laws have presented additional difficulties. For example, it was reported that in 1952 it took a truckload of merchandise seven days to travel 975 kilometers from Beirut to Teheran. The trip required six sets of customs formalities and documents, loading and reloading the goods onto four different trucks, and four successive drivers—a Lebanese, a Syrian, an Iraqi, and an Iranian. Under such circumstances, freight rates were found to be unavoidably high, and additional breakage and loss resulted from repeated handling. [14] A transit agreement signed on December 9, 1959, by the U.A.R. (Syrian and Egyptian Regions), Lebanon, Jordan, and Saudi Arabia was intended to eliminate such transloading requirements with regard to transit trade between those countries. [15] However, inter-Arab trade and transit trade through many of the Arab countries are still encumbered by transportation requirements and formalities.

Private and public monopolies that exist in the nonsocialist Arab countries, government purchasing policies, subsidies, differences in excise taxes, and various other factors have also constituted impediments to economic integration. As J. E. Meade has pointed out, there are a whole host of domestic economic arrangements that must be examined in attempting to effect economic integration. Although such arrangements may constitute impediments to economic integration, they may, on the other hand, also be perfectly legitimate instruments of policy for the attainment of certain other perfectly legitimate domestic objectives. Consequently, what is required is a selection and coordination of domestic economic policies that are effective for the attainment of the major aims of economic policy in the countries involved and also are compatible with regional integration.[16]

The Arab Economic Unity Agreement addresses itself to most of the aforementioned factors by providing in general terms that the parties to the agreement shall undertake to coordinate their fiscal legislation; unify their transport and transit regulations; coordinate their policies relating to agriculture, industry, and domestic commerce and unify their economic legislation in a way that will ensure uniform opportunities for their citizens; coordinate their economic development programs; and participate in joint Arab development projects. However, such measures have yet to be drafted and agreed to by the Arab countries that are presently participating in the Arab common market undertaking, and regional financial and development institutions have yet to be established to aid in the implementation of such measures.

OPPORTUNITIES

While there are a number of difficulties involved in Arab economic integration, there are also a number of opportunities for economic gains that could be derived therefrom. Such integration could result in the creation of a wider market for Arab industrial products, effect a greater and more economic utilization of regional resources for regional purposes, and lead to a larger flow of capital into the region and to additional markets for Arab products outside the region. In this section, these various aspects of Arab integration will be considered after a few comments have been made regarding the general rationale that has tended to evolve for economic integration among underdeveloped countries.

Rationale

The general rationale, which has evolved outside the static framework of traditional international trade and customs union theory,[17] rests primarily on the importance of industrialization to the underdeveloped countries. It consists essentially of two principles: (1) Protection is a necessary condition for economic development at the national level; and (2) group protection offers advantages over national protection in accelerating the rate of economic growth.[18] In support of the first principle, the underdeveloped countries have maintained for some time that they need to industrialize and that they would be unable to do so without furnishing their existing and contemplated establishments with protection from foreign producers—since such producers in the industrialized countries are much more advanced than are or would be their own—and without restricting the importation of many consumer products—since they must conserve their foreign exchange in order to buy the machinery and other capital goods that they need to industrialize. They have contended that their need for industrialization is obvious in view of the structural deficiencies in their economies, reflected by the limited amounts of cultivated and cultivable land within their borders, the existence of large numbers of underemployed and unemployed persons, and the low marginal productivity in agriculture caused by the population pressure on the land under cultivation. They have also contended that productivity is generally higher in industry than in agriculture, that demand for many of their products in foreign markets is inelastic, that their terms of trade have declined over the years, and that they have encountered balance-of-payments problems because of the fluctuations in the prices for agricultural commodities and their own increased demand for industrial products. Based on such contentions, their conclusion has been that industrialization, albeit fraught with difficulties, could result in an increase in their rate of economic growth and eventually in their standard of living.

In support of principle (2), the main contentions that have been made are that the domestic markets of the underdeveloped countries are exceedingly limited, that group protection could create a wider market for the products of the underdeveloped countries, and that such a market could better enable these countries to establish diversified and economically viable industrial structures and thereby accelerate their rate of economic growth. One writer summarizes these contentions as follows:

> Those who favor regional groupings of underdeveloped countries do so because they see great advantages in securing, for the agricultural and

industrial producers of each country, protected access to a region-wide market, instead of being confined within the limitations of narrow national markets. Such protected access would make it possible (a) for countries to use their existing agricultural and industrial capacities more fully in supplying one another's needs; (b) for new investment to take place in industries that would not be viable if confined to individual national markets; (c) for both old and new industries to reduce costs by benefiting from the economies of scale and specialization: in some cases this might help the industries concerned in the process of becoming fully competitive in world markets, including the markets of the developed countries.[19]

Whatever the criticisms of the contentions made in support of these two principles (and there have been many), the first principle has become generally accepted in the field of international trade and has been recognized as such by the contracting parties to the General Agreement on Tariffs and Trade.[20] With regard to the second principle, there appears to be a growing realization that the development of heavy industry in the underdeveloped countries, which is considered by many of these countries as the key to substantial economic progress, requires a broad market and that one of the ways of creating such a market is through regional integration.[21] The plausibility of this general rationale is dependent, however, on the implicit condition therein that measures can be adopted and means employed by underdeveloped countries participating in regional schemes to avail themselves of access to a broader market. Consequently, in evaluating regional integration it becomes necessary to expand the scope of inquiry. The economic gains from Arab integration would appear to be contingent not only on the creation of a wider market for Arab products but also on the implementation of a program of regional development and coordination as a part of the integration process and on the effecting of alterations in Arab trade and economic relations with third countries and international institutions as an outgrowth thereof.

Wider Market

The Arab countries, like other underdeveloped countries, have small internal markets which have hampered the growth and diversification of industrialization and which in turn have reflected the absence of a broad industrial base. There have been a number of factors responsible for the limited markets in the Arab countries for industrial products, including low per capita incomes, small and widely dispersed populations, and poor transportation facilities.

With regard to industrialization in Libya, the International Bank Mission to Libya in 1959 stated in its report:

> The Libyan market is much too small and widely dispersed for the development of manufacturing on a large scale. . . . This market is small, not only because of Libya's limited population, but even more because of the uneven distribution of the people among the main settled regions, divided from each other by large uninhabited areas. Social and economic differences between the nomadic, the settled rural and the urban populations and the considerable differences in their purchasing power and patterns of consumption have further split up the market, restricting the scope for large industrial units and narrowing down the range of products for which local manufacture is economic.[22]

Similar statements are contained in the International Bank reports on Jordan[23] and Syria.[24] In the report on Syria, it was stated:

> The expansion and, above all, the diversification of industrial output in Syria is restricted by the rather small domestic market. In a country of only 3.6 million people with low purchasing power it is generally possible to manufacture only a limited range of articles which are used widely enough to warrant production on an economic scale. Broader industrial opportunities are likely to emerge only if a larger market is initially available.[25]

The markets in the other Arab countries are also small and for much the same reasons. Although the U.A.R. has a relatively large population, its domestic market has been limited by a number of factors, including a very low per capita income. Charles Issawi has observed:

> The Egyptian population is sufficiently big to support most industries at an adequate scale. But this is largely offset by the low per-capita income owing to the small percentage of the population engaged in the labour force and the low productivity per man, especially in agriculture and some services. As a result, the total output of Egypt is probably not much larger than that of a city like Baltimore with a million inhabitants. . . . The purchasing power available for industrial goods is, however, much smaller than that of Baltimore.[26]

The small markets in the Arab countries have constituted an impediment to industrialization with regard both to the establishment of new industries and to the operation of existing industries. The absence or slow development of a petrochemical industry in the Arab countries is especially noticeable in view of the keen interest shown in such an industry by many of the Arab countries due to the existence in the region of large supplies of petroleum. The Little report, submitted to the Iraqi Government during the 1950's as a plan for industrial development in Iraq, stressed that the Iraqi market was far too small to justify a substantial program of industrial expansion, particularly if Iraq was to make use of its chemical resources. The report stated that the domestic market for chemicals was so limited that even medium-size chemical plants, in order to be economically successful, would be fairly large in comparison with domestic consumption. The report pointed out the complexities of a chemical industry and of the interdependence of plants within such an industry. Not only are production costs closely related to plant size, but one plant often produces a number of joint products or by-products, and it is generally not economically sound to build a plant unless there is a potential market for all of its products. Despite its large sale of products to other industries, today's chemical industry is its own best customer. In most countries it consists of a number of complex, interdependent plants. The Little report emphasized that Iraq could not escape conformity with this pattern.[27]

Similar statements are contained in a report on Saudi Arabia by the International Bank:

> The development of a petrochemical industry in Saudi Arabia is a special problem that should be handled entirely separate and apart from general industrial development and in much the same way that the oil industry is handled. Petrochemicals require a huge plant with a high rate of productivity, a diverse range of products that necessitates a wide market to sustain, and a large and experienced management and staff.[28]

Much the same reasoning would appear to apply to the development of an iron and steel industry, a machinery and machine tool industry, and various other industries—including a number of industries that produce heavy consumer products. The capital-output ratio for such industries would be exceedingly high if they were to depend solely on the internal Arab markets. Although the U.A.R. has established an iron and steel industry and has begun to produce certain machinery, its production of such articles has been quite small and its costs have been quite high.

The traditional industries in the Arab countries have also been adversely affected by the limited outlets for their products. Syria, for example, had a great deal of excess capacity in many of its industries during the 1950's even though it had been pursuing a protectionist policy for many years. The International Bank report on Syria pointed out that various industries were overequipped in relation to the market outlets for their products and to the available raw material supply. The following statement from the report will give some idea of the problems involving excess capacity that Syrian industries have encountered:

> Some industries . . . seem as a whole to be overequipped . . . . A striking example is the installed capacity in the cotton ginning industry, which could handle two and three times the present cotton crop. . . . The government has accordingly prohibited the importation of cotton gins. [Another example is] the vegetable oil industry. . . . As a complement to the protection of local cotton seed, the government has also placed an embargo on the importation of vegetable oils. A third instance of overequipment is in the glass industry: the Damascus factory was designed and installed on the basis of the rather ambitious notion that it should serve most of the needs of the Middle East. Some of its machinery, as for instance that for the manufacture of electric bulbs, has never been in operation. Although most of the items it produces may not be imported into Syria and although recently exports to Lebanon and Jordan, where its glass is admitted duty free, have been increasing, the plant is running much below capacity. A fourth instance is the match industry, which has a capacity much in excess of the requirements of the home market. This industry is also protected by an embargo on imports but prospects for increasing exports are practically non-existent; European matches are of better quality and have captured the Jordan market, Lebanon produces its own and Iraq is putting up a match factory. [29]

The U.A.R., notwithstanding its larger population, has had much the same problems involving many of its traditional industries. In a United Nations study prepared during the 1950's, the following observation was made:

> Despite the relatively limited extent of industrialization . . . there exist . . . a number of industries with excess capacity. . . . A number of enterprises, such as breweries and fruit and vegetable canneries, were either founded or expanded during the war to meet the demand of the Allied forces, and thereafter had to face a much smaller market. [30]

The industries that have been established in the other Arab countries have also been and will probably continue to be hampered by their limited domestic markets. In effect, the smallness of the Arab markets, in conjunction with various other factors, has prevented many of the domestic firms from achieving various internal economies of scale, from either establishing minimum efficient size plants or of operating such plants at an optimum level of production, from undertaking fully integrated production of a line of products, and from achieving possible external economies of scale that could accompany industrial diversification and expansion.

There appears to be little question that the establishment of an Arab common market could increase the opportunities for more diversified and economic industrialization within the region. The combining of a number of small markets does not necessarily result in a large market but it does result in a larger market. To what extent such opportunities would increase, of course, would depend in part on the eventual size of an Arab common market. And the size of such a market would depend not only on the number of participating countries, regional purchasing power, and adequate regional transportation facilities, but also to a large extent on the external control framework for such a market, the establishment of a payments mechanism to finance inter-Arab trade, and the trade policies of the socialist Arab countries. However, a wider market, regardless of its size, constitutes only one of the factors to be considered in determining the opportunities for economic gains to be derived from Arab economic integration. Access to a wider market is significant for the Arab countries only insofar as they are or would be in a position to avail themselves of such access. Hence, in determining such opportunities, it is necessary to consider the other facets of regional economic integration heretofore mentioned.

Regional Development and Coordination

The greatest opportunities for economic gains that could be derived from Arab economic integration would appear to emanate not simply from the establishment of a wider market but from the establishment of a wider market as a concomitant of a program of regional development and coordination. The benefits to be derived from a wider market would depend in large part on the increases and diversification in industrial and agricultural production in the Arab countries, but most of these countries possess inadequate amounts of foreign exchange to sustain a large-scale, national pro-

gram of rapid economic development.[31] They are heavily dependent on foreign sources of supply for machinery, parts, raw materials, and various other products, and they have outlets in such
countries for only a small number of their own products. Hence,
the establishment of a wider market among the Arab countries
might generate only a limited amount of economic growth.

However, if a substantial portion of the supplies of foreign exchange of all of the Arab countries, especially those of the oil-
producing states, were to be used as a part of a program of regional development and coordination within the framework of a customs union, then the opportunities for economic gains to be derived from Arab economic integration become more apparent for a
number of reasons. First and foremost, more funds could be made
available to expand output in existing industries, to establish new
industries, to increase production on land being cultivated, to
bring under cultivation additional land, and to create a regional
infrastructure; and second and almost equally important, there
could be a more rational and economic utilization of such funds
on a regional basis than on a national basis.

With well over $2 billion per year in ever-increasing oil revenues
accruing to certain of the Arab countries and with additional large
sums that have already accrued and that have been invested outside the region, the amounts of foreign exchange that could be
made available for regional development could be quite substantial. By utilizing such funds within the broader framework of
planned regional development and coordination, much of the industrial duplication that is contemplated by the Arab countries
could be avoided; the construction of larger and integrated regional firms and an integrated regional infrastructure could be undertaken, rather than the piecemeal construction that could result
from national planning; a fuller utilization of plant capacity for
regional needs could be effected; land with potentially high re-
turns could be improved, rather than resorting to submarginal land
that would require very large investments and produce relatively
low yields; and concomitant savings in foreign exchange could be
utilized for further industrial and agricultural expansion. Moreover, the use of such funds to implement a plan for regional development and balanced economic growth could accelerate the
effecting of a larger regional market, which in turn could act as a
stimulus to further industrialization.

In addition, in view of the difficulties heretofore mentioned, there is some question whether an Arab common market could be effected or, if effected, could remain in existence for very long without a program of regional development and coordination. For the Arab countries to function within the broader framework of regional integration would appear to necessitate the establishment of strong regional institutions which would be instrumental in formulating and giving a sense of direction to a program of regional development and coordination and which would be in a position to utilize or to oversee the utilization of a substantial portion of the region's funds for the implementation of such a program. Although the Arab Economic Unity Council has been given the task of coordinating the economic development of the countries presently participating in the Arab common market undertaking and of preparing programs for the realization of joint development projects in such countries, it has not yet been endowed with the financial institutions that could enable it to effectively perform such functions.[32] One of the primary weaknesses in the Arab common market undertaking, as of 1967, lay in the fact that the Arab countries that were in the best position to make significant financial contributions toward regional economic integration—namely, Kuwait, Saudi Arabia, and Libya—were not parties to the undertaking. [33]

Trade and Economic Relations with Third Countries and International Institutions

Although the utilization on a broad scale of regional funds for regional development and the creation of a wider market could present many opportunities for economic gains, the Arab countries still would require additional capital and outlets to establish and maintain a well-diversified and economically viable industrial structure. An Arab common market probably would not be adequate initially to sustain a fully integrated petrochemical industry, nor apparently would regional funds be adequate to fulfill all of the regional requirements for machinery, parts, raw materials, and other articles not produced within the region. Hence, in attributing opportunities for economic gains to Arab integration, one must also consider the effects that such integration could have on the trade and economic relations of the Arab countries with third countries and international institutions.

There appear to be two principal effects that integration could have on such relations. First, by negotiating as an economic entity, the Arab countries could strengthen their bargaining position in trade and economic negotiations with other countries and blocs. Second, by creating a larger, single market, undertaking a program of regional development and coordination, and functioning as a regional economic entity, they could place themselves in a position to receive larger sums of economic aid from private and public sources and could encourage the investment of larger sums within the region by private companies.

As small, underdeveloped countries, the individual Arab states have not carried much weight in the multilateral trade and commercial negotiations in which they have participated, nor have they been in a position to extract many concessions from the industrialized countries in their bilateral negotiations. The existence of large supplies of oil in some of these countries and their strategic or former strategic location have at times improved their bargaining position, but their position basically has been one of weakness rather than of strength.

For example, in order to gain additional outlets in the industrialized countries for their own manufactured and primary products, the Arab countries (together with other underdeveloped countries) have called upon the industrialized countries—as at the 1964 United Nations Conference on Trade and Development[34]—to remove various import restrictions, to grant preferential treatment to their manufactured products, to enter into international commodity arrangements, and to adopt various other measures. The underdeveloped countries have maintained that their own economic growth would contribute to that of the industrialized or developed countries and have sought unilateral tariff and quota concessions from the latter to enable the underdeveloped countries to earn the foreign exchange needed to diversify their economies. However, although these efforts have resulted in the adoption of some favorable recommendations by the United Nations Conference and in the issuance of favorable statements by some of the developed countries, they have not resulted in the adoption of many substantive measures by the developed countries.

It would appear that the Arab countries would be in a much better position to obtain their objectives in multilateral and bilateral negotiations with the industrialized countries if they were to negotiate as a single entity rather than as separate entities. By negotiating as a single entity able to speak for the entire region and its resources, they could assume a much more important position in international trade and commerce. Imports of any one commodity into any one of the Arab countries might be relatively small, but imports of such a commodity into all of them might be rather substantial. Likewise, exports of petroleum from one of the Arab countries might be more important to that country as a source of revenue than they might be to other countries as a source of supply, but there is little doubt regarding the importance of the total supply of Arab oil to the Western European and various other countries. In effect, by grouping their markets and resources, the Arab countries could assume a position of supply and demand that could enhance their role at the bargaining table.

Similarly, the establishment of a common market as a part of a program for regional development and the concomitant evolution of a regional economic entity could place the Arab countries in a position to receive more substantial loans and grants from various national and international sources. It would appear that loans and grants would be more readily forthcoming from foreign governments, private banks and institutions, and the World Bank and other international agencies for regional projects considered to be economically feasible than for similar national projects of doubtful economic feasibility. Moreover, the credit standing of the region as a whole, with its large oil revenues, would be much better than that of many of the individual Arab countries. For such reasons and others, there could well be a greater willingness by international and national agencies to grant or channel funds to or through a regional development bank or other regional institutions than there has been to grant or channel such funds to or through national institutions in many of the Arab countries. In this connection, it is to be noted that the United States and various other industrialized countries have made substantial contributions to the capitalization of the Asian Development Bank which was established in 1966 and that the United States has been the principal contributor to the capital funds of the Inter-American Development Bank.

Arab economic integration could also encourage the investment of foreign private capital within the region by giving rise to expectations of an acceleration in regional development. Whether and to what extent such investment would increase would depend in large part on the climate for private investment in an Arab common market. The climate for investment in the Arab common market as presently constituted would not appear to be such as to result in any substantial inflow of foreign private capital.

CONCLUSIONS

Four basic conclusions become apparent in evaluating Arab economic integration: (1) Such integration could prove to be a very effective instrument for the acceleration of regional economic growth if it were to involve the utilization on a broad scale of regional resources for regional development; (2) any such comprehensive undertaking would require a wide community of political and economic interests and aspirations; (3) such a wide community of interests and aspirations has been lacking among the Arab countries; and (4) underlying its absence has been the growth of political and economic nationalism in the Arab world and the virtual absence of Arab political and economic rapport.

Undoubtedly, the economic significance of Arab integration lies essentially in the utilization of the vast oil revenues of the region within a framework of regional planning and development. Such oil revenues could go a long way toward furnishing the continuing supply of foreign exchange that would be needed both to resolve the economic difficulties that could be encountered in the integration process and to create a viable regional entity. When considered in the light of such revenues and the region's large known oil reserves, balance-of-payments problems do not appear insurmountable, and industrial expansion and diversification assume much more realistic proportions. Without the utilization of these oil revenues within a regional development framework, many of the difficulties heretofore mentioned acquire much more significance and in turn tend to minimize the significance of the creation of a wider geographical market.

Although the presence of Arab socialism has changed the nature of Arab economic integration and could, in the absence of substantial transformations within the region, place limitations on the extent of such integration, it need not detract from the potential benefits that could accrue to the Arab countries from a regional approach. What it necessitates is a greater degree of regional planning and coordination on their part.

Any such comprehensive undertaking, however, would require a wide community of political and economic interests and aspirations to effect the mobilization of the necessary capital, the establishment of the requisite institutional structure, the adoption and implementation of the essential economic measures, and the concomitant compromises and adjustments. Implicit in such a broad undertaking would be a willingness on the part of the participating countries to surrender a substantial amount of their freedom of action with regard to the many matters involved in creating a regional economic entity.

But such a wide community of interests and aspirations has been the very ingredient lacking among the Arab countries. The evolution of separate and distinct Arab political and economic entities, possessing different political and economic systems and having vested political and economic interests, has created a situation in which the Arabs have found it exceedingly difficult to compromise their national interests for regional purposes. The geographical proximity and the ethnic and social factors that these countries have in common—including similarities in religion, language, and culture—have not been sufficient to supply the impetus. The political and economic factors have been the controlling factors, and although at times these factors have been such that the Arab countries have been willing to pay more than lip service to regional integration, they have not been such that these countries have been willing to pursue a course of action to effect it. It remains to be seen whether the vested domestic interests and political and economic differences within the Arab world will tend to proliferate and solidify so as to further impede Arab economic integration, or whether future political and economic developments will facilitate or create an impetus for such integration.

APPENDIXES

APPENDIX I

TRADE AGREEMENT APPENDIX

TABLE 1

CHRONOLOGICAL LISTING OF INTER-ARAB
BILATERAL TRADE AND PAYMENTS AGREEMENTS,
1920-63[a]

Countries	Type of Agreement	Date Concluded	Date of Entry into Force
Palestine-Syria	Trade	10/1/21	b
Syria-Transjordan	Trade	5/10/23	3/15/23
Iraq-Syria	Transit	1/16/25	4/1/25
Hejaz & Nejd-Syria	Trade	3/19/26	b
Palestine-Transjordan	c	2/26/28	b
Egypt-Syria	Trade	6/13/28	1928[b]
Egypt-Palestine	Trade	6/21/28	6/21/28
Palestine-Transjordan	Transit	9/26/28	10/1/28
Palestine-Syria	Trade	5/18/29	6/1/29
Egypt-Syria	Trade	3/11/30	3/11/30
Egypt-Palestine	Trade	1930[b]	6/11/30
Egypt-Transjordan	Trade	8/21/30	8/21/30
Egypt-Syria	Trade	10/11/34	10/21/34
Egypt-Palestine	Trade	8/18/36	8/18/36
Iraq-Palestine	Trade	12/14/36	2/14/37
Egypt-Iraq	Trade	5/16/38	5/16/38
Lebanon-Palestine	Trade	11/39[b]	12/1/39
Palestine-Syria	Trade	11/39[b]	12/1/39
Lebanon-Syria	Customs Union	10/1/43	1944[b]
Egypt-Yemen	Trade	9/27/45	b
Egypt-Transjordan	Trade	4/21/47	4/21/47
Egypt-Saudi Arabia	Trade & Payments	5/31/49	5/31/49
Saudi Arabia-Syria	Trade	1/29/50	3/12/50
Egypt-Syria	Trade	8/20/50	8/20/50
Iraq-Lebanon	Trade & Payments	2/20/51	4/11/52
Egypt-Jordan	Trade	8/5/51	8/5/51
Egypt-Lebanon	Trade & Payments	9/2/51	9/2/51
Lebanon-Syria	Trade	2/4/52	3/8/52
Jordan-Lebanon	Trade	8/27/52	3/10/53
Jordan-Syria	Trade	2/18/53	4/29/53
Lebanon-Syria	Trade	3/5/53	3/28/53
Egypt-Libya	Trade	6/25/53	6/25/53
Iraq-Jordan	Trade	9/30/53	6/22/54
Egypt-Saudi Arabia	Payments	9/5/55	9/5/55

Countries	Type of Agreement	Date Concluded	Date of Entry into Force
Saudi Arabia-Syria	Trade	11/9/55	3/16/56
Egypt-Syria	Trade & Payments	1/29/56	10/24/56
Egypt-Libya	Trade & Payments	5/26/56	2/14/57
Egypt-Lebanon	Trade & Payments	6/27/56	6/11&12/57
Egypt-Sudan	Payments	4/7/57	4/8/57
Iraq-Saudi Arabia	Trade & Payments	5/15/57	12/20/57
Egypt-Tunisia	Trade & Payments	7/2/57	12/31/57
Saudi Arabia-U.A.R.	Trade	2/21/58	9/21/58
Morocco-U.A.R.	Trade & Payments	7/31/58	11/6/58
Iraq-U.A.R.	Payments	10/11/58	10/11/58
Iraq-U.A.R.	Trade	11/15/58	1/17/59
Morocco-U.A.R.	Trade & Payments	7/13/59	7/13/59
Sudan-U.A.R.	Trade & Payments	11/8/59	7/1/59
Sudan-U.A.R.	Trade	11/8/59	12/7/59
Iraq-Tunisia	Trade & Payments	1/28/60	12/5/60
Iraq-Morocco	Trade	5/9/60	5/9/60
Libya-U.A.R.	Trade & Payments	5/12/60	6/1/60
Iraq-Syria	Trade & Payments	11/3/61	12/21/61
Saudi Arabia-Syria	Trade	11/16/61	9/10/62
Tunisia-U.A.R.	Trade & Payments	3/1/62	3/1/62
U.A.R.-Yemen	Trade & Payments	1/8/63	1/8/63
Algeria-U.A.R.	Trade & Payments	4/24/63	4/24/63
Algeria-Morocco	Trade	4/30/63	7/1/63
Algeria-Tunisia	Trade	1963[b]	11/1/63
Jordan-Saudi Arabia	Trade	1963[b]	1963[b]

Note: The dates in this table are set forth in month-day-year order.

[a]This table does not contain a complete listing of the bilateral trade and payments agreements concluded between the Arab countries from 1920 through 1963, nor does it contain a listing of the various amendments and protocols to such agreements.

[b]Exact date not ascertained.

[c]Exact nature of agreement not ascertained.

CONVENTION

FOR FACILITATING TRADE EXCHANGE AND REGULATING

TRANSIT TRADE BETWEEN THE STATES

OF THE ARAB LEAGUE, AS AMENDED[1]

The Governments of:

The Hashemite Kingdom of Jordan
The Syrian Republic
The Kingdom of Iraq
The Kingdom of Saudi Arabia
The Lebanese Republic
The United Kingdom of Libya
The Republic of Egypt
The Mutawakkilite Kingdom of Yemen

Being desirous of fostering economic ties between the States of the Arab League and of carrying out Article 2 of the Pact of the League of Arab States which emphasizes the necessity for close cooperation between States of the Arab League in financial and economic matters, including trade, customs, agriculture, and industry,

Have agreed upon the following:

Article 1

A. Exchange of Agricultural and Animal Products and Natural Resources.

Agricultural and animal products and natural resources included in List A annexed to this Convention shall be exempt from customs import duties, provided that they originate from the territory of a contracting party.

B. Exchange of Industrial Products.

Industrial products originating from the territory of a contracting party shall be accorded preferential treatment with regard to customs import

---

[1]By the first three amendments to the Convention.

duties. They shall be subject to a customs tariff reduced by the following percentage:[2]

1. Twenty-five percent of the ordinary tariff applicable in the importing Arab country for the products included in List B annexed to this Convention.

2. Fifty percent of the ordinary tariff applicable in the importing Arab country for the products included in List C annexed to this Convention.

C. Agricultural, animal, and industrial products produced in the territory of a contracting party and imported into the territory of another contracting party shall not be subject to internal taxes exceeding those imposed by the importing country on similar domestic products or on their component raw materials.

D. The Arab countries shall grant most-favored-nation treatment to each other with regard to import and export licenses, provided that import licenses for perishable agricultural products in Sections 7 and 8 of List A annexed to this Convention shall be granted readily and quickly.

E. Due observance shall be paid to the above without infringing on other privileges provided for in bilateral agreements already concluded, or to be concluded in the future, between the Arab countries.

F. All merchandise benefiting from a tariff exemption or preference must be accompanied by a certificate of origin from a designated Governmental agency. With regard to industrial products mentioned in List B or C, the certificate of origin shall conform to the following model: I certify that these articles are of _____ origin and that the percentage of Arab raw materials and domestic labor is not less than 50 percent of the total cost of production.

Article 2

Articles Subject to Government Monopoly

The provisions of this Convention shall not be applicable to articles subject to Government monopoly.

---

[2] Products assembled in the contracting countries and of which the cost of domestic labor or Arab raw materials, or both, comprised not less than 20 percent of their total cost were, if specified by the Arab League Economic Council, to be subject to a 20 percent reduction in customs import duties.

Article 3

Goods, the Importation or Exportation
of Which Is Prohibited

Goods, the importation of which is prohibited or becomes prohibited into the territory of a contracting party according to the regulations of that country, are liable to confiscation if imported from other countries unless a transit permit, bearing a customs seal, has first been obtained for their transfer to foreign countries. The goods shall not be returned to the exporting country.

Goods, the exportation of which is prohibited from the territory of a contracting party, shall be confiscated if imported into the territory of another contracting party. The customs authorities in the importing country shall be responsible for their return to the exporting country.

Article 4

Transit

A. The following are considered as being in transit across the territory of a contracting party: goods and personal effects—whatever their origin, whether or not transferred from one means of transportation to another, whether or not in storage, whether or not subject to alterations—the transport of which constitutes a complete transport, beginning and ending outside the frontier of the country crossed. Also considered in transit are new cars being transported by their own means, as well as livestock being transported by vehicle or on foot on the road from one of the contracting parties to another contracting party, provided such transit is in conformity with the laws and customs regulations.

B. Goods in transit across the territory of a contracting party shall be permitted to be transported by automobile, truck, or any other means of transportation without any restriction or discrimination as to their kind or nationality and without hindrance of any kind. Means of transportation registered in a contracting country shall be permitted to cross, without hindrance or discrimination, the territory of another contracting party for the purpose of transporting goods belonging to any one of the contracting parties.

C. Goods, personal effects, and their means of transportation belonging to nationals of a contracting party shall, while in transit across the territory of another contracting party, be exempt from customs duties, transit fees, and any other fees except what is reasonable for services rendered. Such fees shall not under any condition exceed those imposed on imported products by that country. Such goods, personal effects, and their means of transportation shall not be subject to any impediments.

D. Means of transportation belonging to a contracting party shall be granted sufficient facilities to enter and cross the territory of any other contracting party. The drivers shall also be granted reasonable facilities as to transit and residence. Such vehicles, however, shall not engage in internal transportation between any two localities within the country of transit. The special facilities to be accorded drivers shall not apply to persons whose entry into the territory of a contracting party is forbidden for security or health reasons.

E. Goods and personal effects sent from the territory of one contracting party to the territory of another shall be accompanied by a manifest of the transport company or its accredited representative. The manifest shall be approved by the customs authorities of the country of origin and shall be accepted by the country of destination when the goods and personal effects cross its frontier and when the customs authorities there are assured, in conformity with the regulations in force, of the validity of the customs seal affixed to the goods and the means of transportation.

F. The contracting parties shall, before the preceding provisions come into force, agree among themselves on the manner of implementing these provisions, on the proportions of the transit trade to be distributed among the vehicles of the contracting parties, and on the transit service fees and other fees.

Article 5

Goods liable to deterioration which are dispatched by transit across the territory of a contracting party to a third country must be exported or withdrawn from the customs within thirty days of their entry into customs custody. Unless this is done, the goods may be confiscated and sold by public auction, or destroyed, in accordance with the laws in force.

RATIFICATION OF THIS CONVENTION

Article 6

The Convention shall be ratified by the signatory countries in accordance with their constitutional procedures in the shortest possible time. The instruments of ratification shall be deposited with the Secretariat-General of the League of Arab States, which shall make a record of the deposit of the instrument of ratification of each country and shall notify the other contracting countries.

Article 7

The Arab League countries that are not signatories to this Convention may adhere to it by sending a notice to the Secretary-General of the Arab League who shall inform the other participating countries of such adherence.

Article 8

This Convention shall become effective one month after the deposit of the instruments of ratification of three of the signatory countries and shall become effective for each other country one month after the deposit of its instrument of ratification or its adherence.

Article 9

This Convention shall be binding for a period of one year from the date of its entry into force and shall automatically be renewed from year to year unless a contracting party shall, at least two months before the expiration of any annual period, notify the Secretary-General of the League of Arab States, in writing, of its desire to modify or withdraw from the Convention. The Secretary-General shall then notify the other contracting parties. The provisions of the Convention shall remain in force with regard to the other contracting parties and shall remain binding with regard to imports or exports made before the expiration of the annual period.

ANNEX NO. 1

List A: Articles Exempted from Customs Import Duties[3]

Section 1

1. Horses, mules, asses, and their offspring.
2. Cows, bulls, buffaloes, and their offspring.
3. Sheep, goats, and their offspring.
4. Poultry and game birds.

---

[3]Most of the product descriptions contained in Lists A and B were obtained from the translation of the Convention by the Arab Information Center in *Basic Documents of the League of Arab States*, Document Collections Number 1 (New York, 1955), pp. 30-35.

5. Bees.
6. Camels and camel colts.
7. Animals imported specially for the improvement of animal stock.
8. Livestock neither specified above nor included elsewhere.

Section 2

1. Fresh, chilled, or frozen meats.
2. Flesh of poultry and game birds.
3. Spiced or prepared meats.
4. Other meats neither specified above nor included elsewhere.
   N.B.—This section does not include meats imported in cans, pots, or jars, hermetically sealed.

Section 3

1. Fresh or frozen fish.
2. Dried, salted, or smoked fish.
3. Fresh crustaceans and molluscs (shellfish).
   N.B.—This section does not include fish imported in cans, pots, or jars, hermetically sealed.

Section 4

1. Fresh, skimmed, or dehydrated milk.
2. Fresh cream.
3. Eggs.
4. Honey.

Section 5

1. Animal materials, nonedible (such as guts, stomachs, bladders), either fresh, salted, or dried.
2. Sinews, scrapings of hides and skins used in glue-making, and cattle blood.
3. Raw skins and feathers of birds.
4. Bones, horns, hoofs, claws, and beaks.
5. Ivory, mother-of-pearl, raw coral, and yusr wood.
6. Sponges.

Section 6

1. Bulbs, tubers, onions, and roots of flower or foilage plants.
2. Cuttings, grafts, and berries.
3. Forest and ornamental plants and fruit-bearing plants.
4. Cut flowers for ornamental use.
5. Foilage, leaves, herbs, and moss for ornamental use.

Section 7

1. Mushrooms, fresh, dried, or truffled.
2. Fresh olives.
3. Salted olives.
4. Tomatoes.
5. Onions and garlic.
6. Edible roots and tubers:
   a) Potatoes for food.
   b) Potatoes for cultivation.
   c) Other.
7. Other edible vegetables and plants:
   a) Asparagus and artichoke.
   b) Cauliflower and cabbage.
   c) Lettuce.
   d) Haricot and other beans, peas, and other pulses.
   e) Cucumber, marrow, pumpkin, watermelon, and other melons.
   f) Edible vegetables and plants not specified above nor included else-
      where.
8. Pulses in the form of dried grains:
   a) Haricot and other beans and peas.
   b) Lentils.
   c) Vetches.
   d) Other.
   N.B.—This section does not include the abovementioned articles when
   imported in cans, pots, or jars, hermetically sealed.

Section 8

1. Dates (including stuffed) and natural molasses (treacle).
2. All fruits, fresh or dried.
   N.B.—The second item of this section does not include the articles mentioned if imported in cans, pots, or jars, hermetically sealed.

Section 9

Coffee beans, not roasted.

Section 10

Cereals:
a) Wheat.
b) Barley.
c) White maize.
d) Yellow maize.
e) Rice.
f) Other.

Section 11

1. Oleaginous seeds:
   a) Sesame.
   b) Aniseed.
   c) Cottonseed.
   d) Other.
2. Other seeds:
   a) Seeds of lettuce, spinach, turnip, beetroot, cucumber, carrot, yellow melon, radish, onion, cabbage, pepper, and parsley.
   b) Other.
3. Industrial and medicinial plants (tobacco and tombac (pressed leaves) excepted):
   a) All the various kinds of roots, flowers, herbs, leaves, barks, algae (seaweed, green moss, sea moss), and seeds used in medicine and not specified elsewhere.
   b) Other.
4. Herbs not specified nor included elsewhere:
   a) Thyme.
   b) Other.
5. Straw and fodder:
   a) Grain bark.
   b) Green and dried fodder and pods.
   c) Beetroot and grass roots.
   d) Other.

Section 12

1. Plants and their parts, fruits, pods, berries, walnuts, and seeds for dyeing and tanning, including powdered (ground) forms:
   a) Woods for dyeing (logwood, yellow wood, red wood, sumach, etc.) in stalks, sawdust or ground; and roots, scraps, leaves, berries, herbs, and twigs for dyeing.
   b) Barks for tanning, and barks, leaves, and twigs of sumach trees.
   c) Roots, herbs, leaves, blossoms, berries, grains, and plants for tanning.
   d) Gallnuts, acorns, and myrobalans.
   e) Henna in leaves or powder.
2. Gums, gum resins, resins, and natural balsams:
   a) Gum dragon and gum arabic.
   b) Natural balsams.

Section 13

1. Vegetable materials for wickerwork and mats.
2. Hard grains, husks (pips), and walnuts for carving.

3. Vegetable materials for padding, including those plaited.
4. Vegetable materials for making brooms and brushes, including those plaited, crude, decolorized, or dyed.
5. Other crude materials of vegetable origin not specified nor included elsewhere.

Section 14

1. Chalk and pigment powder:
    a) Ground chalk for building.
    b) Crude pigment powder.
2. Salt.
3. Sulphur.
4. Emery, pumice stone, and similar products, ground or unground.
5. Marble, alabaster, and crude granite.
6. Other crude stones for carving and building.
7. Gypsum.
8. Calcium.
9. Scrapings and fragments of pottery.
10. Carnelian.
11. Mineral materials not specified nor included elsewhere:
    a) Talc for industry.
    b) Other kinds of talc.
    c) Crude mica and quartz and glass sand.
    d) Ratbane.
    e) Asphalt for roads.
    f) Other.

Section 15

1. Wood for fuel, in round faggots or stacks, in twigs or bundles, wood scrapings, and sawdust.
2. Logs, rough, planed, or notched with spade.
3. Charcoal, in briquettes or pulverized.

Section 16

Raw hides and skins, cocoons, and raw wool, hair, and fiber.

Section 17

Cotton, flax, and hemp.

ANNEX NO. 2

List B: Products Subject to a 25 Percent Reduction in Customs Import Duties

Section 11

1. Cereal flour.
2. Potato starch.
3. Grain starch.
4. Bran of all kinds.

Section 15

1. Cottonseed oil.
2. Sesame oil (tahina).
3. Terebinth pistachio oil.
4. Linseed oil.
   All these oils in solid or liquid form.

Section 16

1. Preserved meat and meat products (pork excluded).
2. Preserved fish and fish products.

Section 17

1. Glucose.
2. Molasses.
3. Confectionery.

Section 18

Chocolate made with sugar from Arab countries.

Section 19

1. Products made of Italian paste (macaroni of all kinds).
2. Biscuits, with or without cocoa, fruit, or sugar.

Section 20

1. Preserved vegetables and vegetable products.
2. Preserved fruits and fruit products.
3. Other preserved plant products.

Section 22

Ethyl alcohol.

Section 23

Inedible molasses.

Section 25

1. Cement, other than white or colored.
2. Yemeni mineral salt.

Section 28

1. Anhydrous carbonic acid, compressed or liquefied by compression.
2. Oxygen gas, compressed or liquefied by compression.
3. Sulphuric acid.
4. Glycerine.
5. Patent medicines and pharmaceutical preparations.

Section 29

Positive and developed reels of film.

Section 30

1. Varnish, clear or mixed with coloring substances.
2. Paints and oil colors.

Section 31

1. Pure natural essential oils from plants of Arab origin.
2. Orange flower water and rose water.

Section 32

Household soap, in blocks or in flakes, excluding soap made from pure olive oil.

Section 34

Matches of all kinds.

Section 35

1. Manure.
2. Calcium nitrate.
3. Superphosphates.

Section 36

1. Tanned hides and skins.
2. Skins and leather of all kinds, bronzed, gilded, silvered, colored or covered with designs or relief ornaments or the like.
3. Dyed skins and straps, varnished or lacquered.

Section 37

Articles of leather.

Section 40

1. Walnut wood veneers.
2. Plywood.
3. Mosaic woodwork.
4. Wooden furniture of all kinds.

Section 42

Furniture of bamboo or wicker.

Section 44

1. Paperboard, without designs, rolled or in sheets, whose weight exceeds 300 grams per square meter.
2. Packing and printing paper.
3. Writing pads and exercise books made of paper of Arab origin.

Section 46

1. Artificial silk yarn of continuous fibers.
2. Artificial silk yarn of noncontinuous fibers.
3. Natural silk embroideries.
4. Trimmings of natural silk.
5. All other kinds of natural silk fabrics, pure or interwoven with other textile material of any kind.
6. Artificial silk lace.
7. Embroideries of artificial silk.

8. Tapestries of artificial silk.
9. Trimmings of artificial silk.
10. Fabrics made of artificial silk yarn of noncontinuous fibers, pure or interwoven.
11. Fabrics made of artificial silk yarn, pure or interwoven, when printed, designed or ornamented or jacquard-figured, whatever be the weight of a square meter thereof.
12. Fabrics made of artificial silk yarn of continuous fibers, pure or interwoven.

Section 47

1. Woolen yarns of all kinds.
2. Woolen carpets and rugs of all kinds.
3. Fabrics of pure wool, if of Arab woolen yarn.
4. Carded wool from Yemen.

Section 48

1. Cotton yarn No. 40 and above, nonglazed.
2. Cotton yarn below No. 40, nonglazed.
3. Cotton laces of all kinds.
4. Embroideries of cotton.
5. Ribbons of cotton.
6. Trimmings of cotton.
7. Floor carpets of cotton.
8. Other woven fabrics of pure cotton of any kind, whose weight per square meter does not exceed 110 grams.
9. Other woven fabrics of pure cotton of any kind, whose weight per square meter is more than 110 grams.
10. Woven cotton fabrics, interwoven with other textile material of any kind.

Section 50

1. Cotton, carded or combed.
2. Antiseptic cotton.

Section 52

1. Clothing fabrics of "tricot" for dresses of all kinds.
2. All other knitted articles, including underclothing, stockings, and socks.

Section 53

1. Clothing and parts of clothing made of any textile material.
2. Sheets of all kinds made of any textile material.

3. All other articles of Arab textile material, including blankets, towels, and tent cloth.

Section 54

1. Boots and shoes of all kinds made of leather of Arab origin.
2. Rubber boots and shoes.

Section 56

Parasols and umbrellas.

Section 58

1. Articles of Arab marble or Arab alabaster.
2. Articles of cement or ferro-concrete.
3. Articles of asbestos cement.

Section 59

1. Refractory bricks.
2. Ceramic tiles.
3. Sanitary ware, pipes, and fittings of terra cotta.
4. Artificial teeth.

Section 61

Yemeni carnelian products.

Section 62

Cooking stoves and heaters using fuel oil, made of cast iron, iron, or steel.

Section 63

Beds, tables, chairs, and other furniture of iron or cast iron.

Section 64

Brass taps.

Section 71

Printing type.

Section 72

1. Electric elevators, except for their motors.
2. Agricultural pumps, except for their motors.
3. Refrigerators of 20 cubic feet or more.

Section 73

1. Electric lamps with bulbs of Arab origin.
2. Automobile batteries with component parts of Arab origin.

Section 80

Military arms.

Section 81

Military ammunition.

Section 82

Plastic manufactures, except toys and ornamental and other objects listed under Chapters 83 and 84 of the League of Nations Nomenclature.

Section 83

Clothes brushes, shoe brushes, and paint brushes of all kinds.

Section 85

1. Metal threads used in textile materials.
2. Metallized yarn.

ANNEX NO. 3

List C: Products Subject to a 50 Percent Reduction in Customs Import Duties

Section 4

1. Butter.
2. Kashkawal cheese.
3. White cheese of all kinds.

Section 8

1. Apricot paste.
2. Raisin paste.
3. Date paste.

Section 9

Roasted and ground coffee, in containers, from Yemen.

Section 15

Olive oil.

Section 17

Sugar of Arab origin.

Section 20

Dehydrated onions and dehydrated garlic.

Section 23

1. Beetroot dregs.
2. Vegetable oil cake.
3. Artificial fodder.

Section 27

Asphalt, tar, emulsion, and similar petroleum products.

Section 32

Household soap made of pure olive oil.

Section 33

Glue of animal origin.

Section 40

Manufactures and statues of olive wood.

Section 46

Natural silk yarn and yarn of silk waste.

Section 49

Jute fabrics of domestic or imported fibers.

Section 50

Twine, cordage, rope, and cable of Arab textile material.

Section 60

1. Glass and crystal, sheet or rolled, of all kinds.
2. Glassware and crystalware, blown or pressed.
3. Bottles, phials, and flasks of all kinds.
4. Laboratory glassware.
5. Hollow glassware, table glassware, and toilet glassware (other than crystal or semicrystal).
6. Glass bulbs (for kerosene lamps).
7. Electric light bulbs entirely of Arab manufacture.

Section 82

Mother-of-pearl articles.

Section 85

Metal fasteners for shoes, clothes, and leather articles.

ECONOMIC UNITY AGREEMENT

BETWEEN THE STATES

OF THE ARAB LEAGUE

The Governments of:

The Hashemite Kingdom of Jordan
The Republic of Tunisia
The Republic of Sudan
The Republic of Iraq
The Kingdom of Saudi Arabia
The Syrian Arab Republic
The United Arab Republic
The Republic of Lebanon
The United Kingdom of Libya
The Mutawakkilite Kingdom of Yemen
The Kingdom of Morocco
The State of Kuwait

Being desirous of organizing their economic relations and of strengthening them on a basis that conforms with the natural and historic ties that exist between their countries and of realizing the best conditions for the prospering of their economies and the development of their resources so as to ensure the well-being of their inhabitants have agreed, in accordance with the following provisions, to establish complete economic unity among themselves and to realize it gradually but with the utmost possible speed that will ensure the evolution of their countries without prejudicing their vital interests:

Chapter 1: The Aims and Means

Article 1

There shall be established between the states of the Arab League complete economic unity that will ensure for these countries and their citizens on an equal basis:

1. The freedom of movement of persons and capital.

2. The freedom of exchange of domestic and foreign goods.

3. The freedom of residence, work, employment, and exercise of economic activity.

4. The freedom of transport and transit and of the use of the means of transportation and of the ports and civil airports.

5. The right to own, bequeath, and inherit.

Article 2

In order to achieve the unity specified in the preceding article, the contracting parties shall:

1. Make their countries a single customs entity with a unified administration and a common customs tariff and common customs laws and regulations.

2. Unify their import and export policies and regulations.

3. Unify their transport and transit regulations.

4. Conclude jointly trade and payments agreements with other countries.

5. Coordinate their policies relating to agriculture, industry, and domestic commerce and unify their economic legislation in a way that will ensure uniform opportunities for their citizens engaged in agriculture, industry, and services.

6. Coordinate their labor and social security legislation.

7. (a) Coordinate their governmental and municipal fiscal legislation and all other taxes and fees relating to agriculture, industry, commerce, real property, and capital investment, in a way that will ensure equality of opportunity.

   (b) Avoid double taxation of their citizens.

8. Coordinate their monetary and financial policies and regulations as a prelude to the unification of their currencies.

9. Standardize their statistical classifications.

10. Take any other action necessary for the achievement of the objectives mentioned in Articles 1 and 2.

In certain cases or as to certain countries, the principle of unification may be bypassed with the approval of the Arab Economic Unity Council provided for in Article 3 of this Agreement.

Chapter 2: Administration

Article 3

A permanent body denominated the Arab Economic Unity Council shall be established with the functions and duties prescribed by the provisions of this Agreement.

Article 4

1. The Council shall be composed of one or more full-time delegates from each of the contracting parties.

2. Cairo shall be the permanent site of the Arab Economic Unity Council, and the Council shall have the right to convene in any other place it decides.

3. Each of the contracting parties shall assume in turn the chairmanship of the Council for a period of one year.

4. The Council shall adopt its resolutions by a two-thirds majority of the votes of the contracting parties, with each country having one vote.

Article 5

1. The Council shall be assisted in carrying out its duties by economic and administrative committees, which shall work under its supervision on a permanent or temporary basis. The functions of these committees shall be determined by the Council.

2. The following permanent committees shall be established initially:

   (a) The Customs Committee to deal with technical and administrative customs matters.

   (b) The Monetary and Financial Committee to deal with monetary, exchange, tax, fee, and other financial matters.

   (c) The Economic Committee to deal with agricultural, industrial, commercial, transport, communications, labor, and social security matters.

   The Council may form other committees when necessary.

3. Each of the contracting parties shall appoint its representatives to the aforementioned committees, and each party shall have one vote.

Article 6

1. A permanent technical advisory office shall be established, composed of experts and technicians appointed by the Arab Economic Unity Council, and shall function under the supervision of the Council.

2. The permanent technical advisory office shall study matters referred to it by the Council or its committees and shall submit studies and suggestions to ensure the harmonization and coordination of the work undertaken by the Council.

3. The Council shall establish a central statistical office, which shall collect, analyze, and publish statistics as needed.

Article 7

1. The Arab Economic Unity Council and the organs under it shall constitute a single entity enjoying financial and administrative independence and having a separate budget.

2. The Council shall prepare its own regulations and the regulations of the organs under it.

Article 8

Within one month from the entry into force of this Agreement, the contracting parties shall designate their representatives to the Council and the committees provided for in Paragraph 2 of Article 5 of this Agreement, and the Council shall begin its work as soon as it is formed. The Council, as soon as it begins to function, shall proceed to form the organs to be under it.

Article 9

The Arab Economic Unity Council shall exercise all of the functions and powers provided for it in this Agreement and its protocols or necessary for the implementation of this Agreement. It shall have in particular the following tasks:

1. Administrative

    (a) Working on the implementation of the provisions of this Agreement and its protocols and all of the regulations and decisions issued pursuant to the Agreement and its protocols.

(b) Supervising the committees and other organs under it.

(c) Appointing employees and experts to the Council and the organs under it in accordance with the provisions of this Agreement.

2. Organizational and Legislative

(a) Preparing the tariffs, regulations, and laws for the creation of a unified Arab customs area and any necessary amendments to these tariffs, regulations, and laws.

(b) Coordinating the foreign trade policies so as to ensure the harmonization of the regional economy with the world economy and the realization of the goals of economic unity at which the Agreement is directed.

The conclusion of trade and payments agreements with other countries shall be subject to the approval of the Arab Economic Unity Council.

(c) Coordinating economic development and preparing programs for the realization of joint Arab development projects.

(d) Coordinating the policies relating to agriculture, industry, and domestic commerce.

(e) Coordinating the financial and monetary policies so as to effect monetary unification.

(f) Preparing unified transport and transit regulations in the contracting countries and coordinating the policies pertaining thereto.

(g) Preparing unified labor and social security laws and amendments thereto.

(h) Coordinating fiscal legislation.

(i) Preparing other legislation with regard to the matters mentioned in this Agreement and its protocols which is necessary for their realization and implementation.

(j) Preparing and adopting the budget of the Council and the organs under it.

Article 10

The expenses of the Council and the organs under it shall be covered by the joint revenues. During the period which precedes the realization of such revenues, the expenses shall be paid by the Governments in proportions that shall be determined by the Council.

Article 11

The joint revenues of the Council shall be divided among the contracting parties, by agreement between them, on the basis of a study to be carried out by the Council before the coming into force of the customs union.

Article 12

The Council shall exercise its powers under this Agreement and its protocols through decisions that shall be implemented by the member countries in accordance with their constitutional procedures.

Article 13

The Governments of the contracting parties undertake not to issue in their territories laws, regulations, or administrative decisions which would be contrary to this Agreement or its protocols.

Chapter 3: Transitional Provisions

Article 14

1. This Agreement shall be implemented in stages with the utmost possible speed.

2. The Economic Unity Council shall formulate, as soon as it is formed, a practical plan for the stages of implementation and shall determine the legislative, administrative, and technical measures for each stage, taking into consideration the special protocol to this Agreement ("Necessary Steps for the Achieving of Arab Economic Unity"), which constitutes an integral part of the Agreement.

3. The Council, in performing its functions specified in this Agreement, shall take into consideration the special conditions existing in some of the contracting countries without impairing the aims of Arab economic unity.

4. The Council and the contracting parties shall implement the measures specified in Paragraph 2 of this article in accordance with the provisions of this Agreement.

Article 15

Two or more of the contracting parties may conclude economic agreements between themselves aimed at realizing economic unity greater in scope than provided for under this Agreement.

Chapter 4: Ratification of, Adherence to, and Withdrawal from the Agreement

Article 16

The Agreement shall be ratified by the signatory countries in accordance with their constitutional procedures in the shortest possible time. The instruments of ratification shall be deposited with the Secretariat of the League of Arab States, which shall make a record of the deposit of the instrument of ratification of each country and shall notify the other contracting countries.

Article 17

The Arab League countries that are not signatories to this Agreement may adhere to it by sending a notice to the Secretary-General of the Arab League who shall inform the other participating countries of such adherence.

Article 18

Arab countries that are not members of the Arab League may adhere to this Agreement, upon approval of the participating countries, by sending a notice to the Secretary-General of the Arab League who shall inform the contracting countries to secure their approval.

Article 19

Any contracting party may withdraw from this Agreement after the lapse of five years from the end of the transition period. A withdrawal shall become effective one year after the Secretariat of the Arab League has been informed by the country of its desire to withdraw.

Article 20

This Agreement shall become effective three months after the deposit of the instruments of ratification of three of the signatory countries and shall become effective for each other country one month after the deposit of its instrument of ratification or its adherence.

SPECIAL PROTOCOL
REGARDING BILATERAL ECONOMIC AGREEMENTS WITH COUNTRIES NOT PARTIES TO THIS AGREEMENT

With reference to Paragraph 4 of Article 2 and Paragraph 2(b) of Article 9 (Organizational and Legislative) of the Economic Unity Agreement between the States of the Arab League signed in Cairo on June 6, 1962, the contracting parties are in agreement that the provisions of that Agreement shall not impair the right of any of the contracting countries to conclude separately for exceptional political or defense purposes bilateral economic agreements with a country not a party to that Agreement provided such agreements do not prevent the attainment of the objectives of that Agreement.

SPECIAL PROTOCOL
REGARDING THE NECESSARY STEPS FOR THE ACHIEVING OF ARAB ECONOMIC UNITY

Pursuant to Paragraph 1 of Article 14 of the Arab Economic Unity Agreement, which provides that that Agreement shall be implemented in stages with the utmost possible speed, the contracting parties have agreed on the following:

1. The Arab Economic Unity Council provided for in Article 3 of the aforementioned Agreement shall be established within the period specified in Article 8 of that Agreement.

2. The Council shall study during a preparatory period not exceeding five years the steps necessary for the coordination of the economic, financial, and social policies and the realization of the following objectives:

   (a) The freedom of movement of persons and the freedom of work, employment, residence, ownership, bequest, and inheritance.

   (b) The freedom of transit trade from any restriction or condition or discrimination with regard to the kind or nationality of the means of transportation.

(c) The facilitation of the exchange of Arab goods and products.

(d) The freedom of the exercise of economic activity, taking into consideration the avoidance of injury to the interests of some of the contracting parties at this stage.

(e) The freedom of the use of ports and civil airports so as to ensure their development.

The Council may, if necessary, recommend to the Governments of the contracting parties that the preparatory period be extended for a period not exceeding five more years.

3. The Council shall study the steps necessary for the achieving in suitable stages of the other objectives of economic unity and shall submit its proposals to the contracting countries for ratification in accordance with their constitutional procedures.

4. Two or more contracting parties may terminate the preparatory stage or any other stage and move directly to complete economic unity.

ARAB COMMON MARKET RESOLUTION

In carrying out the provisions of the Economic Unity Agreement between the States of the Arab League, the Arab Economic Unity Council, being desirous of achieving social progress and economic prosperity in the countries that are parties to that Agreement and of establishing economic unity on economic development bases that are sound, harmonious, and lasting and in conformity with the natural and historical ties that exist between them, and

Being desirous of achieving complete economic unity between the contracting parties and of uniting their efforts to achieve the best conditions for the development of their resources, the raising of their standard of living, and the improvement of their working conditions,

Has decided upon the establishment of an Arab Common Market with the aim of achieving the following objectives:

1. The freedom of movement of persons and capital,

2. The freedom of exchange of domestic and foreign goods and products,

3. The freedom of residence, work, employment, and exercise of economic activity,

4. The freedom of transport and transit and of the use of the means of transportation and of the ports and civil airports,

in accordance with the following provisions:

Chapter 1: Terms and Definitions

Article 1

The following terms shall be interpreted, wherever they appear, as follows:

1. Contracting parties: Member countries of the Arab Economic Unity Council.

2. Restrictions: Administrative restrictions imposed by any of the contracting parties on imports and exports, including import and export prohibitions, quotas, and licensing, and other trade restrictions.

178

3. Customs duties and other duties: Customs duties are those contained in the customs tariff schedule. Other duties are any other duties and taxes, whatever their designation, imposed on imported commodities. The following are not considered as duties or taxes:

(a) Duties, taxes, or fees imposed for services.

(b) Duties or taxes imposed on products or their raw materials imported from the contracting parties if similar domestic products or raw materials are subject to equivalent duties or taxes.

4. Agricultural and animal products and natural resources: Agricultural and animal products and natural resources of which the country of origin is one of the contracting parties and which are imported in their natural state.

5. Industrial products: Products manufactured in the territory of a contracting party, of which the domestic cost of production entering into their manufacture is not less than 40 percent of their total cost of production. Included in the domestic cost of production are imported materials which originate from any of the contracting parties and which enter into such production.

Chapter 2: General Principles

Article 2

There shall be the freedom of exchange of agricultural and animal products, natural resources, and industrial products between the contracting parties in accordance with the provisions of the following articles.

Article 3

The restrictions and various duties and taxes on importation and exportation presently in force in each of the contracting parties are fixed insofar as each party is prohibited from imposing new duties, taxes, or restrictions, or increasing those already in existence, on the exchange of agricultural or animal products, natural resources, or industrial products with the other parties.

Article 4

The Governments of the contracting parties shall apply to each other the most-favored-nation principle as to that which relates to their trade with countries not parties to the Economic Unity Agreement, provided that the provisions of this article shall not be applicable with regard to agreements presently in force.

Article 5

The Governments of the contracting parties are prohibited from imposing internal duties or taxes on agricultural and animal products, natural resources, and industrial products exchanged between the contracting parties in excess of those imposed on similar domestic products or on their raw materials.

Article 6

Agricultural and animal products, natural resources, and industrial products exchanged between the contracting parties shall not be subject to customs export duties.

Article 7

1. The reexportation to foreign markets of agricultural and animal products, natural resources, and industrial products exchanged between the contracting parties is prohibited without the prior consent of the country of origin unless they are subject to industrial transformations giving them the character of domestically produced industrial products of the importing country.

2. The reexportation to any contracting party of domestic agricultural and animal products, natural resources, and industrial products exchanged between the contracting parties is prohibited if they have been subsidized by the country of origin and if there exists similar production in the country to which they are intended to be reexported.

Article 8

No contracting party shall subsidize the exports of its national products to another contracting party if there exists similar production in the importing country.

Article 9

Existing concessions and monopolies in the territories of the contracting parties shall not be altered, except in conformity with the provisions of the Arab Common Market.

Chapter 3: Exchange of Agricultural and Animal Products
and Natural Resources

Article 10

Until specific schedules for the Arab Common Market providing for more favorable treatment are drafted by a technical committee appointed by the Economic Unity Council, the following provisions shall apply:

1. Agricultural and animal products and natural resources of which the country of origin is one of the contracting parties and which are contained in List A annexed to the Convention for Facilitating Trade Exchange and Regulating Transit Trade between the States of the Arab League, as modified by the first three amendments to the Convention, shall be exempt from customs duties and other duties. Customs duties and other duties on agricultural and animal products and natural resources not contained in the aforementioned list shall be reduced at an annual rate of 20 percent, commencing January 1, 1965.

2. The contracting parties shall work toward the removal of the restrictions on these products in five annual stages, commencing January 1, 1965, at the annual rate of 20 percent of these products.

Chapter 4: Exchange of Industrial Products

Article 11

Until specific schedules for the Arab Common Market providing for more favorable treatment are drafted by a technical committee appointed by the Economic Unity Council, the following provisions shall apply:

1. The customs duties and other duties on industrial products of which the country of origin is one of the contracting parties shall be reduced at an annual rate of 10 percent, commencing January 1, 1965.

The industrial products which are contained in List B annexed to the Convention for Facilitating Trade Exchange and Regulating Transit Trade, as modified by the first three amendments to the Convention, and which presently benefit from a 25 percent reduction in customs duties and the industrial products which are contained in List C and which presently benefit from a 50 percent reduction in customs duties shall be subject to the following reductions:

Date of Reduction	Rate of Reduction in the Customs Duties and Other Duties on the Industrial Products Contained in List B	Rate of Reduction in the Customs Duties and Other Duties on the Industrial Products Contained in List C
1/1/1965	35%	60%
1/1/1966	45%	70%
1/1/1967	55%	80%
1/1/1968	65%	90%
1/1/1969	75%	100%
1/1/1970	85%	. .
1/1/1971	95%	. .
7/1/1971	100%	. .

2. The contracting parties shall work toward the removal of the restrictions on these industrial products exchanged between them in ten annual stages, commencing January 1, 1965, at the annual rate of 10 percent of these products.

Chapter 5: Common Provisions

Article 12

Each contracting party shall deposit with the Economic Unity Council two months prior to the beginning of each annual stage:

1. A list of the agricultural and animal products and natural resources which shall be effectively exempted from restrictions during the coming stage and which shall represent 20 percent of such products.

2. A list of the industrial products which shall be effectively exempted from restrictions during the coming stage and which shall represent 10 percent of such products.

Article 13

Each of the contracting parties shall deposit with the Economic Unity Council prior to November 1, 1964, the following lists:

1. A comprehensive list of the restrictions imposed on the importation or exportation of:

Agricultural and animal products and natural resources.

Industrial products.

2. A comprehensive list of the customs duties and other duties imposed on imports or exports.

3. A comprehensive list of the domestic taxes imposed on industrial, agricultural, and animal products.

4. A comprehensive list of the taxes imposed for services.

5. A comprehensive list of the national products which are subsidized in any way, as well as the amount of the subsidy.

Each of the contracting parties shall inform the Economic Unity Council of any alterations in these lists.

Article 14

Each of the contracting parties may, for very justifiable reasons, request of the Economic Unity Council that certain products be reserved from the exemptions from or reductions in the customs duties and other duties and from the removal of restrictions. The Economic Unity Council is authorized to approve such exceptions and to fix the period of time for which each exception shall be allowed, which shall not exceed that of the implementing stages.

Article 15

All merchandise benefiting from a tariff exemption or preference must be accompanied by a certificate of origin from a designated Governmental agency.

With regard to industrial products, the certificate of origin shall conform to the following model:

"I certify that the commodities herein listed are of_____ origin and that the domestic cost of production, including Arab materials of which the country of origin is one of the countries participating in the Arab Common Market, is not less than 40 percent of the total cost of production."

The customs authorities of each of the contracting parties shall adopt the necessary measures to ensure that the commodities correspond with the certificate of origin.

Chapter 6: The Settlement of Current Transactions
Between the Contracting Parties

Article 16

Pending the institution of an Arab Payments Union and an Arab Monetary Fund for the contracting parties so that their currencies can become convertible between them, the following provisions shall apply:

1. The payments for goods and services exchanged between the contracting parties shall be made in accordance with the bilateral payments agreements in force between these countries.

2. In the case of the absence of a bilateral payments agreement between two of the contracting parties, the payments mentioned in the preceding paragraph shall be made in United States dollars, pounds sterling, or any other convertible currency agreed to by the two parties, and both of the parties shall undertake to permit the transfer of all amounts due to the exporting country without delay.

Chapter 7: Implementing Provisions

Article 17

In accordance with the provisions of Article 12 of the Economic Unity Agreement between the States of the Arab League, the contracting parties shall implement the provisions contained in this resolution in accordance with their constitutional procedures.

APPENDIX **II**

STATISTICAL APPENDIX:
CHRONOLOGICAL TABLES OF VALUE OF INTER-ARAB TRADE OF
IRAQ, JORDAN, LEBANON, SYRIA, AND THE U.A.R.

TABLE 2

IRAQ'S TOTAL IMPORTS AND IMPORTS FROM ARAB LEAGUE COUNTRIES, 1939-65

(Value in million Iraqi dinars)[a]

Imports c.i.f.

Countries	1939	1944	1951	1952	1953	1954	1955	1956	1957	1958	1959	1960	1961	1962	1963	1964	1965
Total Imports	8.16	14.22	50.87	61.78	68.40	72.68	97.16	113.43	121.78	109.80	116.48	138.91	145.67	128.76	114.00	147.45	160.93
Syria	0.16[b]	2.31[b]	1.73	1.38	1.18	1.19	1.40	2.34	2.50	1.84	1.22	0.11	0.53	2.04	2.53	2.26	0.33
Lebanon			0.21	0.26	0.33	0.35	0.81	1.01	2.19	1.23	1.94	3.93	2.33	1.63	1.85	2.82	3.70
Palestine	0.01[c]	0.58[c]															
Jordan	0.18	0.13	0.01	0.03	0.05	0.12	0.27	0.26	0.32	0.28	0.10	0.10	0.71	0.53	0.66	0.92	0.76
U.A.R. (Egypt)	0.01	0.01	0.13	0.11	0.14	0.18	0.25	0.42	0.75	0.31	0.18	0.02	0.10	0.19	0.33	0.98	1.21
Saudi Arabia	d	0.02	d	d	0.01	0.01	0.01	0.01	d	0.01	0.01	0.01	d	d	0.10	0.35	0.38
Sudan	d	d	d	0.01	d	d	d	d	0.49	0.52	0.63	1.11	1.13	0.27	0.33	1.07	1.09
Libya	d	d	d	d	d	d	0.01	d	d	d	d	d	d	d	0.01	d	d
Morocco	d	d	d	d	d	d	0.02	0.01	0.01	d	0.01	0.07	0.04	d	0.02	0.20	0.21
Tunisia	d	d	d	d	d	0.01	0.09	d	d	d	d	d	d	d	d	d	0.18
Algeria	d	d	0.02	0.10	0.06	0.01	0.07	0.04	0.06	0.07	0.02	d	d	d	d	d	d
Kuwait	0.01	0.04	0.01	0.03	0.01	0.07	0.05	0.07	0.01	d	0.01	0.01	0.01	0.01	d	0.01	0.01
Yemen	d	0.05	0.01	d		d	d	d	0.01	d	d	d	d	d	d	d	d

[a]Rounded to the nearest I.D. 10,000.
[b]Includes imports from Lebanon.
[c]Includes imports from Jordan.
[d]Less than I.D. 5,000.

Source: Derived from Iraq, *Bulletin of Foreign Trade Statistics* (annual) and United Nations, *Yearbook of International Trade Statistics.*

TABLE 3

IRAQ'S TOTAL EXPORTS AND EXPORTS TO ARAB LEAGUE COUNTRIES, 1939-65

(Value in million Iraqi dinars)[a]

Countries	Exports f.o.b.																
	1939	1944	1951	1952	1953	1954	1955	1956	1957	1958	1959	1960	1961	1962	1963	1964	1965
Total Exports[b]	3.52	9.17	27.01	18.77	19.07	17.97	15.92	13.17	12.88	14.25	11.46	7.98	7.87	19.32	16.73	15.29	18.12
Syria	0.10[c]	0.65[c]	0.51	0.71	0.96	1.08	0.64	0.65	0.45	0.68	0.60	0.46	0.27	0.58	0.45	0.55	0.73
Lebanon			2.24	1.02	0.64	0.54	0.91	0.76	0.61	0.56	0.98	0.85	1.14	1.79	2.20	2.55	2.54
Palestine	0.28[d]	1.62[d]															
Jordan			1.43	0.50	0.41	0.32	0.61	0.45	0.43	0.47	e	0.01	0.10	0.19	0.34	0.15	0.10
U.A.R. (Egypt)	0.04	0.04	0.76	0.51	0.55	0.26	0.25	0.10	0.34	0.33	0.16	0.07	0.07	0.12	0.07	0.39	1.95
Saudi Arabia	0.05	0.13	0.13	0.36	0.53	0.51	0.62	0.61	0.68	0.87	0.61	0.10	0.52	0.92	0.78	0.65	1.03
Sudan	e	e	0.04	0.04	0.07	0.04	0.09	0.05	0.04	0.02	0.03	0.06	0.05	0.07	0.12	0.07	0.06
Libya	e	e	e	e	e	e	0.06	e	e	e	e	e	e	e	e	e	e
Morocco	0.01	e	e	0.01	0.01	0.03	0.05	0.02	e	0.01	0.01	e	0.02	e	0.03	e	e
Tunisia	e	e	e	e	e	e	e	e	e	e	e	0.02	0.09	e	e	e	e
Algeria	e	e	e	e	e	e	e	e	e	e	e	e	e	e	e	0.02	e
Kuwait	0.05	0.14	0.59	0.75	1.47	1.11	0.68	0.90	1.43	1.16	1.13	0.86	0.65	0.01	1.30	1.59	1.62
Yemen	0.02	e	e	e	0.02	0.05	0.01	0.04	e	e	0.05	0.11	0.07	0.09	0.23	0.42	0.27

[a]Rounded to the nearest I.D. 10,000.

[b]Excluding petroleum.

[c]Includes exports to Lebanon.

[d]Includes exports to Jordan.

[e]Less than I.D. 5,000.

Source: Derived from Iraq, *Bulletin of Foreign Trade Statistics* (annual) and United Nations, *Yearbook of International Trade Statistics*.

TABLE 4

JORDAN'S TOTAL IMPORTS AND IMPORTS FROM ARAB LEAGUE COUNTRIES, 1938-66

(Value in thousand Jordanian dinars)[a]

Imports c.i.f.

Countries	1938	1944	1951	1952	1953	1954	1955	1956	1957	1958	1959	1960	1961	1962	1963	1964	1965	1966
Total Imports	1229	2986	15672	17335	18395	19841	27059	27819	30486	34029	40328	42935	41910	45629	50927	53558	56052	68212
Syria	176[b]	235[b]	1911[b]	1931	2713	2202	1811	1670	1940	2816	2958	2836	2084	2329	4863	2820	2835	3438
Lebanon				671	944	853	909	1191	1590	1204	1714	2219	1830	2129	2157	2554	3658	3773
Iraq	106	388	1775	738	759	666	1039	869	659	1274	212	49	442	753	596	305	271	1727
Palestine	46	689	c	c	c	c	c	c	c	c	c	c	c	c	c	c	c	c
U.A.R. (Egypt)	c	126	354	170	84	515	759	910	1175	1050	735	802	911	822	1218	1454	1278	1285
Saudi Arabia	4	76	301	386	408	453	732	1195	1641	739	531	2242	1246	1313	1733	1955	2135	2436
Sudan	c	c	c	c	c	8	10	3	7	105	322	263	272	229	303	311	176	374
Libya	c	c	c	c	c	c	2	c	3	c	12	27	28	8	81	40	4	10
Morocco	c	c	c	c	c	c	3	c	c	c	20	c	c	3	c	c	c	306
Tunisia	c	c	c	c	c	c	15	58	19	1	c	1	2	1	58	53	48	52
Algeria	c	c	c	c	c	c	c	1	c	1	7	3	c	4	5	7	5	28
Kuwait	c	c	c	c	c	c	c	c	c	c	c	c	150	c	c	c	c	c
Yemen	c	c	c	c	c	c	c	c	c	c	c	c	c	c	c	c	c	c

[a] Values in thousand Palestinian pounds for the years 1938 and 1944. Values rounded to the nearest L.P. 1,000 or J.D. 1,000.

[b] Includes imports from Lebanon.

[c] Less than L.P. 500 or J.D. 500.

Source: Derived from Jordan, *Statistical Yearbook* and United Nations, *Yearbook of International Trade Statistics.*

TABLE 5

JORDAN'S TOTAL EXPORTS AND EXPORTS TO ARAB LEAGUE COUNTRIES, 1938-66

(Value in thousand Jordanian dinars)[a]

Exports f.o.b.

Countries	1938	1944	1951	1952	1953	1954	1955	1956	1957	1958	1959	1960	1961	1962	1963	1964	1965	1966
Total Exports	472	1457	1041	1280	1900	2434	2619	4379	4302	3139	3098	3481	4252	4929	5523	7012	7753	8759
Syria	28[b]	15[b]	955[b]	567	687	683	708	1144	1197	971	718	658	814	856	957	817	833	1308
Lebanon		2	17	496	924	1202	719	1765	999	327	386	521	549	840	1022	1219	1981	1143
Iraq	c			51	139	339	438	443	465	305	179	148	353	505	607	736	570	1287
Palestine	445	1430							1					1	c	2	2	1
U.A.R. (Egypt)	c	c	24	c	3	13	9	5	1	5	1	1	1	1	c	2	2	c
Saudi Arabia		10	13	103	38	73	50	166	295	255	347	321	388	439	643	894	908	795
Sudan							c	c	c	c	c	c	c	c	c	c	c	c
Libya						1	1	1	1	1	1	1	1	c	3	1	4	1
Morocco													c	c	c	c	c	c
Tunisia													c	c	c	c	c	c
Algeria													c	c	c	1	c	c
Kuwait					5	18	45	118	209	263	398	461	501	763	789	972	1029	1078
Yemen												c	c	c	c	1	c	c

[a] Values in thousand Palestinian pounds for the years 1938 and 1944. Values rounded to the nearest L.P. 1,000 or J.D. 1,000.

[b] Includes exports to Lebanon.

[c] Less than L.P. 500 or J.D. 500.

Source: Derived from Jordan, *Statistical Yearbook* and United Nations, *Yearbook of International Trade Statistics.*

TABLE 6

LEBANON'S TOTAL IMPORTS AND IMPORTS FROM ARAB LEAGUE COUNTRIES, 1938-66[a]

(Value in million Lebanese pounds)[b]

Imports c.i.f.

Countries	1938	1944	1951	1952	1953	1954	1955	1956	1957	1958	1959	1960	1961	1962	1963	1964	1965	1966
Total Imports	70.81	93.66	320.99	343.91	363.76	485.13	529.57	561.19	626.57	518.33	699.83	854.60	1061.36	1049.56	996.59	1194.88	1791.87	2003.11
Syria	2.35	17.17	59.11	63.86	91.70	108.79	86.71	111.08	92.16	54.91	62.76	52.57	43.50	100.59	111.51	122.61	195.27	202.50
Iraq	0.23	0.30	23.69	17.79	15.12	16.99	23.21	20.78	22.76	21.84	15.55	9.43	8.55	18.80	27.10	28.19	48.28	58.73
Jordan			1.95	2.83	5.18	9.99	4.50	8.77	8.77	3.45	4.69	5.86	5.44	17.85	7.71	12.42	19.78	12.40
Palestine	4.33	13.02																
U.A.R. (Egypt)	1.91	4.11	4.60	2.39	2.99	5.13	7.37	10.26	12.78	8.71	12.07	32.15	51.68	9.55	12.32	13.63	20.12	14.18
Saudi Arabia	0.03	0.05	2.31	4.19	8.55	6.71	18.71	20.89	27.22	24.14	33.74	56.57	46.70	34.42	33.01	34.33	36.09	38.62
Sudan	c	c	0.27	0.66	0.67	0.17	0.28	0.64	0.49	1.30	1.09	0.96	3.00	1.49	2.83	2.63	2.98	5.87
Libya	c	c	0.27	0.44	0.04	0.09	0.09	0.04	0.32	0.61	0.07	0.06	0.09	0.12	0.13	0.23	0.13	0.20
Morocco	c	c	0.48	0.39	0.42	0.89	3.17	0.58	0.40	0.57	0.69	1.72	0.68	0.17	0.69	1.49	0.57	0.82
Tunisia	c	c	0.02	0.06	d	0.02	0.10	0.35	0.44	0.68	0.91	5.15	0.09	0.08	0.08	0.07	0.18	0.04
Algeria	c	c	0.37	0.53	0.83	0.41	1.08	0.85	1.16	0.39	0.67	0.53	0.39	0.65	1.23	0.20	0.62	2.27
Kuwait	c	c	7.28	0.82	0.43	0.58	0.94	1.14	1.70	0.66	1.88	1.47	6.25	1.72	1.86	1.92	1.41	2.17
Yemen	c	c	0.04	0.05	0.03	0.04	0.07	0.02	0.04	0.05	0.04	0.04	0.04	0.52	0.04	0.02	0.03	0.36

[a]The import values shown for 1938 and 1944 are the values of imports of Lebanon and Syria.
[b]Rounded to the nearest L.L. 10,000.
[c]Not obtained.
[d]Less than L.L. 5,000.
Source: Derived from Lebanon, *Statistiques du Commerce Extérieur* (annual) and United Nations, *Yearbook of International Trade Statistics.*

TABLE 7

LEBANON'S TOTAL EXPORTS AND EXPORTS TO ARAB LEAGUE COUNTRIES, 1938-66[a]

(Value in million Lebanese pounds)[b]

Exports f.o.b.

Countries	1938	1944	1951	1952	1953	1954	1955	1956	1957	1958	1959	1960	1961	1962	1963	1964	1965	1966
Total Exports[c]	29.28	46.20	97.59	77.59	86.68	105.60	120.60	145.80	152.33	110.51	139.10	218.04	397.27	192.04	196.33	216.05	324.06	369.47
Syria			22.02	16.62	13.74	14.97	13.37	16.33	18.26	19.32	20.66	18.60	20.78	28.20	21.71	24.20	22.65	24.00
Iraq	0.96	6.12	2.62	2.74	4.50	4.59	6.70	4.75	9.07	5.15	9.78	16.13	10.85	9.34	6.81	12.61	23.12	29.26
Jordan	1.23	1.44	3.64	3.34	6.09	5.28	5.74	7.85	10.87	9.95	12.14	17.39	31.61	17.53	19.45	19.72	27.14	28.89
Palestine	8.07	8.00																
U.A.R. (Egypt)	1.66	2.83	9.42	6.60	5.99	8.76	6.70	6.05	5.18	1.89	2.21	1.76	2.19	2.98	2.01	3.25	3.44	4.05
Saudi Arabia	0.26	0.47	8.08	7.28	9.94	11.94	11.72	16.45	19.37	13.49	17.40	43.36	79.26	23.33	23.84	34.91	83.64	78.92
Sudan	d	d	1.24	0.97	0.05	0.40	0.45	0.64	0.94	0.19	1.94	1.22	0.87	2.50	1.96	2.84	1.97	1.53
Libya	d	d	0.01	0.31	0.62	0.49	0.20	0.22	0.16	0.28	0.41	0.72	0.49	0.72	1.10	1.66	8.27	17.32
Morocco	d	d	0.35	0.03	0.03	e	0.07	1.10	0.42	0.29	0.25	0.14	0.17	0.25	0.54	0.41	0.40	0.57
Tunisia	d	d	0.01	0.38	0.13	e	0.11	0.60	0.14	0.16	0.11	0.01	0.19	0.16	0.13	0.21	0.19	0.24
Algeria	d	d	0.02	0.04	0.21	0.41	2.09	0.23	0.37	0.28	0.14	0.16	0.20	0.56	0.41	0.38	0.44	0.81
Kuwait	d	d	0.78	1.99	5.35	11.49	15.08	13.56	13.39	8.42	16.47	40.96	121.41	18.39	16.63	18.76	18.49	28.49
Yemen			e	e	e	e	e	e	e	0.03	0.02	0.04	0.12	0.01	e	0.01	0.01	0.04

[a]The export values shown for 1938 and 1944 are the values of exports of Lebanon and Syria.

[b]Rounded to the nearest L.L. 10,000.

[c]Includes reexports.

[d]Not obtained.

[e]Less than L.L. 5,000.

Source: Derived from Lebanon, *Statistiques du Commerce Extérieur* (annual) and United Nations, *Yearbook of International Trade Statistics.*

191

TABLE 8

SYRIA'S TOTAL IMPORTS AND IMPORTS FROM ARAB LEAGUE COUNTRIES, 1938-66[a]

(Value in million Syrian pounds)[b]

Imports c.i.f.

Countries	1938	1944	1951	1952	1953	1954	1955	1956	1957	1958	1959	1960	1961	1962	1963	1964	1965	1966
Total Imports	70.81	93.66	303.95	313.33	307.05	408.11	430.53	449.28	616.06	752.62	678.49	858.28	711.32	862.28	896.23	898.42	812.21	1103.44
Lebanon	2.35	17.17	34.09	35.72	33.38	38.57	25.32	40.19	24.60	37.31	29.05	28.67	22.99	30.95	39.57	52.28	37.78	37.07
Iraq	0.23	0.30	8.93	8.53	8.33	6.17	26.53	28.31	34.02	24.22	14.98	44.76	47.00	49.52	55.14	65.02	66.60	69.69
Jordan			4.35	6.00	8.31	9.08	9.44	10.08	12.59	10.34	7.65	7.46	9.03	10.03	11.60	8.82	9.86	15.27
Palestine	4.33	13.02																
U.A.R. (Egypt)	1.91	4.11	3.70	1.37	0.83	4.79	6.82	8.34	14.26	25.51	41.80	52.48	67.66	3.22	12.52	15.71	8.02	6.16
Saudi Arabia	0.03	0.05	3.56	7.91	11.86	14.72	14.90	22.36	30.78	18.75	5.24	2.92	1.31	1.91	1.95	2.43	1.63	1.18
Sudan	c	c	0.05	0.43	0.39	0.33	0.31	0.37	0.53	1.05	1.98	1.48	0.67	0.87	3.65	2.04	1.96	2.96
Libya	c	c	d	0.04	0.01	0.01	0.58	0.04	0.04	0.14	0.17	0.14	0.03	0.09	0.13	0.30	0.11	0.07
Morocco	c	c	0.12	0.24	0.23	0.34	0.10	0.19	0.06	0.09	0.26	0.77	0.22	0.20	0.12	0.10	0.10	0.18
Tunisia	c	c	0.22	0.03	d	0.01	0.01	0.05	0.02	0.08	0.54	1.87	0.27	0.07	0.52	0.03	0.08	d
Algeria	c	c	0.12	0.87	0.24	0.48	0.49	0.75	1.74	1.34	0.29	0.31	0.19	1.01	0.78	0.53	0.27	1.02
Kuwait	c	c	0.17	0.03	0.10	0.40	0.50	0.18	1.48	3.70	2.00	1.76	0.86	0.88	11.54	7.96	4.29	0.51
Yemen	c	c	0.03	0.09	0.03	0.03	0.04	d	0.02	d	d	d	d	d	d	d	d	d

[a]The import values shown for 1938 and 1944 are the values of imports of Syria and Lebanon.

[b]Rounded to the nearest L.S. 10,000.

[c]Not obtained.

[d]Less than L.S. 5,000.

Source: Derived from Syria, Statistiques du Commerce Extérieur (annual) and United Nations, Yearbook of International Trade Statistics.

TABLE 9

SYRIA'S TOTAL EXPORTS AND EXPORTS TO ARAB LEAGUE COUNTRIES, 1938-66[a]

(Value in million Syrian pounds)[b]

Countries	Exports f.o.b.																	
	1938	1944	1951	1952	1953	1954	1955	1956	1957	1958	1959	1960	1961	1962	1963	1964	1965	1966
Total Exports[c]	29.28	46.20	277.13	319.39	375.83	465.74	473.54	515.92	547.99	436.70	424.60	405.19	394.73	617.16	720.92	672.59	643.74	661.39
Lebanon			59.45	70.28	90.38	123.81	101.14	120.67	92.96	56.85	52.46	48.48	41.02	92.62	111.35	116.26	139.80	117.75
Iraq	0.96	6.12	20.25	17.18	17.36	16.26	21.82	28.94	25.77	19.11	11.76	2.53	8.92	21.64	25.73	26.06	5.26	7.60
Jordan	1.23	1.44	12.35	16.85	21.71	20.94	17.24	15.09	17.77	22.70	23.62	24.07	19.13	21.98	40.95	26.00	25.16	32.12
Palestine	8.07	8.00																
U.A.R. (Egypt)	1.66	2.83	7.20	4.33	3.43	3.06	5.17	9.03	31.79	16.58	68.38	60.98	42.74	5.26	0.38	0.29	2.02	3.16
Saudi Arabia	0.26	0.47	8.49	10.33	12.19	12.00	10.79	19.31	22.34	24.92	20.39	26.82	15.12	18.36	19.02	27.04	34.42	23.67
Sudan	d	d	0.22	0.41	0.38	0.21	0.28	0.21	0.39	0.46	0.65	0.16	0.44	0.82	0.92	0.66	0.88	0.74
Libya	d	d	e	0.03	0.59	0.16	0.14	0.38	0.54	0.04	0.11	0.49	0.52	0.47	1.25	5.83	3.87	4.10
Morocco	d	d	0.10	0.15	0.69	0.15	1.24	0.57	1.10	0.05	0.01	0.10	0.13	0.12	0.18	e	0.10	0.01
Tunisia	d	d	0.08	e	0.24	0.08	0.13	0.51	0.11	0.29	0.01	0.01	e	0.03	e	e	0.01	0.01
Algeria	d	d	0.07	0.06	0.74	0.21	0.08	1.27	0.02	e	0.02	e	e	3.32	0.25	0.16	0.32	0.30
Kuwait	d	d	1.20	1.68	1.91	3.83	12.19	14.72	8.76	11.29	12.80	11.62	6.40	7.26	7.45	8.01	10.41	9.46
Yemen	d	d	0.04	0.04	e	e	e	e	e	e	0.01	0.02	e	e	0.08	0.04	0.06	0.01

[a]The export values shown for 1938 and 1944 are the values of exports of Syria and Lebanon.

[b]Rounded to the nearest L.S. 10,000.

[c]Includes reexports.

[d]Not obtained.

[e]Less than L.S. 5,000.

Source: Derived from Syria, *Statistiques du Commerce Extérieur* (annual) and United Nations, *Yearbook of International Trade Statistics*.

TABLE 10

U.A.R.'S (EGYPT'S) TOTAL IMPORTS AND IMPORTS FROM ARAB LEAGUE COUNTRIES, 1938-65

(Value in million Egyptian pounds)[a]

Countries	Imports c.i.f.																
	1938	1944	1951	1952	1953	1954	1955	1956	1957	1958	1959	1960	1961	1962	1963	1964	1965
Total Imports[b]	36.93	51.01	279.80	225.80	175.22	161.42	182.92	186.13	182.56	240.17	222.17	232.48	243.78	300.92	398.36	414.62	405.88
Syria	0.20[c]	0.43[c]	1.07	0.48	0.62	0.65	0.91	1.42	3.46	1.92	7.74	7.40	5.72	0.79	0.22	0.13	0.80
Lebanon			1.98	1.45	0.77	0.92	1.27	0.81	2.10	0.91	0.73	0.36	0.59	0.59	0.66	0.96	0.91
Palestine	0.28[d]	2.29[d]															
Jordan			0.04	0.02	0.02	0.03	0.02	0.01	0.04	0.01	0.01	e	0.01	e	0.01	0.01	0.01
Iraq	0.16	4.08	3.21	2.98	0.75	0.30	0.34	0.33	0.53	0.41	0.27	0.06	0.13	0.11	0.23	0.32	3.58
Saudi Arabia	0.14	0.45	2.84	3.45	4.97	5.62	5.24	4.08	5.99	5.14	5.87	8.03	7.14	7.59	11.60	9.80	10.23
Sudan	0.82[f]	2.60[f]	3.02[f]	3.45[f]	2.18[f]	3.11[f]	4.33[f]	4.68	4.91	2.73	1.80	2.50	3.35	3.30	6.15	3.30	3.58
Libya	0.01	0.16	0.68	0.44	0.42	0.49	0.46	0.38	0.68	0.96	1.39	0.37	0.07	0.06	0.06	5.47	5.38
Morocco	0.01	e	0.50	0.24	0.28	0.19	0.22	0.15	e	0.06	0.22	0.29	e	0.25	0.38	0.38	0.31
Tunisia	0.04	e	0.20	0.07	0.08	0.07	0.08	0.21	0.02	0.17	0.03	e	e	0.01	0.27	0.45	0.39
Algeria	0.03	0.01	0.38	0.25	0.37	0.15	0.19	0.06	e	e	e	0.03	e	e	e	0.99	1.14
Kuwait	g	g	g	g	g	g	g	g	g	g	g	0.09	0.06	5.01	7.50	11.20	5.23
Yemen	0.03	0.04	0.02	0.06	0.03	0.04	0.05	0.03	0.03	0.05	0.18	0.07	0.04	0.02	0.17	0.05	0.06

[a]Rounded to the nearest L.E. 10,000.
[b]Excluding imports from the Sudan prior to 1956.
[c]Includes imports from Lebanon.
[d]Includes imports from Jordan.
[e]Less than L.E. 5,000.
[f]Includes all merchandise arriving from the Sudan.
[g]Not reported separately.

Source: Derived from U.A.R. (Egypt), *Annual Statement of Foreign Trade* and United Nations, *Yearbook of International Trade Statistics.*

TABLE 11

U.A.R.'S (EGYPT'S) TOTAL EXPORTS AND EXPORTS TO ARAB LEAGUE COUNTRIES, 1938-65

(Value in million Egyptian pounds)[a]

Exports f.o.b.

Countries	1938	1944	1951	1952	1953	1954	1955	1956	1957	1958	1959	1960	1961	1962	1963	1964	1965
Total Exports[b]	29.34	26.95	200.64	142.85	135.86	136.71	137.01	140.94	170.26	165.10	159.14	196.49	167.44	157.45	226.80	234.38	263.13
Syria	0.25[c]	0.17[c]	0.55	0.14	0.12	0.81	0.93	1.31	1.41	2.47	6.09	5.89	7.47	0.40	1.44	1.70	0.85
Lebanon			0.60	0.70	0.66	1.48	1.38	2.01	3.47	1.85	2.45	1.88	2.31	2.19	3.10	3.20	3.41
Palestine	0.41[d]	1.31[d]															
Jordan	0.07	0.12	0.42	0.12	0.07	0.39	0.61	0.90	0.98	0.37	0.49	0.58	0.76	0.84	1.48	0.75	1.50
Iraq	0.12	0.25	0.07	0.08	0.09	0.12	0.14	0.08	0.12	0.19	0.09	0.07	0.26	0.16	0.53	1.17	1.42
Saudi Arabia	0.12	0.25	0.54	0.68	1.42	1.81	1.99	1.75	3.35	2.96	2.61	2.90	3.02	2.49	1.43	1.48	1.58
Sudan	1.11[e]	1.86[e]	4.26[e]	5.06[e]	5.21[e]	5.58[e]	7.62[e]	9.06	7.38	5.50	5.57	4.81	4.99	5.84	2.80	4.29	2.52
Libya	0.01	0.05	0.41	0.40	0.46	0.67	0.85	0.95	0.95	0.71	0.40	0.60	0.66	0.54	0.77	0.74	0.84
Morocco	0.03	f	0.04	0.06	0.03	0.02	0.04	0.05	0.43	0.06	0.08	0.13	0.67	0.69	1.41	0.29	0.10
Tunisia	0.01	f	0.05	0.03	0.03	0.03	0.08	0.24	0.04	0.15	0.02	0.02	0.04	0.08	0.39	0.45	0.59
Algeria	0.01	f	0.08	0.01	0.02	g	0.05	0.01	f	f	g	f	f	0.02	0.88	0.51	0.52
Kuwait	g	g	g	g	g	g	g	g	g	g	g	0.61	0.49	0.68	1.03	1.15	0.79
Yemen	f	f	f	f	0.02	0.02	0.01	f	0.03	0.02	0.06	0.01	0.07	0.02	0.31	0.66	0.59

[a]Rounded to the nearest L.E. 10,000.

[b]Excluding exports to the Sudan prior to 1956. Includes reexports in 1963, 1964, and 1965.

[c]Includes exports to Lebanon.

[d]Includes exports to Jordan.

[e]Includes all merchandise sent to the Sudan.

[f]Less than L.E. 5,000.

[g]Not reported separately.

Source: Derived from U.A.R. (Egypt), *Annual Statement of Foreign Trade* and United Nations, *Yearbook of International Trade Statistics.*

NOTES

NOTES

1. There were, in addition, a number of internal duties that were applicable to articles destined for export, as well as to imported products consumed within the Empire. See *The Economic History of the Middle East 1800-1914*, ed. and trans. Charles Issawi (Chicago: University of Chicago Press, 1966), p. 38.

2. The 12 percent ad valorem duty consisted of the customary 3 percent export duty plus an additional 9 percent duty that was imposed in lieu of the internal duties. Foreign products on which the customary 3 percent import duty plus an additional 2 percent in import taxes had been paid could be sent to any part of the Empire free of any further duties. This placed domestic producers of similar products at a decided disadvantage since they continued to have to pay a number of internal duties. *Ibid.*, pp. 38, 46, 54, and 188.

3. For examples of the treaties concluded during 1861 and 1862, see the text of the treaty concluded between the Ottoman Empire and the United States on February 25, 1862, in *Treaties, Conventions, International Acts, Protocols and Agreements Between the United States of America and Other Powers 1776-1909*, comp. William M. Malloy (2 vols.; Washington: Government Printing Office, 1910), Vol. II, pp. 1321-1341; and the text of the treaty concluded between the Ottoman Empire and France in 1861 in: Egypt, Direction Générale des Douanes, *Code de l'Administration des Douanes* (Première Édition; Alexandria, 1902) Appendix A, pp. III-IX. Article V of the treaty with the United States provided that "the duties to be imposed on every article the produce or manufacture of the United States of America imported into the Empire and possessions of His Imperial Majesty the Sultan shall in no case exceed one fixed rate of eight per cent ad valorem, or a specific duty, fixed by common consent, equivalent thereto." Article XIV provided for an exception to the foregoing provision with regard to tobacco in any shape whatsoever and with regard to salt. In accordance with Article V and pursuant to Article XXII, representatives of the United States and the Ottoman Empire completed, on February 28, 1862, the preparation of the list of specific duties to be applicable to various articles. For an example of the capitulations granted by the Ottoman Empire during the seventeenth century, see the Capitulations of 1675 extending certain privileges to British subjects. Great Britain, Foreign Office, *Handbook of Commercial Treaties, & C., Between Great Britain and Foreign Powers* (1st ed.;

comp. Gaston de Bernhardt; London: His Majesty's Stationery Office, 1912), pp. 947-970. For the text of the Anglo-Turkish Commercial Convention of 1838, see Issawi, *op. cit.*, pp. 39-40.

4. A customs union was established between France and Algeria in 1867.

5. The Ottoman standard of currency was 1 piaster equal to 40 paras, but there were many modifications within the Empire, and practically every nation in Europe contributed to the coinage in use in the various parts of the Empire.

6. With regard to Egypt's unsuccessful attempts to industrialize on a large scale during the first half of the nineteenth century, see Issawi, *op. cit.*, pp. 390-402.

7. Great Britain, Foreign Office, *Turkey in Asia (II)* ("Peace Handbooks," Vol. XI; London: His Majesty's Stationery Office, 1920), No. 63 ("Mesopotamia"), pp. 96-98.

8. The region generally referred to as Syria before World War I included approximately the area which is presently within the boundaries of Israel, Jordan, Lebanon, and Syria.

9. For example, the earliest available official statistics show that in 1884 about two-thirds of Egypt's exports went to Great Britain and over one-third of its imports came from there, while about one-eleventh of its exports went to and about one-ninth of its imports came from France. Imports from other parts of the Ottoman Empire also appear to have been substantial, accounting for about one-fifth of Egypt's imports. Egypt, Direction Générale des Douanes, *Le Commerce Extérieur de l'Égypte Pendant l'Année 1910* (Alexandria, 1911). For a description of the trade of Iraq, Syria, and Arabia in the 1800's, see Issawi, *op. cit.*, Parts III, IV, and V.

10. Also in 1912 Morocco was divided between France and Spain.

11. For the text of this arrangement, see Egypt, *Code de l'Administration des Douanes, op. cit.*, pp. 147-156. By an Imperial Firman (Decree) of 1873, Egypt was given the right to conclude commercial conventions with foreign countries, and beginning in 1884, two years after the occupation of its territory by Great Britain, Egypt proceeded to conclude such conventions, or protocols of adherence, with most of the countries that had commercial treaties with the Ottoman Empire. These conventions constituted a replacement of the Ottoman tariff capitulations with Egyptian tariff capitulations. Whereas the Ottoman Empire in its treaties of 1861 and 1862 agreed not to impose on imports a rate of duty higher than 8 percent ad valorem, Egypt in the conventions that it concluded during the last two decades of the nineteenth century agreed not to impose on imports of most products a rate of duty higher than 10 percent ad valorem. The application of the higher rate of duty was suspended, however, pending the adherence to these conventions of, or the conclusion of conventions with, all of the countries with which the Ottoman Empire had treaty commitments. France did not conclude a convention with Egypt until 1902, and in that convention Egypt agreed not to impose an

import duty of more than 8 percent ad valorem. For some of the provisions of the Firman of 1873, see the preface to *ibid*. For the texts of the conventions and protocols concluded during the 1880's and 1890's, see *ibid*., pp. 3-118. For an extract from the Franco-Egyptian convention of 1902 (ratifications were not exchanged until October 25, 1906), see *The International Customs Journal-Egypt* (No. 36, 11th supplement to 1st ed.; Brussels: International Customs Tariffs Bureau, 1906). For a history of Egypt's customs regime and conventions prior to World War I, see Egypt, Ministry of Finance, *Annual Statement of Foreign Trade 1945* (Cairo: Government Press, 1946), pp. 5-13. During the 1880's, Egypt also adopted a new system of currency of one Egyptian pound equal to 100 piasters. In addition, the British sovereign became legal tender and the main currency in circulation in Egypt.

12. The difficulties that the Ottoman Empire encountered in its treaty relations with the so-called Great Powers and the conditions under which these Powers finally agreed to the increase in the Ottoman tariff from 8 percent to 11 percent are commented upon briefly in: Great Britain, Foreign Office, *The Balkan States* ("Peace Handbooks," Vol. III; London: His Majesty's Stationery Office, 1920), No. 16 ("Turkey in Europe"), pp. 128-129. For the text of the agreement, see Great Britain, Foreign Office, *Handbook of Commercial Treaties, op. cit.*, pp. 976-978.

13. For the text of this agreement, see Great Britain, Foreign Office, *British Possessions, II: The Congo* ("Peace Handbooks," Vol. XVI; London: His Majesty's Stationery Office, 1920), No. 98 ("Anglo-Egyptian Sudan"), pp. 165-167.

14. Article 7 provided:

Import duties on entering the Sudan shall not be payable on goods coming from Egyptian territory. Such duties may, however, be levied on goods coming from elsewhere than Egyptian territory; but in the case of goods entering the Sudan at Suakin, or any other port on the Red Sea littoral, they shall not exceed the corresponding duties for the time being leviable on goods entering Egypt from abroad.

Duties collected by Egypt on imports of foreign products destined for the Sudan were retained by Egypt, while duties collected by the Sudan on foreign products destined for Egypt were retained by the Sudan. This constituted a source of revenue for Egypt, which, however, was more than offset by the annual grants in aid from the Egyptian Government to the Sudan. These contributions from 1899 to 1913 totaled the equivalent of $25,993,500. In 1913, the budget of the Sudanese Government showed a surplus for the first time under the Anglo-Egyptian condominium, and the annual Egyptian contribution was discontinued. It was agreed that the Sudan would be reimbursed for duties collected at Egyptian ports on exports from the Sudan destined for other countries and on imports from other countries destined for the Sudan. Pending the carrying out of the arrangements necessary to put the agreement into effect, it was agreed that the equivalent of $425,000 would be paid annually by Egypt to the Sudan. United States, Department of Commerce, *The Anglo-Egyptian Sudan: A Commercial Handbook*, by North Winship ("Trade Promotion Series," No. 49; Washington: Government Printing Office, 1927), p. 22. The Egyptian pound was the unit of currency in the Sudan.

15. A rate of duty of 5 percent ad valorem was applied to products of Eritrea, Belgian Congo, French Congo, and Uganda. For the Sudanese customs tariff of 1913, see *The International Customs Journal-Sudan* (No. 73, 1st ed.; Brussels: International Customs Tariffs Bureau, 1914). For the customs regime that was applicable in the Sudan in 1902 and for the special arrangements made by the Sudan with the aforementioned four countries, see *The International Customs Journal-Egypt* (1st ed., 7th supplement [1902] and 8th supplement [1904]). Products of these countries entering Egypt from the Sudan were charged with the difference between the Sudanese duty and the duty imposed under the Egyptian tariff.

16. Although the network of railroads and roads in Syria was rather extensive, there was a lack of uniformity of gauge on the various railroad lines, and the roads, except for those in Lebanon, were generally very defective prior to 1914. In addition to the network of railroads and roads within Syria, there was also a railroad connection between Syria and Arabia following the completion of the southern section of the Hejaz railroad in 1908, and Egypt and the Sudan were connected by rail and boat.

17. Great Britain, Foreign Office, *Mohammedanism: Turkey in Asia (I)* ("Peace Handbooks," Vol. X; London: His Majesty's Stationery Office, 1920), No. 60 ("Syria and Palestine"), p. 153. Egypt and the rest of the Ottoman Empire each accounted for about 22½ percent of these exports. Most of the exports to Egypt and the rest of the Empire were from Alexandretta and Jaffa. Most exports from Beirut went to France. *Ibid.*, p. 152.

18. *Ibid.*, p. 132.

19. Egypt, Ministry of Finance, *Annual Statement of Foreign Trade 1929* (Cairo: Government Press, 1931), p. 16.

20. Great Britain, Foreign Office, *British Possessions, II: The Congo, op. cit.*, pp. 142-152.

21. Great Britain, Foreign Office, *Mohammedanism: Turkey in Asia (I), op. cit.*, pp. 121-125.

22. The term "Fertile Crescent" refers to the territory now included in Iraq, Syria, Lebanon, Israel, and Jordan.

23. The policy followed by these countries was one of developing appendages to the metropolitan economies. In Tunisia, the French monetary system had been introduced in 1891, with the Tunisian franc replacing the Tunisian piaster as the unit of currency, and in 1898 the Ottoman rate of duty had been replaced by a new customs tariff which provided for preferential, duty-free treatment for many products of French origin. Such treatment was subsequently extended to additional French products, and substantial increases were made in the margins of preference. Finally, in 1928 a customs

union was established between France and Tunisia. In Morocco, closer trade ties were effected with the parent countries within what was supposed to have been a nonpreferential customs framework. Morocco, like the Ottoman Empire, had entered into commercial conventions during the nineteenth century with Great Britain, France, and other countries, and in those conventions had agreed that the rate of duty levied by it on the products of such countries would not exceed 10 percent ad valorem. In the Anglo-French Declaration of 1904 Respecting Egypt and Morocco, the principle of economic equality or the so-called open door principle was enunciated. This principle was confirmed in general terms by the Act of Algeciras to which Morocco, France, Spain, Great Britain, United States, and various other countries were parties in 1906. A special tax of 2½ percent ad valorem, which was to be imposed by Morocco in addition to the 10 percent import duty, was established on February 17, 1908, in accordance with Article 66 of the Algeciras Act. These nonpreferential rates were continued following World War I as the parent countries proceeded to change the monetary systems in their respective zones to make them conform to their own systems. The Moroccan franc, which was based on and tied to the French franc, became the official currency in the French zone, replacing the Moorish or Hassani silver currency; the Spanish peseta became the official currency in the Spanish zone, with French francs and Hassani currency also in circulation; and the Moroccan franc and Spanish peseta were the principal currencies in circulation in the international zone of Tangier. In Libya, the Italian lira had become the unit of currency prior to World War I, and Italian products had received preferential treatment by being assessed for customs duties at only 50 percent of their invoice value. Following the war, a more formal preferential framework was established for Italian imports.

NOTES TO CHAPTER 1

1. Included within the French Mandate at one time or another during the interwar period were the State of Syria, the State of Greater Lebanon, the Government of the Alawis (Latakia), the Sanjaq of Alexandretta, and the State of Jabal al-Duruz.

2. An agreement had been concluded between Great Britain and Kuwait on January 23, 1899.

3. "Normal duties" was the term used to designate the rates of duty applicable to merchandise of countries which were members of the League of Nations or with which or with regard to which Syria had concluded trade agreements or issued special decisions providing for the application of such rates. "Conventional duties," which could be, and were in many cases, lower than the "normal duties," were applicable to products of contiguous countries with which Syria had concluded trade agreements. "Maximum duties"

were applicable to countries which were not members of the League of Nations and with which or with regard to which Syria had not concluded trade agreements or issued special decisions or had concluded agreements providing for such rates on certain products.

4. For Syria's tariff changes during the 1920's, see *The International Customs Journal-Syria and Great Lebanon* (No. 193, 1st ed. with 8 supplements; Brussels: International Customs Tariffs Bureau, 1925).

5. From 1918 until 1927 the Egyptian pound had been the unit of currency in Palestine.

6. The rate of duty of 11 percent was generally applied until 1922. In that year an additional duty of 1 percent was imposed on most imported articles. British *Board of Trade Journal*, May 11, 1922, pp. 523-524. For Palestine's tariff changes during the 1920's, see subsequent issues of that publication and *The International Customs Journal-Palestine* (No. 194, 2d ed. and the first two supplements to that edition; Brussels: International Customs Tariffs Bureau, 1927).

7. For the Transjordan Customs and Excise Ordinance of 1926, as amended, see Palestine, Department of Customs, Excise and Trade, *The Commercial Bulletin*, September 1, 1927, pp. 276-289. See also A. Konikoff, *Transjordan: An Economic Survey* (2d ed.; Jerusalem: Economic Research Institute of the Jewish Agency for Palestine, 1946), p. 92.

8. For Iraq's tariff changes during the 1920's, see the issues for that period of the British *Board of Trade Journal*.

9. Kuwait imposed a customs duty of 4 percent ad valorem on all imports. Great Britain, Department of Overseas Trade, *Economic Conditions in the Persian Gulf*, by Lieutenant Commander Forester (London: His Majesty's Stationery Office, 1929), p. 24. At Hodeida in 1930 a rate of duty of 15 percent was imposed on imports of silk, scents, and other valuable articles, while a rate of duty of 8 percent was imposed on imports of all commodities of average or slight value. The rate of duty on the latter commodities had been increased from 4 percent to 8 percent in 1930.

10. Under the "Hejaz-Nejd Coinage Regulation," provision was made for a monetary unit, the silver riyal, weighing 24.055 grams, .830 fine, the pure silver content being 19.965 grams. This unit was termed the "Arab dollar." *Tate's Modern Cambist* (28th ed., ed. William F. Spalding; London, 1929), pp. 409-410.

11. In many places on the Arabian coast the Maria Theresa silver dollar was a popular coin and a common medium of exchange among the traders. The Indian silver rupee was also used. *Ibid.*, pp. 412-413. See also Great Britain, Department of Overseas Trade, *Economic Conditions in the Persian Gulf, op. cit.*, p. 25.

12. The Mandate for Palestine included Transjordan, but many of its provisions were not applicable to Transjordan. Among those that were applic-

able were the no-discrimination provisions regarding imports and the exceptions thereto, which were contained in Article 18 of the Mandate.

13. For the text of the British Mandate for Palestine, see United States, Department of State, *Mandate for Palestine* (Washington: Government Printing Office, 1927), pp. 107-113. For partial texts of the 1922 Treaty of Alliance and subsequent British-Iraqi Treaties of Alliance and the French Mandate for Syria, see Great Britain, Foreign Office, *Handbook of Commercial Treaties, & C., Between Great Britain and Foreign Powers* (4th ed.; London: His Majesty's Stationery Office, 1931), pp. 1057-1070 and 1080-1082.

14. The agreement was signed by Palestine on May 4, 1929, and by Syria on May 18, 1929, and came into force on June 1, 1929. For the text of this agreement as amended to October 25, 1937, see Palestine, Department of Customs, Excise and Trade, *Customs Ordinance: Rules, Regulations, Orders and Notices Made Thereunder* (Jerusalem: Government Printing Press, 1937), pp. 209-214.

15. Norman Burns, *The Tariff of Syria 1919-1932* (Beirut: American Press, 1933), p. 67, Footnote 4.

16. The agreement was silent with regard to the imposition by either party of quantitative restrictions. However, there were provisions in the agreement that provided for the confiscation of any article whose exportation or importation was prohibited.

17. The turning over of the duties collected by the reexporting country to the country of destination was not specifically provided for in the agreement. This arrangement had been the practice in the past and apparently continued to be the practice. *Ibid.*, p. 69, Footnote 3.

18. Under the agreement, merchandise in transit from one country to the other was authorized and exempted from duty only if such merchandise was transported by rail or sea. These transit restrictions were due to the substantial amount of smuggling between Syria and Palestine. Large quantities of tobacco, spirituous liquors, petroleum, sugar, gold, and certain other products were involved in this smuggling trade.

19. The agreement was concluded on May 10, 1923. Great Britain, Colonial Office, *Report by His Majesty's Government to the Council of the League of Nations on the Administration of Palestine and Transjordan for the Year 1938* (London: His Majesty's Stationery Office, 1939), p. 352. See also Sections 6 through 9 of the Transjordan Customs and Excise Ordinance of 1926. At the end of March 1923, a law enacted by the Transjordanian Administration, which provided for the imposition of customs duties on goods entering Transjordan from Syria, caused some stir among the merchants in Damascus and led to the negotiation of the 1923 convention. Great Britain, Department of Overseas Trade, *Report on the Trade, Industry and Finance of Syria*, by H. E. Satow (London: His Majesty's Stationery Office, 1923), p. 11.

20. Article 7 of the Agreement of February 26, 1928, between Great Britain and the Amir of Transjordan. Konikoff, *op. cit.*, pp. 68-69.

21. See Sections 10 and 11 of the Transjordan Customs and Excise Ordinance of 1926.

22. Konikoff, *op. cit.*, p. 69. The two countries also concluded a transit agreement on September 26, 1928, which came into force on October 1, 1928. The provisions of the transit agreement, like the transit provisions of the Syrian-Palestinian agreement, were very limited. Transit through Palestine was authorized and exempted from duty only with respect to goods arriving at the port of Haifa by sea and goods arriving by rail from Egypt. In each case, the goods had to be forwarded to Amman by rail in sealed cars containing transit goods only. For the text of this transit agreement, as amended, see Palestine, Department of Customs, Excise and Trade, *Customs Ordinance ...*, *op. cit.*, p. 215.

23. Camels and horses were to be subject to a rate of duty of 50 piasters paper per head, sheep to a rate of duty of 15 piasters per head, and butter, rugs, and wool to a rate of duty of 1½ percent ad valorem. Burns, *op. cit.*, p. 101, Footnote 3.

24. A transit agreement was concluded by Syria and Iraq on January 16, 1925, which provided in Article 1:

> Goods of whatever origin, including goods of Syro-Lebanese origin and of Iraqi origin, passing through Syria or Iraq or through both countries, shall not be subject to the payment of import duties if they are transported through the country or countries of transit within six months from the date of their entry into the country, under the conditions determined by each contracting country and laid down in its own regulations. A transit duty of half percent of the value of the goods thus transported shall be levied on these goods in the country or in each of the countries through which they pass, within the period of six months referred to above. No preferential duty shall be accorded to the goods of any country.

This agreement was a sequel to the opening of the transdesert auto route between Beirut and Baghdad and Teheran. It was hoped by the French that the opening of this route would result in the shipment of a considerable quantity of French silks, perfumes, and other articles to Iraq and Persia. Prior to the effective date of this agreement, Syrian merchandise crossing Iraq paid transit duties ranging from 15 to 50 percent. *Ibid.*, p. 93. For the text of this agreement, see League of Nations, *Treaty Series,* Vol. XLIX (Geneva, 1926), pp. 9-27.

25. The agreement between Egypt and Syria was concluded on June 13, 1928, and went into effect the latter part of that year. It was subject to termination upon three months' notice by either party. Burns, *op. cit.*, p. 83. The agreement between Egypt and Palestine was concluded on June 21, 1928, and went into force on the same date. It was also subject to termination upon three months' notice by either party. It was provided in the agreement that most-favored-nation treatment would also apply to Palestinian tobacco imported into Egypt, which would be given the benefit of the differ-

ential tariff, and that the treatment granted by Egypt to Sudanese products would not be extended to Palestinian products and the treatment granted by Palestine to Syrian products would not be extended to Egyptian products. A similar provision was contained in the Egyptian-Syrian agreement. For the texts of the notes constituting the agreement between Egypt and Palestine, see League of Nations, *Treaty Series*, Vol. LXXX (1928), pp. 279-281.

26. It should be noted, however, that these statistics did not reflect all of the inland trade that was carried on between the Arab countries. The statistics that were kept at the inland customs stations were incomplete, and a great deal of smuggling took place between the Arab countries.

27. The trade percentages set forth in this section were based on statistics obtained from the annual government statistical publications in the cases of Egypt, Palestine, and the Sudan. For Syria and Iraq, statistics were obtained from the British Department of Overseas Trade reports on those countries. Some trade statistics for Kuwait and some of the other territories in the Arabian Peninsula are contained in the British Department of Overseas Trade report on the Persian Gulf territories.

28. Great Britain, Department of Overseas Trade, *Report on Economic and Commercial Conditions in Egypt*, by G. H. Selous (London: His Majesty's Stationery Office, 1937), p. 14.

29. *Ibid.*

30. It also devalued its currency in September 1931.

31. For Egypt's tariffs and tariff changes during the 1930's, see *The International Customs Journal-Egypt* (4th ed. with 28 supplements; Brussels: International Customs Tariffs Bureau, 1931); and Egypt, Ministère des Finances, *Tableau des Droits Inscrits au Tarif des Douanes* (Cairo, 1931 and 1936). The decree establishing the new customs tariff of 1930 and the new customs tariff schedules annexed to that decree are set forth in the British *Board of Trade Journal*, January 9, 1930, pp. I-XXIV (special section to that issue), and February 27, 1930, pp. 305-311. See also subsequent issues of that publication for week-to-week changes in Egypt's import duties during the 1930's.

32. Great Britain, Department of Overseas Trade, *Report on Economic and Commercial Conditions in Egypt, op. cit.*, p. 14.

33. The Bank Misr controlled subsidiary companies that were involved in a variety of industrial and commercial undertakings, including the ginning and export of cotton, the manufacture of cotton goods, silk goods, and linen goods, insurance and shipping, printing, film production, fisheries, and the manufacture of cigarettes and other tobacco products.

34. Great Britain, Department of Overseas Trade, *Economic Conditions in Egypt*, by G. H. Selous (London: His Majesty's Stationery Office, 1933), pp. 86-87.

35. Iraq, Ministry of Finance, *Customs Tariff (1933)* (translation). For earlier increases, see issues of British *Board of Trade Journal* for 1930-33.

36. Great Britain, Department of Overseas Trade, *Economic Conditions in Iraq*, by C. Empson (London: His Majesty's Stationery Office, 1933), p. 29.

37. Great Britain, Department of Overseas Trade, *Economic Conditions in Iraq*, by J. P. Summerscale (London: His Majesty's Stationery Office, 1936), p. 22.

38. Great Britain, Department of Overseas Trade, *Report on Economic and Commercial Conditions in Iraq*, by J. P. Summerscale (London: His Majesty's Stationery Office, 1938), pp. 19-20.

39. *The International Customs Journal-Iraq* (No. 34, 1st ed.; Brussels: International Customs Tariffs Bureau, 1938).

40. For Syria's tariff changes during 1932, see the issues for that year of the British *Board of Trade Journal*.

41. Great Britain, Department of Overseas Trade, *Report on Economic and Commercial Conditions in Syria and the Lebanon*, by G. T. Havard (London: His Majesty's Stationery Office, 1938), p. 3.

42. British *Board of Trade Journal*, November 5, 1936, p. 673.

43. *Ibid.*, May 12, 1938, p. 667. See also Great Britain, Department of Overseas Trade, *Report on Economic and Commercial Conditions in Syria and the Lebanon, op. cit.*, p. 4.

44. Great Britain, Department of Overseas Trade, *Economic Conditions in Palestine*, by C. Empson (London: His Majesty's Stationery Office, 1935), pp. 53-54.

45. For Palestine's tariffs and tariff changes during the 1930's, see *The International Customs Journal-Palestine* (Supplements 4 through 10 to the 2d ed.; 3d ed. [1936]; and 4th ed. [1938]). See also issues for that period of the British *Board of Trade Journal*.

46. Great Britain, Department of Overseas Trade, *Economic Conditions in Palestine, op. cit.*, pp. 53 and 55.

47. Palestine, Department of Customs, Excise and Trade, *Customs Ordinance...*, *op. cit.*, pp. 131-133 and 136-138. These restrictions did not apply to Transjordanian flour, semolina, and wheat but did apply to such Syrian products.

48. Konikoff, *op. cit.*, p. 92. British *Board of Trade Journal*, March 18, 1937, p. 422.

49. Great Britain, Colonial Office, *Report... of Palestine and Transjordan... 1938, op. cit.*, p. 393.

50. British *Board of Trade Journal*, October 24, 1935, p. 586.

51. *Ibid.*, December 3, 1936, p. 822.

52. For Saudi Arabia's tariffs during the 1930's, see issues for that period of the British *Board of Trade Journal*. Kuwait imposed a duty of 4½ percent ad valorem on imports. Great Britain, Department of Overseas Trade, *Report on Economic and Commercial Conditions in the Persian Gulf*, by F. H. Todd (London: His Majesty's Stationery Office, 1937), p. 11.

53. Alcoholic beverages, tobacco and tobacco products, and certain other products were dutiable at much higher rates. For example, the duty on silk fabrics and other articles of silk was 50 percent ad valorem. On October 1, 1939, a new customs ordinance came into effect which provided for higher rates of duty on most products. For the Sudan's tariffs during the period of the 1930's preceding World War II, see *The International Customs Journal-Anglo-Egyptian Sudan* (3d ed. [1931] and 4th ed. [1935]; Brussels: International Customs Tariffs Bureau). See also Great Britain, *Report by the Governor-General on the Administration, Finances and Conditions of the Sudan in 1938* (London: His Majesty's Stationery Office, 1939), pp. 35-38.

54. Egypt had terminated its earlier agreements with Syria and Palestine. Each of the 1930 agreements was concluded by an exchange of notes. The agreement with Syria came into force on March 11, 1930; the agreement with Palestine on June 11, 1930; and the agreement with Transjordan on August 21, 1930. British *Board of Trade Journal*, May 22, 1930, p. 703, and September 18, 1930, p. 348. Great Britain, Colonial Office, *Report . . . of Palestine and Transjordan . . . 1938, op. cit.,* pp. 123 and 356. Like the 1928 agreements, the 1930 agreements excluded from most-favored-nation treatment the preferences granted by these countries in certain other trade agreements.

55. Article 2 contained the proviso that "during the first year dating from the enforcement of the new Tariff, the Minister of Finance is authorized to accord, by Decree, temporary exemptions from the surtax aforesaid, either as a general measure or by special measures." Pursuant to this article, the Minister of Finance issued decrees at various times during 1930 suspending the application of the surtax. See issues for 1930 of the British *Board of Trade Journal.*

56. *Ibid.,* issues for the years 1930 through 1932. Burns, *op. cit.,* p. 85.

57. *Ibid.*

58. British *Board of Trade Journal,* May 18, 1933, p. 794.

59. *Ibid.,* September 14, 1933, p. 379.

60. *Ibid.,* November 29, 1934, p. 803.

61. *Ibid.*

62. *Ibid.,* issues for 1935.

63. These percentages were calculated from figures which included re-exports and transit exits. These figures are contained in the British Department of Overseas Trade reports on Syria and the Lebanon which were published in 1930, 1932, 1934, 1936, and 1938.

64. Egypt's total imports also decreased substantially during the 1930's, as did its total exports (mainly cotton). See Egypt, Ministry of Finance, *Annual Statement of Foreign Trade.*

65. Such as sheep, lambs, butter, leather, oranges, lemons, limes, citrons, grapes, haricot beans, chickpeas, bananas, raisins, dried figs and apricots,

walnuts, almonds, pistachio nuts, olive oil, liquorice root, cotton fabrics, cotton handkerchiefs and certain other cotton products, silk fabrics, artificial silk fabrics, and hemp rope and cordage.

66. For example, imports of oranges had decreased from over 2½ million kilograms valued at approximately L.E. 15,000 in 1929 to about 25,000 kilograms valued at approximately L.E. 260 in 1938. Imports of pistachio nuts had decreased from about 160,000 kilograms valued at approximately L.E. 18,000 to about 46,000 kilograms valued at approximately L.E. 5,000. Imports of dried apricots had dropped from about 2 million kilograms valued at approximately L.E. 45,000 to about 137,000 kilograms valued at approximately L.E. 4,000. And imports of butter had decreased in volume and value by about 90 percent. The only products that were imported in 1938 into Egypt from Syria in amounts exceeding L.E. 5,000 were sheep, lambs and certain other live animals, butter, dried currants and raisins, walnuts in the shell, apricot paste, liquorice root, aromatic seeds, olive oil, certain other oils used in the manufacture of soap, cinema films, and natural silk yarn.

67. For example, exports of cottonseed oil decreased from about 800,000 kilograms valued at approximately L.E. 32,000 in 1929 to about 77,000 kilograms valued at approximately L.E. 3,000 in 1938. Imports of cottonseed oil into Syria had become subject to license in 1933. Exports to Syria of grey cotton fabrics, which during 1929 amounted to L.E. 11,000, practically ceased during the 1930's.

68. *The International Customs Journal-Palestine* (4th supplement to 2d ed.).

69. Palestine Department of Customs, Excise and Trade, *Customs Ordinance . . . , op. cit.*, pp. 131-135.

70. The agreement also came into force on August 18, 1936. For the texts of these notes, see League of Nations, *Treaty Series*, Vol. CLXXVI (1937), pp. 178-184. According to the terms of the agreement, the Egyptian customs duty on imported soap manufactured in Palestine and made exclusively from unadulterated olive oil could not exeed 500 milliemes per hundred kilograms gross; the duty on Palestinian watermelons imported during July and August could not exceed ·1 Egyptian pound per ton; the duty on Palestinian grapefruit could not exceed 1½ Egyptian pounds per ton for a two-year period; the duty on Palestinian oranges imported between May 1 and September 30 could not exceed 2 Egyptian pounds per ton; and the railway tariff on Palestinian household soap transported by the Egyptian State Railways was to be at the same rate as that charged for the transport of household soap of Egyptian manufacture, excluding the special export tariff and flat rates. Palestine promised in the agreement not to impose a duty higher than 1 Palestinian pound per ton on Egyptian watermelons and other melons imported during May and June; to reduce the duty on Egyptian sugar from 10 Palestinian pounds to a rate which would be subsequently established but which would not be lower than 5 Palestinian pounds per ton; to

remove the import restrictions on Egyptian mangoes; and to reduce the railway tariff on Egyptian tibn (chopped straw) transported by the Palestine Railways by one class. It was made clear in the agreement that the reduced rates contained therein were not intended to be preferential rates of duty. Certain of these reductions came into force in advance of the formal exchange of notes. British *Board of Trade Journal*, October 22, 1936, p. 594.

71. These percentages were calculated from the figures contained in the official trade statistics of Palestine. See Palestine, Department of Customs, Excise and Trade, *Statistics of Imports, Exports and Shipping*, and Palestine, *Blue Book* (Jerusalem: Government Printer).

72. While Palestine's exports to Egypt decreased substantially during the 1930's, its total exports increased from about L.P. 2 million in 1930 to about L.P. 5 million in 1938. Most of the increase in Palestine's total exports was accounted for by the large quantities of oranges that Palestine sold to European countries (mainly Great Britain). Production of oranges increased substantially in Palestine during the 1930's, and Palestinian producers found a good market for their oranges in Great Britain and other European countries.

73. Whereas in 1929 imports of Palestinian soap into Egypt amounted to about 3½ million kilograms valued at approximately L.E. 165,000, in 1938 they amounted to 1⅓ million kilograms valued at approximately L.E. 57,000. Likewise, imports of Palestinian oranges decreased from about 4½ million kilograms valued at approximately L.E. 22,000 in 1929 to about 65,000 kilograms valued at approximately L.E. 700 in 1938; imports of Palestinian watermelons dropped from about 37 million kilograms valued at approximately L.E. 79,000 in 1929 to about 172,000 kilograms valued at approximately L.E. 530 in 1938; and imports of Palestinian raisins dropped from about 420,000 kilograms valued at approximately L.E. 10,000 in 1929 to about 28,000 kilograms valued at approximately L.E. 560 in 1938.

74. Egypt's exports to Palestine during the second half of the 1920's had also been about L.E. 400,000 annually but had constituted a larger percentage of Palestine's total imports. Total imports into Palestine more than doubled in value during the 1930's, amounting to about L.P. 14 million in 1938.

75. Exports from the Sudan to Egypt included such products as sheep, cattle, salted fish, butter, untanned hides and skins, millet, lupines, sesame, dates, ground nuts, gum arabic, garad (tanning pods), melon seeds, chilies, maize, and chickpeas. Exports from Egypt to the Sudan included such products as sugar, cheese, rice, fresh fruits, wheat flour, cottonseed oil, cigarettes and tobacco, cement, household soap, leather and manufacturers thereof, confectionery, macaroni, asphalt and bitumen, certain cotton fabrics, certain fabrics of cotton and artificial silk (mixture), and certain wearing apparel. Sudan, *Annual Report of the Department of Economics and Trade 1938* (Khartoum, 1939).

76. Konikoff, *op. cit.*, p. 72.

77. The agreement, which involved an exchange of notes, was concluded and came into force on May 16, 1938. For the texts of these notes, see League of Nations, *Treaty Series*, Vol. CXC (1938), pp. 183-185. It was specified in the agreement that its provisions would not apply:

(a) To advantages which are at present or may in future be granted by Iraq to a border State to facilitate traffic; to those resulting from any customs union that Iraq may conclude; to any special customs advantages that Iraq may grant to the natural or manufactured products of Turkey or of a country whose territory, in 1914, was wholly comprised within the Ottoman Empire in Asia;

(b) To the regime granted Sudanese products or which may be granted to the products of certain border countries under regional agreements.

78. The agreement, which involved an exchange of notes, was concluded on December 14, 1936, and came into force on February 14, 1937. For the texts of these notes, see *ibid.*, Vol. CLXXVII (1937), pp. 222-239. In the agreement, Palestine promised to accord certain free trade zone facilities to Iraq in the port of Haifa, and to reduce its customs duties on the following commodities of Iraqi origin imported into Palestine by the Baghdad-Haifa land route: rice, other than unhusked (from 1½ mils per kg. to ¾ mil per kg.), rice, unhusked (from 1 mil per kg. to ½ mil per kg.), dates, fresh (from 1 mil per kg. to ½ mil per kg.), dates, dried (from 5 mils per kg. to ½ mil per kg.), and dates, compressed (from 1½ mils per kg. to ½ mil per kg.). Palestine, however, reserved the right to raise or lower the duty on rice with the understanding that Iraqi rice imported into Palestine by the Baghdad-Haifa land route would be subject to only 50 percent of the general Palestine duty on rice in force at any time. Barley and butter of Iraqi origin imported into Palestine by the Baghdad-Haifa land route were to be exempt from duty, subject, in the case of barley, to such temporary measures of general application as might be necessary to protect the Palestine crop, and subject, in the case of butter, to any restrictions that might from time to time be applicable to butter imported from Syria. Palestine also promised not to alter the then prevailing duties (set forth in parentheses) on the following articles without giving Iraq six months' notice of its intention to do so: animals, live (free), eggs, in the shell (20 mils per 100 eggs), eggs, without shells (12 percent), fish, fresh (5 mils per kg.), hides, raw or dried (free), tanned hides (30 mils per kg.), meat, frozen or chilled (free), chickens, live (free), chickens, frozen (12 percent), linseed (free), cotton, raw (free), ground nuts, decorticated (free), ground nuts, unshelled (2½ mils per kg.), and wool, raw (free).

79. In addition to the free zone facilities to be accorded by Palestine to Iraq within the port of Haifa, the 1936 agreement provided that Palestine would exempt from import duties motor vehicles, tires, tubes, and gasoline imported into Palestine by transportation companies using the Baghdad-Haifa land route. Provision was also made for special reduced vehicle license fees and reduced wharfage dues.

80. See Sa'id Himadeh, *Al-Nizam al-Iqtisadi fi al-'Iraq* (Beirut, 1938), pp. 414-416.

81. Imports from Syria consisted mainly of soap and artificial silk fabrics and smaller amounts of cigarette paper, certain cotton fabrics, certain wearing apparel, raw silk, cement, and leather.

82. See Appendix II. For detailed statistics on Iraqi trade during the second half of the 1930's, see the annual issues for that period of: Iraq, Ministry of Finance, Department of Customs and Excise, *Foreign Trade Statistics* (Baghdad: Government Press).

83. *Ibid.*

84. Most of Iraq's exports to Egypt consisted of sheep and lambs and date paste, and most of its exports to Syria consisted of sheep and other live animals and tanned hides and skins and smaller amounts of such products as eggs, wool, dates, gall nuts, and butter.

85. Imports into Palestine from Iraq during 1938 amounted to about L.P. 170,000. On the other hand, exports from Palestine to Iraq amounted in 1938 to only about L.P. 8,000.

86. In Appendix II, a fairly substantial amount of imports into Transjordan from Iraq is shown for 1938. However, about L.P. 103,000 of the L.P. 106,000 shown consisted of animals imported in connection with the work on the construction of the Haifa-Baghdad road. Great Britain, Colonial Office, *Report... of Palestine and Transjordan... 1938, op. cit.*, p. 392. Recorded imports into Transjordan from Iraq in 1937 amounted to only about L.P. 7,000. *Ibid.*

87. Konikoff, *op. cit.*, p. 71.

88. Great Britain, Department of Overseas Trade, *Economic Conditions in the Persian Gulf, op. cit.*, p. 24.

89. Burns, *op. cit.*, pp. 101-103. Syria and Hejaz and Nejd signed a Treaty of Friendship on November 10, 1931, which came into force on June 24, 1932, and in which the countries agreed to proceed with negotiations for an agreement on all customs and other economic questions arising between them. *Ibid.*, p. 102, and British *Board of Trade Journal* October 6, 1932, p. 458. However, apparently no such agreement was concluded.

90. See Appendix II.

91. In 1937, Palestine's imports of manufactured articles from Syria amounted to about L.P. 671,000, whereas its exports of manufactured articles to Syria amounted to about L.P. 147,000. Total imports into Palestine from Syria during that year were approximately L.P. 1,375,000, and total exports from Palestine to Syria were about L.P. 625,000.

92. Konikoff, *op. cit.*, p. 70.

93. For the texts of these agreements, see *Palestine Gazette Extraordinary*, November 30, 1939, Supplement No. 2, pp. 1339-1392. These agreements came into force provisionally on December 1, 1939, by an exchange of

letters between the High Commissioners for Palestine and the states of Syria and Lebanon. Each agreement was subject to the right of either party to terminate the agreement by giving one month's notice.

94. The exceptions included wheat other than hard wheat, meat (live animals were included in the list), cheese, milk, lemons, cucumbers, eggplants, and tomatoes. The duty-free admission of hard wheat (triticum durum) into the territory of either contracting party was limited to 5,000 tons in any one year. In addition, only potatoes imported during the period from September 1 to March 31, inclusive, and eggs, in the shell, imported during the period from July 1 to November 30, inclusive, were entitled to duty-free admission.

95. Included in the duty-free list were certain marble slabs and blocks; sulphur; asphalt; sand and stones; woolen and worsted yarn; silk yarn; artificial silk yarn; flax, hemp, jute and linen yarn; certain cotton yarn; fertilizers; straw; colored straw braids; straw mats and certain other straw manufactures; certain metal wire and wire netting; soap; dentifrices and other toilet preparations; jewelry; printed matter, including books, newspapers, and periodicals; and dyes, paints, colors, and certain other chemicals. Although there was a substantial amount of yarn produced in Syria, there was very little yarn produced in Palestine during this period. Consequently, imports of cotton, wool, silk, artificial silk, flax, hemp, jute and linen yarns from whatever origin were exempted from duty by Palestine.

96. Syrian exports to Palestine included such articles as barley, wheat, wheat flour, sheep, lambs, poultry, eggs, cheese, butter, various fruits and vegetables, confectionery, industrial olive oil, cement, furniture, artificial silk fabrics, cotton fabrics, woolen fabrics, leather, shoes, socks, stockings, shirts and other wearing apparel, macaroni, paper and cardboard, and silk yarn. Palestinian exports to Syria included such articles as watermelons and other melons, oranges, edible oils, confectionery, sesame seeds, hides and skins, intestines, certain cotton and artificial silk fabrics, dresses, knitted wear and other wearing apparel, envelopes and other paper manufactures, leather purses and wallets and other leather products, and soap. A detailed statistical analysis of trade between Palestine and Syria from 1927 through 1937 was published by the Government of Palestine in February 1939. See Palestine, Office of Statistics, *Trade Between Palestine and Syria 1927-1937*, Special Trade Bulletin No. 1/1939 (Jerusalem, 1939).

97. The independence of these states was proclaimed in 1941. See Chapter 3.

NOTES TO CHAPTER 2

1. For example, imports into Palestine from Syria and Lebanon decreased from about L.P. 1,355,000 in 1939 to about L.P. 500,000 in 1940

and about L.P. 400,000 in 1941, while exports from Palestine to those territories decreased from about L.P. 390,000 in 1939 to about L.P. 245,000 in 1940 and about L.P. 150,000 in 1941. These decreases reflected the very small amount of trade that was carried on between these countries during the second half of 1940 and the first half of 1941. Palestine, Department of Statistics, *Statistical Abstract of Palestine 1943* (Jerusalem: Government Printing Press, 1944), p. 101.

2. United States, Department of Commerce, "Economic Conditions in Turkey, Syria, and Iran in 1940 and Early 1941," *International Reference Service*, Vol. I, No. 31 (1941), p. 5.

3. Egypt did not license imports until November 1941.

4. The anti-British, pro-Nazi government in Iraq was also ousted by British forces.

5. The Exchange Office of Syria and Lebanon was to sell upon request sterling bloc currencies to residents of Syria and Lebanon. Currency thus bought could be transferred to London or to any other center within the sterling bloc or could be used to buy goods and services from the sterling countries. Although this privilege was not officially extended to residents of Syria and Lebanon until May 30, 1943, large sums were transferred by residents of the two countries to sterling countries before that date. Elias S. Saba, *The Foreign Exchange Systems of Lebanon and Syria 1939-1957* (Beirut: American University of Beirut, 1961), pp. 42-43.

6. Middle East Supply Centre, *Some Facts about the Middle East Supply Centre* (Cairo: The Nile Press, 1944), p. 3.

7. Fred Winant and John P. Dawson, "The Middle-East Supply Program," *Foreign Commerce Weekly*, April 1, 1944, p. 38.

8. Supply Centre, *op. cit.*, p. 5.

9. With regard to the administration, functions, procedures, and structure of the Middle East Supply Center, see the following articles and publications: Guy Hunter, "Economic Problems: The Middle East Supply Centre," *Survey of International Affairs 1939-1946: The Middle East in the War*, by George Kirk (London: Oxford University Press, 1952), pp. 169-193; Martin W. Wilmington, "The Middle East Supply Center: A Reappraisal," *The Middle East Journal*, Vol. VI (Spring, 1952), pp. 144-156; Richard Grew, "Organization of Trade in the Middle East: Setup and Functions of the Middle East Supply Centre and Its Results Since Being Established in 1941," *Canadian Exporter*, Vol. XIV (November 1944), p. 12 et seq.; *The Economist*, March 13, 1943, pp. 319-321; James M. Landis, "Anglo-American Co-operation in the Middle East," *The Annals of the American Academy of Political and Social Science*, Vol. CCXL (July 1945), pp. 64-72.

10. See Hunter, *op. cit.*, pp. 180-183; and Wilmington, *op. cit.*, p. 150.

11. *Ibid.*, p. 185 and pp. 157-158, respectively. Also Francis Boardman, "Civilian Requirements from War to Peace: The Middle East Supply Center," *The Department of State Bulletin*, December 23, 1945, p. 998.

12. Among the products which were manufactured in Palestine on a fairly large scale were glass, carbonic acid, sulphuric acid, brass and steel castings, precision instruments, boots and shoes, sole leather, packing boxes, electric batteries, and plastics. Not all of these were new, wartime products, but the increased scale of production was such that in most cases they were described as wartime innovations. Artificial teeth, dental burrs, and razor blades were also produced in fair quantities for home consumption and for export to neighboring countries, and the production of various other manufactured articles increased substantially. One of the most significant developments was the wartime growth of the diamond cutting industry. Great Britain, Department of Overseas Trade, *Palestine: Review of Commercial Conditions* (London: His Majesty's Stationery Office, 1945), pp. 16-19. In Egypt, industries were established or expanded which produced glucose, gelatine, dehydrated onions and carrots, calcium carbide, sodium hypochlorite, chromium sulphate, red lead and litharge, battery acid, ferroalloys, asbestos, cooking stoves, oil heating stoves, high pressure cast iron water pipes, dry batteries, corks (paper), refractory bricks, steel castings, cigarette lighters, jute and sisal rope and twine and jute bags, and lead tubes (collapsible). In addition, the production of beer, canned foods, vinegar, refined sugar, certain chemicals, glassware, and various other articles increased significantly. Great Britain, Department of Overseas Trade, *Egypt: Review of Commercial Conditions* (London: His Majesty's Stationery Office, 1945), pp. 37-40.

13. *Ibid.*, p. 15, and Grew, *op. cit.*; United Nations, Department of Economic and Social Affairs, *Review of Economic Conditions in the Middle East 1951-52* (New York, 1953), p. 45.

14. K. A. H. Murray, Foreword to the book by Bernard A. Keen, *The Agricultural Development of the Middle East* (a report to the Director General of the Middle East Supply Centre) (London, 1946).

15. In Egypt, for example, 1,292,000 metric tons of wheat were produced in 1943 compared to the average annual Egyptian production of 1,184,000 metric tons for the period 1934-38. In 1943, however, 805,000 hectares of land were used to grow wheat compared to the annual average of 588,000 hectares for the period 1934-38. For a statistical comparison of the production of cereals and certain other crops in Egypt, Iraq, and Syria during the prewar and war years, see United Nations, Department of Economic and Social Affairs, *Economic Developments in the Middle East 1945-1954* (New York, 1955), p. 32, Table 13; p. 94, Table 26; and p. 183, Table 50. See also United Nations, Food and Agriculture Organization, *Yearbook of Food and Agricultural Statistics-1947* (Washington, 1947).

16. See Appendix II.

17. For example, the cost of living and wholesale price indexes for Egypt show almost a threefold rise in prices from 1940 to 1945, for Iraq about a fourfold rise, for Palestine approximately a threefold rise, and for Lebanon nearly a sevenfold rise. United Nations, Department of Economic and Social

Affairs, *Review of Economic Conditions in the Middle East 1949-50* (New York, 1951), p. 84.

18. For example, imports of household soap from Palestine into Egypt increased in terms of value from L.E. 57,344 in 1938 to L.E. 67,640 in 1944 but decreased in terms of volume from 1,311,711 kilograms to 456,785 kilograms. Exports from Egypt to Palestine of rice increased in terms of value from L.E. 140,964 in 1938 to L.E. 189,172 in 1944 but decreased in terms of volume from 13,644,780 kilograms to 7,144,186 kilograms. Likewise, whereas in 1939 imports into Iraq from Syria of apricot paste, cement, and household soap amounted to 92 tons valued at I.D. 1,653; 3,050 tons valued at I.D. 10,298; and 734 tons valued at I.D. 25,705, respectively, imports of these products in 1944 amounted to 354 tons valued at I.D. 37,575; 4,164 tons valued at I.D. 97,717; and 617 tons valued at I.D. 309,681, respectively.

19. These exports were not included in Iraq's export statistics but were included in Palestine's and Syria and Lebanon's import statistics. The amount of such crude petroleum shown in Syria and Lebanon's import statistics consisted of the petroleum refined in Tripoli for consumption in Syria and Lebanon.

20. These exports were included in Palestine's export statistics and Egypt's and Syria and Lebanon's import statistics. In Egypt's import statistics, most of these petroleum products were listed as imports from Iraq. Large quantities of the petroleum products shipped from Haifa were used in the region in motor vehicles and tractors and in plants and locomotives that were converted to use oil instead of coal.

21. Likewise, a large percentage of the total value of Syria and Lebanon's imports from Iraq in 1944 consisted of crude petroleum.

22. These figures probably include reexports from Syria and Lebanon to Iraq of cotton fabrics of non-Syrian-Lebanese origin.

23. Egypt's imports from Saudi Arabia increased from L.E. 142,099 in 1938 to L.E. 451,039 in 1944, but about 80 percent (L.E. 355,090) of the latter amount consisted of imports of specie (sovereigns).

24. For example, the following import restrictions were in effect in Palestine during the latter part of 1943: (1) Certain items—such as cereals, cereal flour, fertilizers, various metals and metal products, agricultural machinery, metal-working and wood-working machinery, diamonds, dates, dehydrated eggs, hides, cottonseed oil, olive oil, onions, potatoes, quinine, sugar, sesame seeds and oil, cattle, sheep, various chemicals, tea, machine tools, tractors and tractor parts, and tires—could be imported only on government account or through a sole importer designated by the government; no import licenses for such products were issued to private importers; (2) a wide range of commodities was prohibited from being imported from any country except Abyssina, Aden, Arabia, Cyprus, Egypt, Eritrea, Iran, Iraq, Lebanon, Sudan, Syria, Transjordan, Turkey, USSR, and Yemen. Included among these commodities were most vegetables and fruits, beer, bread, brushes, brooms,

butter, buttons, cement, various alcoholic and nonalcoholic beverages, cheese, chocolate, cigars and cigarettes, cosmetics, eggs in the shell, fish, various fruit juices, sheet glass, hollow glassware, glue, hosiery, ice cream, jams and jellies, macaroni, milk, shoes, certain cotton manufactures, certain silk manufactures, soap, sugar candy, silk thread, and artificial silk yarn; (3) another wide range of commodities was permitted to be imported only within quota limits. Included among these commodities were various chemicals; baby foods; bandages; various metal products; drugs; synthetic dyestuffs; sanitary earthenware; certain engines; rubberized fabric and manufactures thereof; felt and felt hoods and shapes; vegetable fibers; haberdashery; insecticides; dental and surgical instruments; musical instruments; jute; jewelry; various machinery and parts; artificial silk, silk, cotton, or wool fabrics; plastic products; pottery; radios; jute sacks; artificial silk, cotton, flax, hemp, jute, or wool thread; tobacco leaf; pipe tobacco; raw wool; vaccines; vitamins; cotton, flax, hemp, jute, or wool yarn; watches; and small household utensils. British *Board of Trade Journal*, April 15, 1944, pp. 144-146. Also see the wartime issues of that publication and the *Foreign Commerce Weekly* with regard to the export restrictions imposed by some of the Arab countries.

25. Great Britain, Board of Trade, *Egypt: Economic and Commercial Conditions in Egypt*, by J. W. Taylor ("Overseas Economic Surveys"; London: His Majesty's Stationery Office, 1948), p. 10.

26. British *Board of Trade Journal*, July 4, 1942, p. 321.

27. *Ibid.*, June 17, 1944, p. 227.

28. Syria and Lebanon, for example, suspended the duties which had been imposed on wheat, barley, and their derivatives.

29. The Middle East Supply Center was dissolved on November 1, 1945. Boardman, *op. cit.*, p. 994.

NOTES TO CHAPTER 3

1. There were two series of notes: One carried at the top the name "Grand Liban," while the other carried the name "Syrie." Notes of both series were, however, considered legal tender throughout the French Mandate.

2. For a full presentation of the customs organization and administration in Syria and Lebanon under the Mandate, see Norman Burns, *The Tariff of Syria 1919-1932* (Beirut: American Press, 1933), pp. 12-39.

3. The complete text of this agreement is contained in a compilation of documents published by the Syrian Government and in a compilation published by the Lebanese Government. Both of these compilations, which pertain to the Syrian-Lebanese Customs Union, were published after the dissolution of that union. Syria, Ministry of Foreign Affairs, *Wathaiq wa Nusus Tatalaq bil Alaqat al-Iqtisadiya bain Suriya wa Lubnan* (Damascus, 1950) (in

Arabic). Lebanon, *Al-Wathaiq wa al-Nusus al-Mukhtasa bil Alaqat al-Iqtisadiya wa al-Maliya bain Suriya wa Lubnan* (Beirut, no date) (in Arabic and French). Hereinafter these compilations will be referred to as the *Syrian Compilation* and the *Lebanese Compilation*.

4. Certain other administrations which under the French Mandate served both Syria and Lebanon, such as the telegraph and mail and general works administrations, were not continued as joint administrations. Article 1.

5. Article 2. The Council was to conduct its business six months of the year in Damascus, where the chairman would be a Syrian national, and the remaining six months in Beirut, where the chairman would be a Lebanese national.

6. Article 5. The Prime Ministers of Syria and Lebanon met on December 28 and 29, 1945, and agreed that the distribution of the net revenues of the joint administrations for the years 1944, 1945, and 1946 would be on the basis of 56 percent for Syria and 44 percent for Lebanon. Minutes of the Meeting of December 29, 1945, *Lebanese Compilation*, pp. 14-15.

7. Article 8.

8. Lebanon's decree was issued on March 16, 1944. The text of this decree (Legislative Decree K/1) is contained in the *Lebanese Compilation*, pp. 10-13.

9. The financial agreement established the following rate of exchange for the Syrian and Lebanese pounds: 1 Syrian or Lebanese pound equals 22.65 French francs at a parity of 200 francs for 1 pound sterling or 883 Syrian or Lebanese piasters (8.83 pounds) equal 1 pound sterling. The rate of exchange of the Syrian and Lebanese pounds vis-à-vis the French franc and the pound sterling was thereby in conformity with the sterling-franc rate of exchange of 200 francs equal 1 pound sterling. The sterling-Syrian-Lebanese pound rate constituted a continuation of the rate that had been established in Syria and Lebanon during the war and that Syria and Lebanon wished to maintain. For the text of this agreement, see *Lebanese Compilation*, p. 25.

10. For the text of this convention, see *Lebanese Compilation*, p. 26. With regard to the distribution of foreign exchange, Syria and Lebanon agreed that until January 1, 1946, 45 percent of the foreign currencies would be allocated to Lebanon and 55 percent of these currencies would be allocated to Syria. After that date, the foreign currencies would be disposed of in accordance with a decision to be made by the Supervisory Committee of the Exchange Control. *Lebanese Compilation*, p. 34. On January 1, 1946, French franc allocations continued to be divided in the same ratio, but export proceeds were divided in the ratio of 25 percent for Lebanon and 75 percent for Syria and remittances (mainly emigrants') in the ratio of 80 percent for Lebanon and 20 percent for Syria. Oil royalties were divided in accordance with the specific agreements that the oil companies had concluded with Syria and Lebanon. Elias S. Saba, *The Foreign Exchange Systems of Lebanon and Syria 1939-1957* (Beirut: American University of Beirut, 1961), p. 189.

11. For the text of this protocol, see *Lebanese Compilation*, p. 28.

12. Syria's decree was issued on April 20, 1944, and Lebanon's decree was issued on May 5, 1944. For the text of Lebanon's decree (Decree No. K/11), see *Lebanese Compilation*, pp. 29-31. The Office of Exchange was to be managed by the BSL subject to control and supervision by the Supervisory Committee of the Exchange Control. The functions of the Office of Exchange were to include the issuance of exchange permits, the setting of the prices for the purchase and sale of foreign currencies (after consultation with the Supervisory Committee), the compilation at the beginning of each year of a list containing the names of the accepted banks and the licensed banks, and the setting of the amount of brokerage permitted the accepted and licensed banks. All of the foregoing functions were to be effected in accordance with the instructions of the respective governments. It was provided in the decrees that the Office of Exchange would have centers in Beirut, Damascus, and Aleppo.

13. For the text of this protocol, see *Lebanese Compilation*, p. 27.

14. Except for the transfers mentioned in this chapter from the French to Syria and Lebanon and the modifications of the working relationship between the Office of Exchange and the BSL, the exchange control system that was established in those two territories in December 1939 continued virtually unmodified until August 1948. United Nations, Department of Economic and Social Affairs, *Economic Developments in the Middle East 1945-1954* (New York, 1955), pp. 198-199. Under this system, all foreign exchange transactions were subjected to license. Export proceeds as well as foreign exchange receipts from invisibles had to be surrendered at official rates to the Office of Exchange, which supplied a certain amount of exchange for licensed imports and other payments. Exports of both foreign exchange and domestic currency required authorization. International Bank for Reconstruction and Development, *The Economic Development of Syria* (Baltimore: The Johns Hopkins Press, 1955), p. 241.

15. For the minutes of the meetings which were held on July 24, 1946; September 13, 1946; December 31, 1946; January 2 and 3, 1947; January 9, 1947; January 15, 16, and 17, 1947; April 30, 1947; July 10, 1947; July 20, 1947; and December 28, 1947, see *Lebanese Compilation*.

16. The duties on these products had been suspended during World War II.

17. MIRA was the name given to the state monopoly established for Syria and Lebanon by the Allied forces in June 1942 for the purpose of providing for the cereal needs of the two territories and the forces stationed there. Its continued existence after the war ended and normal trade relations had been restored was objected to on many occasions by Lebanon. It was liquidated on March 20, 1949. Saba, *op. cit.*, p. 191.

18. At Geneva in 1947, Syria and Lebanon, negotiating as the Syrian-Lebanese Customs Union, granted concessions involving over 200 tariff items

in their customs tariff. Some of these concessions provided for the application of rates of duty which involved reductions in the prevailing rates of duty, whereas other concessions involved the binding of certain rates or the binding of the duty-free status of certain articles. Most of these concessions were on manufactured articles. In return for these concessions, the Customs Union obtained the benefits of the reductions or bindings involved in the concessions which the other contracting parties to the GATT initially negotiated with the Customs Union, or which they negotiated with each other and which were made applicable to products of Syria and Lebanon by virtue of the most-favored-nation treatment provided for in Article I of the GATT. Lebanon signed the Protocol of Provisional Application of the GATT on June 29, 1948, and became a contracting party to the GATT on July 30, 1948; and Syria signed the Protocol on June 30, 1948, and became a contracting party on July 31, 1948. For the Syrian-Lebanese schedule of concessions, the schedules of concessions of the other contracting parties, and the related provisions of the GATT, see the General Agreement on Tariffs and Trade (dated October 30, 1947), the Protocol of Provisional Application of the GATT, and the Final Act Adopted at the Conclusion of the Second Session of the Preparatory Committee of the United Nations Conference on Trade and Employment. United States, *Statutes at Large*, Vol. LXI (1947), Parts 5 and 6. A few additional GATT concessions were granted by Syria and Lebanon at Annecy in 1949. For the schedule of these concessions and the concessions of the other contracting parties, see *ibid.*, Vol. LXIV (1950-51), Part 3. Syria and Lebanon, as well as some of the other Arab countries, were also involved during the early postwar period in the negotiations concerning the proposed Havana Charter for an International Trade Organization. The Charter was drafted in March 1948 but was not put into effect by the signatory countries. For the full text of the Havana Charter, see United States, Department of State, *Havana Charter for an International Trade Organization* (Publication 3117, Commercial Policy Series 113 [Washington: Government Printing Office, 1948]).

19. Minutes of the Meeting of July 24, 1946, *Lebanese Compilation*, pp. 83-84.

20. Minutes of the Meeting of January 2 and 3, 1947, *Lebanese Compilation*, pp. 89-91.

21. See issues of the British *Board of Trade Journal* for 1946 and 1947.

22. The differences in the taxes applicable to petroleum and certain petroleum derivatives seemed to be of the greatest concern to the two countries.

23. Import and export licenses were issued by the Ministry of National Economy in each country. Exchange permits for foreign exchange were obtained from the Office of Exchange.

24. See Saba, *op. cit.*, pp. 64-65. France had maintained at a constant rate the sterling value of Syria and Lebanon's franc assets on two previous

occasions. In January 1944, it credited the BSL in French Government bonds of three months' maturity the equivalent of about 287 million French francs to reflect the increase in the value of the pound sterling vis-à-vis the French franc that had occurred after North Africa had been liberated. Later, in December 1945, the franc was again devalued vis-à-vis the pound sterling, and once again France credited the BSL with the equivalent of enough francs to offset the decline in the sterling value of Syria and Lebanon's franc assets.

25. Some of Syria's objections were that the proposed agreement provided a sterling guarantee for only a part of Syria and Lebanon's franc balances; that the foreign exchange, other than French francs, to be made available under the agreement was too small in amount; that Syria was not in a position to permit the free transfer of capital to the French franc area as provided for in the agreement; and that the clause in the agreement providing for the acceptance of payment in French francs for Syrian and Lebanese exports to the French franc area would deprive Syria of opportunities to earn United States dollars or other hard currencies from its exports of wheat, olive oil, and cotton to countries within the franc area. *Ibid.*, pp. 81-82.

26. On the date of the signature of the agreement, these assets amounted to about 8,985 million francs.

27. *Ibid.*, pp. 70-78. United Nations, *op. cit.*, p. 170.

28. *Lebanese Compilation*, pp. 17-20. Several meetings were subsequently held at which the parties agreed to further time extensions of the specified temporary measures.

29. Capital transfers and payments for invisibles continued to be subjected to prior authorization from the exchange authorities, and exports continued to be subjected to prior licensing, as well as currency prescription. Saba, *op. cit.*, pp. 99-100; and International Bank for Reconstruction and Development, *op. cit.*, pp. 241-242. For the reasons behind the official recognition of a free exchange market in Syria, see Saba, *op. cit.*, pp. 101-104. Some of the factors involved which led to this recognition were the overvaluation of the Syrian currency, the tight foreign exchange situation in Syria, and the black market operations in Syria and Lebanon.

30. Included among these specified currencies were the Belgian franc, Canadian dollar, Egyptian pound, Iraqi dinar, British pound, Swiss franc, and United States dollar. *Ibid.*, p. 105.

31. Foreign currencies bought in the free market could be freely exported from Lebanon, whether in payment for merchandise imports or invisibles or as capital transfers. *Ibid.*, p. 106.

32. British *Board of Trade Journal*, April 16, 1949, p. 795. For the reasons behind the establishment of the free exchange market in Lebanon, see Saba, *op. cit.*, pp. 107-111. Some of the factors involved, such as the overvaluation of the Lebanese pound and the existence of black market operations, were about the same as those that led Syria to recognize a free exchange market. In addition, there were other factors, such as Lebanon's

position as a reexport and transit center and France's decision to discontinue selling foreign exchange to Lebanon in September 1948.

33. In addition to the taxes on various petroleum products, the taxes imposed by the two countries on various sugar products were different. Moreover, their income taxes were also different.

34. Actually, three monetary agreements were concluded—a liquidation agreement dealing with the settlement of Syria's franc balances, an agreement dealing with Syria's debts to France, and a payments agreement.

35. These assets amounted to about 7,015 million francs.

36. French claims amounted to about 23.2 million Syrian pounds for property left in Syria. In an exchange of letters, France promised to convert to European currencies an additional sum, equivalent to about 375,000 pounds sterling, from Syria's guaranteed francs upon release of those francs. United Nations, *op. cit.*, p. 197.

37. Saba, *op. cit.*, pp. 78-84.

38. *Syrian Compilation*, pp. 41-43.

39. *Ibid.*, pp. 119-121.

40. *Ibid.*, pp. 122-127.

41. The duty imposed on rice prior to the agreement was 1 piaster per kilogram.

42. For some of the tariff changes made prior to the dissolution of the Syrian-Lebanese Customs Union, see the British *Board of Trade Journal*, October 8, 1949, p. 704; and *ibid.*, June 10, 1950, pp. 1219-1220.

43. For the text of this agreement, see *Lebanese Compilation*, pp. 47-49.

44. The first solution gave the currency of each country the right of discharge in the other country. The second solution was that referred to in Item 3 of Syria's letter of June 5, 1949, and set forth in detail in Part II of the enclosure with that letter. The third solution involved the adoption of similar policies by both countries with regard to the French franc, which would authorize the freedom, restriction or prohibition of the exchange of both currencies for the franc. The fourth solution dealt with the establishment of a stabilization fund in Lebanese pounds for the account of Syria. The fifth solution involved the free exchange of the two currencies and the use of each of the currencies as a cover for the other within a certain limit. For the text of this report, see *Lebanese Compilation*, pp. 50-55.

45. *Ibid.*, pp. 115-119.

46. *Ibid.*, pp. 120-126.

47. *Ibid.*, pp. 127-129.

48. *Ibid.*, pp. 130-134.

49. *Syrian Compilation*, pp. 101-102. Lebanon in turn prohibited, with certain exceptions, imports from Syria.

50. *Lebanese Compilation*, pp. 135-139.

51. United Nations, *op cit.*, p. 190.

52. See issues of the British *Board of Trade Journal* for 1950 and 1951.

53. For example, wheat, barley, and cereal flours—which were formerly dutiable at 50 percent ad valorem—became free of duty; cattle, sheep, goats, butter, cheese, rye, oats, husked rice, raw cotton, and wool in the mass were also exempted from duty; and the duties on various other articles (including paper, envelopes, silk fabrics, artificial silk fabrics, metals, and chemicals) were either reduced or removed. *Ibid.*

54. During 1951, the two countries also withdrew from the GATT—Lebanon on February 25, 1951, and Syria on August 6, 1951. United Nations, *Treaty Series*, Vol. LXXVII (New York, 1950-51), p. 367; and Vol. XC (New York, 1951), p. 324. The unofficial reason given for Lebanon's withdrawal was that Lebanon had surpluses of locally produced goods, such as tobacco, olive oil, citrus fruits, and silk textiles, and needed freedom of action to dispose of these surpluses. It wanted to enter into bilateral trade agreements with countries in which preferences would be granted and in which the countries would agree to buy stated quantities of certain Lebanese articles. Lebanon hoped that by granting preferences to these countries, they would be induced to buy more Lebanese products. Since such preferences would be contrary to the GATT, Lebanon withdrew. United States, Tariff Commission, *Operation of the Trade Agreements Program*, Fourth Report, July 1950-June 1951 (Washington: Government Printing Office, 1952), pp. 44-45. Little was said, officially or unofficially, regarding Syria's withdrawal from the GATT. Possible reasons were the dissolution of the customs union; Syria's desire to have complete freedom to carry out its economic policies involving the protection of its industries and foreign exchange holdings; its desire to effect closer economic ties with the other Arab League countries, which would involve the granting of preferential treatment not applicable to the other GATT countries; and its feeling that the GATT represented the interests of the industrialized countries and not the underdeveloped countries. At the time of Syria's withdrawal from the GATT, many of the underdeveloped countries were dissatisfied with the provisions in the GATT regarding the use of high tariffs and quantitative restrictions for economic development, as well as with the absence of provisions authorizing the establishment of preferential tariff arrangements for economic development. In 1952, subsequent to Syria's withdrawal, a provision was added to the GATT that would have permitted under certain conditions the establishment of preferential tariff arrangements between the Arab countries that were formerly a part of the Ottoman Empire and that were detached from it on July 24, 1923. In addition, in 1957, the provisions relating to the use of high tariffs and quantitative restrictions for economic development were completely revised and liberalized.

55. United Nations, Department of Economic Affairs, *Customs Unions: A League of Nations Contribution to the Study of Customs Union Problems* (Lake Success, New York, 1947). See also J. E. Meade (ed.), *Case Studies in*

European Economic Union: The Mechanics of Integration (London: Oxford University Press, 1962).

NOTES TO CHAPTER 4

1. International Bank for Reconstruction and Development, *The Economic Development of Iraq* (Baltimore: The Johns Hopkins Press, 1952), p. 162. British *Board of Trade Journal*, November 12, 1949, p. 954.

2. International Monetary Fund, *Second Annual Report on Exchange Restrictions* (Washington, 1951), pp. 111-112.

3. British *Board of Trade Journal*, August 12, 1950, pp. 378-381. *The International Customs Journal-Iraq* (3d supplement to the 1st ed.; Brussels: International Customs Tariffs Bureau, 1950). There had also been a number of tariff increases in 1949. *Ibid.*, June 11, 1949, p. 1232. Included among the products on which duties were increased during 1949 and 1950 were various textiles, wooden furniture, matches, meats, macaroni, pastries, dates and citrus fruits, preserved fruits and vegetables, packing paper, footwear, and various other leather products.

4. Included among these articles were hazel nuts, chestnuts, dried figs, walnuts, vegetable marrow and watermelon seeds for food, dried broad beans, lentils, garlic, fresh tomatoes and various other fresh vegetables, rice flour, refined salt, butter, tomato juice, animal fat, macaroni, spaghetti and vermicelli, beer, ethyl alcohol, honey, sesame seed, linseed, cottonseed, sesame oil, cottonseed oil, various kinds of edible vegetable oils, certain cotton yarns, pajamas of cotton, silk, or wool, raw hides, certain lining pelts and half-tanned hides, paper bags (except cement bags), cement (except kinds not manufactured in Iraq), wooden doors and window frames, bricks and tiles for buildings (except roofing tiles and firebricks), certain iron furniture, and wooden furniture. British *Board of Trade Journal*, September 8, 1951, p. 553.

5. *Ibid.*, p. 552. For a description of the restrictions and exchange controls in effect in Iraq in 1951, see *Ibid.*, pp. 550-553, and International Monetary Fund, *Third Annual Report on Exchange Restrictions* (Washington, 1952), pp. 116-117.

6. In 1946 Great Britain recognized in the Treaty of London the termination of its Mandate and the full sovereignty of Transjordan. The name of the country was changed from "Transjordan" to "The Hashemite Kingdom of Jordan" in that year, but the new name did not come into general use until 1949.

7. British *Board of Trade Journal*, May 20, 1950, p. 1066.

8. On August 5, 1950, Jordan increased its import duties on articles in 221 categories of the 305 listed in the 1950 edition of its tariff. *Foreign Com-*

merce Weekly, November 6, 1950, p. 13. On April 16, 1951, imports into Jordan of lambs, sheep, goats, chickpeas, certain beans, dates, wheat, barley, millet, maize, and cereal flour were exempted from duty. British *Board of Trade Journal*, June 2, 1951, p. 1186.

9. *Ibid.*, June 9, 1951, p. 1222.

10. For a description of the restrictions and exchange controls in effect in Jordan in 1951, see International Monetary Fund, *Third Annual Report . . .*, *op. cit.*, pp. 202-203, and International Monetary Fund, *Fourth Annual Report on Exchange Restrictions* (Washington, 1953), pp. 216-219.

11. Yemen, Persian Gulf Principalities, and Aden were added to the list of excepted countries in July 1952.

12. Included among these commodities were apricot paste, live animals, eggs, animal casings, vegetables, barley, wheat, maize, cottonseed, raw cotton, cotton textiles, liquorice root, silk textiles, raw wool, hemp, olive oil, fruits, tobacco, soap, hides and leather, and footwear. Specified currencies acceptable in payment for these exports included Belgian francs, Egyptian pounds, French francs, pounds sterling, Swiss francs, and United States dollars. The actual currency accepted for exports depended, however, on the destination of the exported commodities. Egyptian pounds could be used only in payment for exports to Egypt. Likewise, when the Lebanese pound became an acceptable currency in December 1952, it could be used only in payment for exports to Lebanon (excluding exports to any of the Lebanese free trade zone areas).

13. For a description of the exportation exchange system in Syria, see International Monetary Fund, *Fourth Annual Report . . .*, *op cit.*, pp. 268-270, and Saba, *op. cit.*, pp. 135-137.

14. *The International Customs Journal-Syria* (No. 50, 1st ed.; Brussels: International Customs Tariffs Bureau, 1951).

15. Included among these articles, in addition to cotton, were intestines, onions, garlic, haricot beans, lentils, cottonseed, sesame, liquorice root, apricot paste, oil cake, tanned sheep and goat skins, and wool in the mass. British *Board of Trade Journal*, September 15, 1951, p. 596.

16. For a description of the restrictions and exchange controls in effect in Syria in 1951, see International Monetary Fund, *Third Annual Report . . .*, *op. cit.*, pp. 146-149.

17. British *Board of Trade Journal*, March 24, 1951, p. 667; June 16, 1951, p. 1283; and December 8, 1951, p. 1199. See also *The International Customs Journal-Lebanon* (No. 49, 1st ed. and 1st and 2d supplements to 1st ed.; Brussels: International Customs Tariffs Bureau, 1951). The ad valorem duties that were imposed by Lebanon, as well as by Syria, were imposed on merchandise values that were obtained by converting the foreign currency values of such imported merchandise into Lebanese, or Syrian, pounds at the official Lebanese, or Syrian, rates of exchange. As has been indicated, both Lebanon and Syria established free exchange markets in 1948, and the free

market rates for both currencies were substantially less than the official rates. Most imports into Lebanon were financed by foreign exchange obtained in the free market. A substantial portion of Syria's imports was financed in a similar manner.

18. International Monetary Fund, *Third Annual Report . . . , op. cit.,* pp. 121-122.

19. British *Board of Trade Journal,* April 3, 1948, p. 686; and April 17, 1948, p. 762.

20. For a description of the restrictions and exchange controls in effect in Egypt in 1951, see International Monetary Fund, *Third Annual Report . . . , op. cit.,* pp. 85-88.

21. *The International Customs Journal-Egypt* (5th ed.; Brussels: International Customs Tariffs Bureau, 1950). The additional duty had initially been imposed in 1932 at the rate of 1 percent ad valorem and had been gradually increased thereafter.

22. *Ibid.* Egypt also imposed a wharfage duty of 10 percent of the amount of the base rate on each item, and a paving duty which, depending on the port of importation, varied from 1½ percent to 3¾ percent of the base rate, the ad valorem rate, the supplementary ad valorem rate, and the excise duty if any.

23. British *Board of Trade Journal,* October 22, 1949, p. 788; October 29, 1949, p. 851; and May 20, 1950, pp. 1064-1065.

24. *Ibid.,* April 21, 1951, pp. 870-871; May 12, 1951, p. 1027; and June 16, 1951, p. 1296. *The International Customs Journal-Egypt, op. cit.,* (Supplements 1 and 2 to 5th ed.).

25. *Ibid.*

26. See issues of the British *Board of Trade Journal* for the period under consideration.

27. Great Britain, Board of Trade, *Sudan: Review of Commercial Conditions* (London: His Majesty's Stationery Office, 1950), pp. 9-10.

28. See issues of the British *Board of Trade Journal.* See also United States, Department of Commerce, "Arabian Peninsula Areas—Summary of Economic Information," *International Reference Service,* Vol. V, No. 92 (1948).

29. *Ibid.*

30. *Ibid.* All articles imported specially for the royal family were exempted from duty.

31. Article 6 of the agreement provided that the agreement would remain in effect for one year commencing from the date of signing. For the Egyptian decree promulgating this agreement, see the *Journal Officiel du Gouvernement Égyptien,* No. 123, September 22, 1949, p. 1.

32. This list contained the following articles: all types of locally manufactured leather and locally manufactured leather items such as shoes, travel bags, belts, and straps; all types of cotton and woolen cloth of local manu-

facture and parts of clothing cut therefrom; all types of silk cloth of local or foreign make and silk clothing if locally tailored and not imported ready-made; locally manufactured glassware, earthenware, pottery, chinaware, and medical instruments; locally manufactured plastics, including beads; rugs, carpets and blankets manufactured locally of wool or cotton; locally manufactured aluminum products; preserved foods and confectionery of local manufacture, not packed in tin containers; and all other local products and manufactures the export of which was not restricted by licensing or did not require hard currency payment.

33. It was provided in the agreement that all payments (credits and debits) would be effected within the limits of the exchange regulations in force in each of the two countries.

34. This list contained the following articles: locally manufactured wooden furniture, including crystal glass parts, mirrors, hinges, locks and keys, upholstery or ticking; locally carpentered wooden doors and windows containing iron, glass, or metal netting; all types of preserved foods and confectionery of local origin, packed in tin containers; locally manufactured electric bulbs; rice; sweets made of dregs of sesame oil; macaroni, biscuits, and all types of agina (a food made of flour, sugar, and various other ingredients); black honey; and cement and cement tiles.

35. The trade agreement with Syria was signed on August 20, 1950; the trade agreement with Jordan was signed on August 5, 1951; and the trade and payments agreement with Lebanon was signed on September 2, 1951. It was provided in each agreement that the agreement would be effective as of the date of signature. For the Egyptian decrees promulgating these agreements, see *Journal Officiel du Gouvernement Égyptien*, No. 113 (Supplement), November 30, 1950, p. 4; No. 102, November 5, 1951, p. 4; and No. 113, December 10, 1951, p. 4. The payments arrangements provided for in the Egyptian-Lebanese agreement did not come into force until April 1952. National Bank of Egypt, *Economic Bulletin*, Vol. V, No. 2 (Cairo, 1952), p. 120.

36. Article 9 of each agreement provided that for purposes of the application of the agreement, certificates of origin issued by competent authorities of each of the contracting parties would be accepted by the other contracting party. Article 4 provided that in case of a change in the import regulations of either of the contracting parties, both parties would consult on the necessity of modifying the terms of the agreement so as to conform to the new situation.

37. Article 1.

38. Articles 7 and 8. In the trade agreement between Egypt and Lebanon, it was specifically provided in Article 8 that Jordan would be regarded as a country contiguous to Lebanon.

39. Article 5.

40. The current payments specified in each annexed list included the following: (1) value of exported articles, plus shipping and insurance costs;

(2) profits on invested capital; (3) expenses of diplomatic, consular, and official missions and Arab League expenses; (4) expenses connected with travel, tourism, health, and commercial trips; (5) expenses connected with student travel and residence and study fees, and salaries of officials and technicians; (6) net profits derived from operations of air lines and other means of communication; (7) periodic settlement of revenues from postal, telegraphic, and other telecommunications; (8) taxes and fees as well as fines and compensations connected with legal and administrative matters; (9) insurance installments; (10) sums due on patents, trademarks, and copyrights in accordance with the provisions of the respective laws of each country; (11) sums due from the showing of films of one contracting country in the other contracting country, subscription fees for newspapers, magazines, and any other publication issued in one country and distributed in the other country.

41. Article 10.

42. The current payments to which the agreement applied were specified in a list annexed to the agreement and were the same as the current payments specified in the lists annexed to the Syrian and Jordanian agreements.

43. Article 10.

44. The list in the agreement with Syria contained the following articles: horses; rams; sheep; goats; butter; eggs; olives; onions; garlic; potatoes; legumes; dried fruits; apricot paste and jams; almonds, walnuts, and pistachio nuts; small raisins of all kinds; fresh fruits; wheat; burghol (ground wheat); wheat flour; barley; liquorice root, liquorice powder, and liquorice root extracts; products for tanning (roots, plants, leaves, flowers, seeds, etc.); olive oil and vegetable oils; fruits preserved naturally or with sugar; concentrated fruit juice, such as concentrated juices from grapes and raisins; arak; tobacco and tombac; asphalt bricks; essential and natural aromatic oils; soap; glue; goat skins and sheep skins (tanned, polished, or gilded); Arabic books; pure or mixed natural silk textiles; pure or mixed artificial silk textiles; pure silk yarns; hosiery; caraway seeds; hemp rope and cordage; glass panes; rasras; embroidery; sweet corn; and locally produced grinding stones for flour.

The list in the agreement with Lebanon contained the following articles: silk or artificial silk textiles; woolen textiles; brushes for cloth or painting, made of vegetable or animal fibers or of plastic; matches; paints; olive oil and vegetable oils; soap made of olive oil or other oil; eau de cologne; biscuits; chocolate; jams; fruit juices; metal buckles for shoes and bags; plumbing fixtures (such as fountain taps, etc.); cement; olives, potatoes, onions, legumes, and other fresh vegetables; apples, pears, oranges, limes, and other fresh fruits; honey; wines; arak; leather; Arabic printed books; hosiery; eggs; dried figs and other dried fruits; macaroni; confectionery; sesame oil; baklawa; and household embroidered linen.

The list in the agreement with Jordan contained the following articles: camels; cows; horses; sheep; goats; butter, cheese, and other dairy products; eggs; beans, lentils, chickpeas, and other fresh vegetables; bananas, melons, grapes, and other fresh fruits; dried vegetables; almonds; walnuts; raw wool; tobacco; tombac; Holy Land products; liquors and other alcoholic drinks; scrap iron, copper scrap, and other scrap metals; marble; alabaster; wheat; barley; white and yellow maize; sesame; oil seeds; plants for tanning and dyeing; olive oil; edible oils and fats; Nabulsi soap; and raw hides and tanned skins.

45. Article 3.

46. The list in the agreement with Syria contained the following articles: domestically produced electric light bulbs; tarbooshes; buttons of all kinds; single or "mezwi" fine cotton yarns (above No. 40); domestically produced carpets and rugs; domestically produced flax yarns and flax products; henna; Arabic printed books; Egyptian motion picture films and records; domestically produced oil products used as insecticides and for certain industrial purposes; goat's hair; and domestically produced essential and aromatic oils.

The list in the agreement with Lebanon contained the following articles: cotton; salt; domestically produced electric light bulbs; tarbooshes; buttons of all kinds; fine cotton yarns (above No. 40); domestically produced flax yarns and flax products; henna; Arabic printed books; Egyptian motion picture films and records; domestically produced oil products used as insecticides and for certain industrial purposes; domestically produced essential and aromatic oils; cotton piece goods; shoes; rice starch; wines; chocolate; domestically produced pharmaceutical products; onions; potatoes; rope and cordage; domestically produced medicated cotton; and domestically produced glass and glassware.

The list in the agreement with Jordan contained the following articles: domestically produced electric light bulbs; tarbooshes; buttons of all kinds; fine cotton yarns; domestically produced carpets and rugs; domestically produced flax yarns and flax products; henna; Arabic printed books; Egyptian motion picture films and records; domestically produced oil products used as insecticides and for certain industrial purposes; cotton textiles and needle work (for not more than 25,000 pounds); leather products; rice starch; domestically produced liquors; chocolate; domestically produced pharmaceutical products; onions; potatoes; rope and cordage; domestically produced medicated cotton; glassware; products of the Egyptian plastics industries; chalk; domestically produced ink; domestically produced printing letters; and cigarettes.

47. It is to be noted that Syria's agreement with Egypt was concluded prior to Syria's withdrawal from the GATT, and, therefore, could not have involved the granting of preferences by Syria to Egyptian products without being in violation of the GATT. As indicated, the GATT did not permit, while Syria and Lebanon were contracting parties, the establishment of new tariff preferences between those countries and the other Arab countries. It did permit the continuation or application of the tariff preferences that were or had been in force between Syria and Lebanon and Transjordan and Pales-

tine, respectively. These preferences could not exceed, however, the margins of preference existing on November 30, 1938, between Syria and Lebanon's normal duties and the preferential duties that were applied to Transjordanian and Palestinian products, and they were subject to elimination by negotiation. The GATT also permitted the formation of customs unions or free trade areas or the adoption of interim agreements necessary for the formation of such unions or areas (Article XXIV). Although the formation of a customs union or free trade area would involve the granting of new preferences, the drafters of the GATT did not regard such unions or areas as being the same as preferential arrangements. See Clair Wilcox, *A Charter for World Trade* (New York: The Macmillan Company, 1949), pp. 70-71.

48. Iraq also concluded a trade and payments agreement with Syria in 1950 that provided for tariff preferences for various Iraqi and Syrian products, but the agreement was not ratified by the two countries. International Monetary Fund, *International Financial News Survey,* May 25, 1951, p. 361; and June 8, 1951, p. 376. International Bank for Reconstruction and Development, *The Economic Development of Syria* (Baltimore: The Johns Hopkins Press, 1955), p. 236.

49. Article 1.

50. Articles 2 and 6.

51. Article 7.

52. It also agreed to reduce the rate of duty applicable to Lebanese green and salted olives, not in hermetically sealed jars, from 54 fils per kilogram net to 40 fils per kilogram net.

53. It also agreed to reduce the rate of duty applicable to Iraqi pure horsehair from 25 percent ad valorem to 20 percent ad valorem. With regard to some of the Lebanese and Iraqi products on the lists attached to the agreement, the concessions which were made involved rather substantial decreases. Lebanese bananas, apples, medlars, cherries, peaches, and certain fruit juices had been dutiable at 33⅓ percent ad valorem when the agreement was negotiated; Iraqi blankets and lentils had been subjected to Lebanon's normal rates of duty of 30 percent and 50 percent, respectively; and Iraqi dates in boxes of 1 kilogram or less, gum tragacanth, and date molasses had been subjected to Lebanon's normal rate of duty of 25 percent ad valorem. On the other hand, Lebanese books and magazines had been entering Iraq free of duty when the agreement was negotiated, and Iraqi goats, sheep, cattle, husked rice, raw hides and skins, magazines and various books, raw wool, and woolen yarn and thread, combed or carded, had been exempted from duty upon importation into Lebanon. Hence, the concessions on these products constituted simply bindings of the prevailing duty-free treatment accorded such articles. Article 4 of the agreement provided that domestically produced commodities originating in one of the contracting countries and exported to the other country had to be accompanied by a certificate of origin issued by the appropriate authorities of the exporting country. Any

product of which at least 50 percent of the value consisted of domestic raw materials and manufacturing costs was to be considered of domestic origin. The agreement also specified that the domestic products that were to be entitled to the reduced rates or duty-free treatment provided for in the agreement had to be exported directly from the territory of one contracting party to the territory of the other contracting party.

54. Instruments of ratification were exchanged on April 10, 1952, and the agreement came into force on April 11, 1952. See Lebanon's official journal, *Al-Jarida al-Rasmiya*, No. 19, May 7, 1952, p. 381.

55. Article 8.

56. The agreement was concluded by an exchange of notes on September 27, 1945. For the Egyptian decree promulgating this agreement, see *Journal Officiel du Gouvernement Égyptien*, No. 155, October 29, 1945, p. 2.

57. The agreement was concluded by an exchange of notes on April 21, 1947, and came into force on that date. For the texts of these notes, see United Nations, *Treaty Series*, Vol. XI (New York, 1947), pp. 3-9.

58. The agreement, which was signed on January 29, 1950, and which came into force on March 12, 1950, was for one year's duration, subject to automatic renewal unless one of the parties expressed its desire to terminate or modify the agreement.

59. See International Bank for Reconstruction and Development, *The Economic Development of Syria, op. cit.*, p. 235.

60. See Appendix II.

61. For a summary of the industrial development in Egypt, Iraq, Lebanon, and Syria during the early postwar period, see United Nations, Department of Economic and Social Affairs, *Economic Developments in the Middle East 1945-1954* (New York, 1955), pp. 36-41, 98-99, 157-163, and 185-189.

62. In Appendix II, a fairly substantial amount of imports into Lebanon from Iraq is shown for 1951. However, over 55 percent of this amount consisted of petroleum products, which were included in Lebanon's import statistics but not in Iraq's export statistics.

63. Over 85 percent of the amount of imports into Egypt from Iraq shown in Appendix II for 1951 consisted of petroleum products.

64. Syria's exports of agricultural products to Jordan consisted predominantly of cereals.

65. These exports of petroleum products (made from crude Iraqi oil entering through the pipeline) from Lebanon to Syria were listed in Lebanon's statistics for 1951 as transit trade with Syria rather than as exports to Syria.

66. The Maghreb countries continued for the most part to be economically removed from the other Arab countries during the early postwar period. Libya was occupied by the British and French until almost the end of 1951, and the other Maghreb countries were in the process of being reinte-

grated into the French economy. Egypt's trade increased with these countries but involved only a few products. Imports in 1951 consisted mainly of beans and olive oil from Tunisia and Algeria, vegetable extracts for soft drinks from Morocco, and livestock and olive oil from Libya, and exports to Morocco, Algeria, and Tunisia consisted mainly of rice. Exports to Libya were more substantial than to the other three Maghreb countries and included, in addition to rice, a rather sizable amount of cotton cloth.

67. The Pact of the League of Arab States came into force on May 10, 1945, fifteen days after the deposit of the fourth instrument of ratification with the Secretary-General of the League, in accordance with Article 20 of the Pact. Following are the dates of deposit of the instrument of ratification and of the entry into force of the Pact in respect to each of the original signatories:

	Date of deposit of instrument of ratification	Date of entry into force
Transjordan	April 10, 1945	May 10, 1945
Egypt	April 12, 1945	May 10, 1945
Saudi Arabia	April 16, 1945	May 10, 1945
Iraq	April 25, 1945	May 10, 1945
Lebanon	May 16, 1945	June 1, 1945
Syria	May 19, 1945	June 4, 1945
Yemen	February 9, 1946	February 24, 1946

The other Arab countries became members of the Arab League after they achieved independence: Libya in March 1953, the Sudan in January 1956, Morocco and Tunisia in October 1958, Kuwait in July 1961, and Algeria in August 1962. The Pact is for a period of unlimited duration with each member retaining the right to withdraw subject to the giving of one year's notice before the effective date of withdrawal. The text of the Arab League Pact appears in United Nations, *Treaty Series*, Vol. LXX (New York, 1950), pp. 237-263.

68. Article 2 of the Pact of the League of Arab States.

69. B. Y. Boutros-Ghali, "The Arab League 1945-1955," *International Conciliation,* Carnegie Endowment for International Peace, Vol. CDXCVIII (May 1954), pp. 433-434. The Council of the League, which was composed of representatives of the member states and which was the principal organ provided for in the Arab League Pact, had very little authority under the Pact to adopt any substantive measures which would be binding on the member states, even if it acted unanimously. The procedure followed in attempting to effect closer economic ties between the member states involved the formulation of draft agreements by the Committee for Financial and Economic Affairs established pursuant to Article 4 of the Pact and their presentation to

the Council for examination before their submission to the member states. The League was not meant to be a supranational organization but rather an organization to provide the member states with an opportunity to air their differences and agree upon various measures, the implementation of which would be left to the individual states. For a study of the Arab League, see Robert W. Macdonald, *The League of Arab States* (Princeton: Princeton University Press, 1965).

70. This treaty was approved by the Council of the League of Arab States on April 17, 1950, and was eventually signed and ratified by all of the original Arab League states. The treaty came into force on August 22, 1952, fifteen days after the deposit of the fourth instrument of ratification with the Secretary-General of the League, in accordance with Article 13 of the treaty. Following are the dates of the signature, of the deposit of the instrument of ratification, and of the entry into force of the treaty in respect to each of the original Arab League states:

	Date of signature	Date of deposit of instrument of ratification	Date of entry into force
Syria	June 17, 1950	October 31, 1951	August 22, 1952
Saudi Arabia	June 17, 1950	August 19, 1952	September 3, 1952
Lebanon	June 17, 1950	December 24, 1952	January 8, 1953
Yemen	June 17, 1950	October 11, 1953	October 26, 1953
Egypt	June 17, 1950	November 22, 1951	August 22, 1952
Iraq	February 2, 1951	August 7, 1952	August 22, 1952
Jordan	February 16, 1952	March 31, 1952	August 22, 1952

The other Arab countries subsequently adhered to the treaty—Morocco on June 13, 1961; Kuwait on August 12, 1961; and Libya, Tunisia, Sudan, and Algeria on September 11, 1964. Article 12 of the treaty provides that after a lapse of ten years from the date of ratification of the treaty, a contracting state may withdraw from it upon giving twelve months' notice to the Secretary-General of the Arab League. For the text of this treaty, see Arab Information Center, *Basic Documents of the League of Arab States*, Document Collections Number 1 (New York, 1955), pp. 21-25.

71. Article 7.

72. Article 8.

NOTES TO CHAPTER 5

1. For the currency and quantitative trade control systems of the Arab countries as of the beginning of 1964, see International Monetary Fund, *Fifteenth Annual Report on Exchange Restrictions* (Washington, 1964). For their systems during the preceding years, see the earlier reports.

2. For general descriptions of these economic development programs, see United Nations, Department of Economic and Social Affairs, *Economic Developments in the Middle East* for 1958-59, 1959-61, and 1961-63 (New York, 1960, 1962, and 1964, respectively).

3. United Nations, Department of Economic and Social Affairs, *Summary of Recent Economic Developments in the Middle East 1952-53* (New York, 1954), pp. 67-84.

4. Imports from Syria and Lebanon had been financed through the free exchange market for some time prior to 1955.

5. The additional ad valorem, supplementary ad valorem, and wharfage duties were consolidated with the base duties. The statistical, pavement, porterage, and excise or consumption duties were retained as separate duties.

6. *UAR Customs Tariff-January 1962*, trans. Tawfik Mohamed Sadek (Cairo: Japan Trade Center, 1962). During 1962 and 1963, further increases were made in some of these rates of duty, as well as in the rates of duty applicable to various other products. For a translation of the U.A.R. Customs Tariff, as amended to December 1964, see *The International Customs Journal-United Arab Republic* (1st ed.; Brussels: International Customs Tariffs Bureau, 1964).

7. For example, under the Syrian tariff act that became effective on January 1, 1963, the duty on most cosmetics was 40 or 50 percent; on various articles of wood, such as fruit bowls, cigarette boxes, and table lamps, 50 percent; on various kinds of textile wearing apparel, 40 or 50 percent or more; on bed and table linens, 35 to 100 percent; on most footwear, 65 percent; on table glassware, 75 percent; and on most iron or steel furniture, 75 percent. In addition, high specific rates subject to high minimum ad valorem duties were applicable to most wooden furniture (minimum ad valorem rate of 50 percent), knitted silk or artificial silk hosiery and certain types of glass (minimum ad valorem rate of 65 percent), most confectionery (minimum ad valorem rate of 50 or 65 percent), most pastry (minimum ad valorem rate of 40 percent), various prepared and preserved fruits and vegetables (minimum ad valorem rate of 65 percent), household and toilet soap (minimum ad valorem rate of 35 percent), and various other products, including fresh oranges, apples, peaches, melons, and certain other fruits, hydrogenated cottonseed oil, beer, prepared hides and skins, and various textile fabrics. Bureau des Documentations Syriennes & Arabes, *Tarif Général Permanent des Douanes de Syrie* (6th ed.; Damascus, 1963). Under the Iraqi tariff act, as of the latter part of 1962, most furniture was dutiable at 100 percent ad valorem; luggage, handbags, and most leather or composition leather wearing apparel were dutiable at 60 percent ad valorem; soft drinks were dutiable at 100 percent ad valorem; alcoholic beverages were subject to very high specific rates of duty; most toilet preparations were dutiable at 75 percent ad valorem; various articles of wood, such as trunks, fruit bowls, cigarette boxes, and table lamps, were dutiable at 60 percent ad valorem; most knitted and crocheted fabrics and most wearing apparel of silk were dutiable at 60 per-

cent ad valorem, of artificial silk at 50 percent ad valorem, and of wool or cotton at 35 or 30 percent ad valorem; and most headwear was dutiable at 50 percent ad valorem. In addition, from 1956 to 1962, the specific rate of duty on butter had been increased from 75 to 225 fils per kilogram net; on olives in brine from 40 to 110 fils per kilogram net; on most prepared and preserved meats from 100 to 250 fils per kilogram net; on various prepared and preserved vegetables from 60 to 120 fils per kilogram net; on fruit jams, jellies, marmalades, and pastes (other than apricot paste) from 60 to 100 fils per kilogram net; on nonalcoholic fruit juices from 50 to 100 fils per kilogram net; and on household soap from 30 to 45 fils per kilogram gross. Duties were also increased on many other products, including fish, cheese, milk, various silk or artificial silk fabrics, pistachio and other nuts, confectionery, pastry, tobacco, and carpets and rugs. Iraq, Ministry of Finance, *Customs Tariff Law-1955* (Baghdad, 1956), and first nine amendments thereto.

8. Included among the articles that were dutiable at a specified rate of 50 percent ad valorem in the tariff schedules (about 35 percent ad valorem based on the free market rate of exchange) were fresh olives, potatoes, tomatoes, onions, and various other fresh vegetables; preserved vegetables; flour of rye, barley, oats, maize, millet, or buckwheat; apricot paste; various fish and animal glues; leather or composition leather gloves; wooden cigarette boxes, fruit bowls, and lamps; cigarette paper in booklet form; certain stationery; certain containers of paper or paperboard; footwear; and wooden furniture. *The International Customs Journal-Lebanon* (2d ed. and 1st and 2d supplements to 2d ed.; Brussels: International Customs Tariffs Bureau, 1961).

9. Included among the articles that were subjected to a specified ad valorem minimum of 50 percent were fresh bananas, oranges, lemons, figs, grapes, apples, pears, peaches, melons, and various other fresh fruits; preserved fruits; most cosmetics; sole leather and machine belting leather; various silk fabrics; various wearing apparel of silk or artificial silk; certain light bulbs; and certain brooms and brushes. *Ibid.*

10. Duties ranging from 50 to 100 percent or more were imposed on footwear, various hydrogenated animal or vegetable fats or oils, tomato puree and other prepared or preserved tomatoes, certain storage batteries, toilet paper, certain wooden containers, alcoholic beverages, leather or composition leather gloves, certain textile wearing apparel, certain chocolate and other confectionery, furniture, and various other articles.

11. Jordan, Ministry of Finance, *Al-Ta'rifa al-Jumrukiya-1962* (Amman, 1962). For a translation of the Jordanian Customs Tariff, as amended to December 1964, see *The International Customs Journal-Jordan* (2d ed.; Brussels: International Customs Tariffs Bureau, 1964).

12. Included among the products on which the Sudan imposed such duties were textile wearing apparel and various other textiles; alcoholic beverages; cosmetics; biscuits; footwear; butter; carpets and rugs; confectionery;

chinaware, pottery, and earthenware; glassware; fresh or prepared or pre-served fruits and vegetables; various other foodstuffs; jewelry; molasses; salt; playing cards; yeast; watches and clocks; essential oil; most vegetable oils; and plasticware. Moreover, the rate of duty of 40 percent ad valorem was appli-cable to many other articles described in the Sudan's tariff schedule, as well as to all articles not described in that schedule. *The International Customs Journal-Sudanese Republic* (5th ed. and 1st, 2d, and 3d supplements to 5th ed.; Brussels: International Customs Tariffs Bureau, 1956). Most of the aforenamed articles were also subjected to high duties by Morocco. *The International Customs Journal-Morocco* (7th ed.; Brussels: International Customs Tariffs Bureau, 1962). Morocco also imposed the following additional duties on imports: a special import tax of 2.5 percent on the value of the product, a customs stamp fee equal to 1 percent of the base duty and the special tax, and a purchase and sales tax of 8 percent on the value of the product plus the base duty and special tax.

13. *The International Customs Journal-Tunisia* (6th ed.; Brussels: Inter-national Customs Tariffs Bureau, 1961). *Tarif des Droits de Douanes d'Importation* (Algiers, 1963). *Libya Customs Tariff Schedules-1962*, trans. Ibrahim Hafez Ramadan (Tripoli, 1962); and *The International Customs Journal-Libya* (2d ed. and 1st supplement to 2d ed.; Brussels: International Customs Tariffs Bureau, 1963). Algeria applied, with certain exceptions, the French tariff until it achieved its independence in 1962. After that, it made certain changes in its duties, and in October 1963 it promulgated a new tariff which provided for the application of rather low rates of duty to most products. In addition, imports from France and the other countries of the European Economic Community were subject to preferential rates of duty, which were substantially lower than the rates on imports from other countries. The preferential treatment accorded to French products, either as exemptions from duty or reduced duties, was greater than that accorded to the products of the other EEC countries. Although Algeria applied rather low import duties to most products, a number were subject to the rather high internal taxes imposed by Algeria. United States, Department of Commerce, "Foreign Trade Regulations of the Republic of Algeria," *Overseas Business Reports,* No. 64-122 (1964), p. 2. Likewise, a number of additional taxes were imposed on imports by Tunisia.

14. United States, Department of Commerce, "Establishing a Business in Kuwait," *Overseas Business Reports*, No. 63-91 (1963), pp. 4-5.

15. At the same time that it reduced or eliminated these duties, it also increased its duties on certain articles to protect its domestic producers. Included among these articles were cement, gypsum, fresh or frozen vege-tables, tiles, and marble. *International Commerce*, August 6, 1962, p. 45.

16. A few articles, such as woolen clothing, carpets, cosmetics, cameras, precious stones, artificial flowers and ornaments, and cigarette lighters, were dutiable at 40 percent ad valorem; and motor vehicles, silk or artificial silk

fabrics and clothing, furs, and cloth and clothing containing metallic substances were dutiable at 50 percent. High customs duties were also imposed on cigarettes and tobacco, and all imported products were subject to a 5 percent defense tax, based on the cost of the product before the assessment of the import duty. *Ibid.*, September 23, 1963, p. 32.

17. There were also a few other inter-Arab bilateral trade and/or payments agreements that were concluded during this period. For example, agreements were concluded by Iraq with Tunisia and Morocco in 1960, by Lebanon with the Sudan in 1962, by the U.A.R. with Yemen in 1963, and by Algeria with Tunisia and Morocco in 1963. These agreements, except for the Algerian agreements, provided primarily for most-favored-nation treatment and for the authorization by the contracting parties of imports and exports from and to each other. The Algerian agreements provided for preferential treatment for various products; however, the agreement with Morocco was a provisional agreement which expired on January 1, 1964.

18. The agreement was concluded on February 4, 1952, and came into force on March 8, 1952. See Lebanon's official journal, *Al-Jarida al-Rasmiya*, No. 11, March 12, 1952, p. 212. The specified duration of the agreement was for one year from the date of its entry into force, subject to renewal from year to year upon request of either party and the approval of the other party.

19. The agreement was concluded on March 5, 1953, and came into force on March 28, 1953. *Ibid.*, No. 13, April 1, 1953, p. 771. The specified duration of the agreement was for six months from the date of its entry into force. However, the duration was extended, and the agreement continued in force during the period under consideration.

20. The agreement was concluded on August 27, 1952, and came into force on March 10, 1953. *Ibid.*, p. 770. The specified duration of the agreement was for one year from the date of its entry into force, subject to automatic renewal annually unless one of the parties indicated its desire three months before the end of any annual period to terminate the agreement.

21. The agreement was concluded on February 18, 1953, and came into force on April 29, 1953. The specified duration of the agreement was the same as that of the 1952 Jordanian-Lebanese agreement. On August 4, 1956, Jordan and Syria signed an agreement that provided for the formation of an economic union between the two countries, but instruments of ratification were not exchanged and the agreement did not come into force.

22. The agreement was concluded on September 30, 1953, and came into force on June 22, 1954. It contained the same duration provision as the 1952 and 1953 Jordanian agreements with Lebanon and Syria.

23. For example, the lists of agricultural and animal products in the Syrian-Lebanese agreements contained such articles as live animals; fresh, chilled, or frozen meats; milk; cheese; eggs; butter; fresh or dried fruits and vegetables; cereals; cereal flour; various seeds; sugar beet; fruit juice; raw tobacco; raw sheep and goat skins; raw wool; and raw cotton. They did not

include animal or vegetable fats or oils; most prepared or preserved meats, vegetables, or fruits; tanned hides or skins; or sugar. Some of these commodities were contained in the lists of industrial products annexed to the agreements, while others were not contained in any of the lists. In the Jordanian agreements with Syria and Lebanon, fresh, salted, or smoked fish, wheat and its by-products, barley and its by-products, lentils, and chickpeas imported into Jordan from Syria or Lebanon and into Syria from Jordan were specifically excepted from the agricultural and animal products that were to be exempt from customs duties and import licenses. Tobacco and salt were also excepted in the Syrian-Jordanian agreement from such exemptions, and tobacco and tombac were specifically excepted from the exemptions for agricultural and animal products in the Iraqi-Jordanian agreement. The Syrian-Lebanese agreements also provided for the assessment by the two countries of unified minimum customs duties on the agricultural and animal products (except wheat and wheat flour) contained in the annexed lists when such products were imported from a third country. Many of these unified duties were substantially higher than the duties that Lebanon had been imposing on such products. The unified duties were not to be applicable to agricultural and animal products of Jordanian origin, nor were those that were in conflict with Lebanon's 1951 trade agreement with Iraq to be imposed on such Iraqi products when imported into Lebanon.

24. Among these products were preserved fruits and vegetables, vinegar, various glass articles, straw mats, cotton carpets, men's hosiery, confectionery, certain brushes, and various ceramic articles. Unified minimum customs duties were to be applied to some of the products, subject to the reservation by each party of the right not to apply such duties, as well as the unified minimum duties provided for agricultural and animal products, if the other party were to ban, restrict, or subject to duty the exportation of such products.

25. Among these products were starch, beer, macaroni and similar articles, women's hosiery, chocolate and chocolate articles, biscuits, wines, certain silk thread and yarn, certain wooden furniture, certain cardboard, certain cement, household soap, and tanned hides and skins.

26. In an exchange of notes annexed to the agreement, the two countries promised to extend most-favored-nation treatment to each other with regard to trade exchanges, the movement of persons between the two countries, the transfer of capital, and the handling of commercial, agricultural, and industrial operations. Syria also promised to authorize, as an exception to its practice of restricting imports to countries of origin, the importation of foreign goods from Lebanon whenever the commercial interests of the two countries required it.

27. The two countries also reserved the right to require an export or import license for the exportation or importation of some of the agricultural and animal products contained in the list of such products annexed to the agreement, but these products were not specified in the agreement.

28. Unified minimum customs duties were specified for the industrial products on the free and reduced-duty lists.

29. Among these items were arak; certain processed leather; wickerwork furniture and bamboo furniture; bottle stoppers; cast iron, iron, or steel stoves and boilers; men's hosiery; certain silk fabrics; certain artificial silk fabrics; and plywood.

30. Among these products were linseed oil, beer, varnishes, toilet soap, leather suitcases, leather soles, rubber soles, sheets of wood, bentwood chairs, certain woolen yarns and textiles, artificial silk hosiery fabrics in the piece, certain cotton textiles, certain footwear, certain cotton hats and caps, umbrellas, and certain cement tiles.

31. The parties also reserved the right to impose, for reasons of organization, an import or export license on the importation or exportation of certain agricultural and animal products contained in the agricultural list attached to the agreement, and to prohibit or restrict the exportation of any agricultural or animal product.

32. The duty-free lists attached to the trade agreement between Jordan and Lebanon included such Jordanian articles as marble, phosphate and phosphate products, coral products, gypsum and sand, olive oil, crushed glass and glass waste, paving stones, potash, mats, and cigarettes; and such Lebanese articles as tar, certain unbleached cotton fabrics, cigarette paper books, agricultural implements, tanned hides and skins, yarns imported for industrial purposes, glass and glassware, animal hair, raw materials for making brushes or brooms, veneers, and cottonseed oil. The duty-free lists attached to the trade agreement between Jordan and Syria included most of the aforementioned Jordanian articles plus a few other Jordanian articles, including cheese; and such Syrian articles as those specified above for Lebanon, as well as yarn, rope, and thread of linen, hemp, or jute; felt; Arab headdress and headbands; apricot paste; asphalt; and certain sulphur.

33. The lists of Syrian and Lebanese articles which were to be subject to import duties equivalent to one-third of the ordinary Jordanian duties included such articles as compressed liquid or solid gases, various fruit or vegetable preparations, drugs and other pharmaceutical preparations, various leather products (excluding shoes), certain wooden boxes, silk and silk fabrics, certain artificial silk fabrics, certain cotton fabrics, underwear, women's hosiery, and copper kitchen utensils. There was no reduced-duty list of Jordanian products attached to the trade agreement between Lebanon and Jordan. The trade agreement between Syria and Jordan contained a list of Jordanian products which were to be subject to import duties equivalent to two-thirds of the normal Syrian duties. This list included such articles as macaroni and similar products, wine, cement bags, vegetable preparations, and fruit preparations.

34. The full-duty lists attached to the two agreements included such Lebanese and/or Syrian products as cement and cement articles, shoes, arak,

macaroni and similar articles, nails, aluminum utensils, brushes and brooms, men's hosiery, distilled alcohol, mirrors, paper articles, various knit goods, various wearing apparel, furniture, tobacco and cigarettes, matches, olive oil, and soap. Jordanian products which were to be subject to full normal duties and to import licenses upon importation into Lebanon included tanned hides and skins, soap, alcohol and alcoholic beverages, macaroni and similar articles, wax, leaf tobacco, and tombac. There was no full-duty list of Jordanian products attached to the trade agreement between Jordan and Syria.

35. In the Syrian-Jordanian agreement, each of the contracting parties also reserved the right to prohibit, restrict, or license the exportation of any agricultural or animal product. In the Lebanese-Jordanian agreement this right was limited to wheat, barley, maize, millet, and their by-products, and to sesame. In both agreements, the contracting parties reserved the right to impose certain excise taxes on animal and agricultural products, as well as on industrial products, imported from each other. The agreements also contained provisions relating to most-favored-nation treatment and to transit and free trade zone privileges, as well as rather elaborate provisions regarding transportation of merchandise by rail and motor vehicles.

36. The lists included such Iraqi products as date syrup; tanned or salted skins; bleached or unbleached sheeting; cotton khaki cloth; dyed cotton yarn; dyed cotton cloth in the piece; winter or summer woolen suitings; rope and cordage; woolen or cotton yarns for industry; certain other woolen articles; and toilet soap; and such Jordanian products as cheese; olive oil soap; phosphate; marble, alabaster, gypsum, and natural stones, crude or polished; canned vegetables; canned fruits; jams; tomato paste; various Holy Land manufactures (mother-of-pearl, olive wood, and embroideries); leather watch straps; salted skins; gravel; tiles; olive oil; and certain olives.

37. Jordan also reserved the right to regulate the importation of barley, rice, wheat, lentils, and chickpeas by means of import licenses when necessary but only for a limited period of time, and both countries reserved the right to prohibit or subject to license the exportation of any agricultural or animal product. The agreement also provided for most-favored-nation treatment with regard to import duties and taxes, import and export licenses, and customs regulations. In addition, it provided that articles in transit across one of the countries to the other would be exempt from duties and taxes.

38. These conventions were called the Convention for Facilitating Trade Exchange and Regulating Transit Trade Between States of the Arab League, and the Convention for the Settlement of Payments of Current Transactions and the Transfer of Capital Between States of the Arab League. They came into force on December 12, 1953, one month after the deposit of the third instrument of ratification with the Secretary-General of the Arab League, in accordance with Article 8 of the trade convention and Article 6 of the payments convention. Following are the dates of the signature, of the deposit of the instrument of ratification, and of the entry into force of the trade convention in respect to each of the original Arab League states:

	Date of signature	Date of deposit of instrument of ratification	Date of entry into force
Lebanon	Sept. 7, 1953	Sept. 17, 1953	Dec. 12, 1953
Jordan	Sept. 7, 1953	Oct. 27, 1953	Dec. 12, 1953
Egypt	Sept. 7, 1953	Nov. 12, 1953	Dec. 12, 1953
Syria	Sept. 7, 1953	June 23, 1954	July 23, 1954
Iraq	Sept. 7, 1953	Dec. 25, 1954	Jan. 25, 1955
Saudi Arabia	Sept. 13, 1953	Feb. 23, 1954	March 23, 1954
Yemen	Dec. 8, 1953		

The dates of signature, deposit, and entry into force in respect to the payments convention are the same as the above dates for each of the aforementioned countries, except that Syria deposited its instrument of ratification of the payments convention on June 13, 1954. The official Arabic texts of these conventions, as well as the texts of other multilateral agreements involving the Arab League countries, are contained in a compilation by the Arab League entitled *Majmu'a al-Mu'ahadat wa al-Ittafaqiyat al-Ma'quda fi Nitaq Jami'a al-Duwal al-'Arabiya wa ma' Ba'd al-Haiat al-Duwaliya* (Cairo, 1966) (in Arabic). Hereinafter this compilation will be referred to as the *Arab League Compilation*. On October 11, 1962, Kuwait acceded to both conventions. The trade convention was for a one-year period from its date of application, subject to automatic renewal from year to year. A party to the convention could withdraw from it by giving notice at least two months before the annual expiration date. The payments convention was of unlimited duration. A contracting party could withdraw from it after the lapse of five years from its entry into force by giving a year's notice.

39. For the text of this convention and its annexed lists of products, see Appendix I.

40. The list of duty-free products annexed to the convention did not include, in addition to various other articles, petroleum; metallic ores; cheese; butter; flour; vegetable oils; tanned hides or skins; or meat, fish, fruits, or vegetables in airtight containers. These commodities, with the exception of petroleum and metallic ores, were included in the list of industrial products annexed to the convention.

41. The list of industrial products annexed to the convention did not include, in addition to various other articles, alcoholic or nonalcoholic beverages; tobacco products; toilet soap; headwear; or most rubber, paper, metal, plastic, or petroleum or other chemical products.

42. The list included the value of goods exported from one contracting party to another contracting party and the cost of their shipping and insurance, commercial profits and dividends accruing from immovable and movable capital, costs of diplomatic missions, tourists' expenses, students' expenses, insurance premiums and indemnities, and various other payments.

43. Asphalt for roads, charcoal in briquettes and pulverized charcoal, and certain dehydrated milk were added to the free list. The industrial products added to the 25 percent list included bran of all kinds; terebinth pistachio oil; chocolate made with sugar from Arab countries; pure natural essential oils from plants of Arab origin; furniture of noncarved wood; furniture of bamboo or wicker; packing paper; printing paper; jute fabrics of local or imported fibers; sanitary wares, pipes, and joints of terra cotta; artificial teeth; beds, tables, chairs, and other furniture of iron or cast iron; printing type; electric elevators, except for their motors; agricultural pumps, except for their motors; electric lamps with bulbs of Arab origin; automobile batteries with component parts of Arab origin; and military arms and ammunition. The 50 percent list included various manufactured products which were formerly on the 25 percent list and some manufactured products which previously had not benefited from any reduction. Included among these products were butter; kashkawal cheese; white cheese of all kinds; apricot paste; raisin paste; roasted and ground coffee, in containers, from Yemen; olive oil; beetroot dregs; vegetable oil cake; artificial fodder; household soap made of pure olive oil; glue of animal origin; manufactures and statues of olive wood; natural silk yarn and yarn of silk waste; twine, cordage, rope, and cable of Arab textile material; glass and crystal, sheet or rolled, of all kinds; glassware and crystalware, blown or pressed; bottles, phials, and flasks of all kinds; laboratory glassware; hollow glassware, table glassware, and toilet glassware (other than crystal or semi-crystal); glass bulbs (for kerosene lamps); electric light bulbs entirely of Arab manufacture; and mother-of-pearl articles.

44. The amendments also added a provision to the trade convention requiring all products benefiting from an exemption from duty or a reduction in duty under the convention to be accompanied by a certificate of origin. The certificate in the case of industrial products had to show that the raw materials of Arab origin and the cost of local labor amounted to at least 50 percent of the cost of the manufacture of the product. Instruments of ratification of these amendments were deposited by Egypt on September 17, 1955; Lebanon on January 22, 1956; Syria on February 29, 1956; Iraq on April 22, 1956; Jordan on June 3, 1956; and Saudi Arabia on April 30, 1961. Kuwait adhered to these amendments on October 11, 1962. *Arab League Compilation*, p. 181.

45. The 1956 amendments added the following items to the 25 percent list: writing pads and exercise books made of Arab paper, certain plastic manufactures, rubber boots and shoes, parasols and umbrellas, brass taps, certain refrigerating storage cabinets, and orange flower water and rose water; and the following items to the 50 percent list: date paste; dehydrated onions; dehydrated garlic; asphalt, tar, emulsion and certain other petroleum products; and fabrics made from jute fibers. Instruments of ratification of these amendments were deposited by Iraq on August 1, 1956; Saudi Arabia on

January 11, 1957; Jordan on February 5, 1957; Egypt on May 9, 1957; Lebanon on October 31, 1959; and Syria (Syrian Region of the U.A.R.) on December 1, 1960. Kuwait adhered to these amendments on October 11, 1962. *Ibid.*, p. 195.

The 1957 amendments added sugar of Arab origin and metal fasteners for shoes, clothes, and leather articles to the 50 percent list. Instruments of ratification of these amendments were deposited by Jordan on March 16, 1958, and the Egyptian and Syrian Regions of the U.A.R. on June 2, 1958. Kuwait adhered to these amendments on October 11, 1962. *Ibid.*, p. 201.

On January 25, 1956, the Economic Council also approved a convention providing for the adoption by the Arab countries of a uniform tariff nomenclature. Instruments of ratification of this convention were deposited by Syria on February 20, 1957; Saudi Arabia on April 6, 1957; Jordan on May 14, 1958; and the Egyptian Region of the U.A.R. on July 5, 1959. *Ibid.*, p. 270.

46. The Economic Council was directed to specify, in the light of economic considerations in the Arab countries, the assembled products to be subject to the 20 percent reduction. On January 14, 1959, the Economic Council approved certain other amendments to the trade convention which provided for an increase in the reduction in import duties on some industrial articles from 25 percent to 35 percent and on certain other industrial articles from 50 percent to 60 percent. However, as of the end of 1965, these amendments had not entered into force. *Ibid.*, p. 212. Amendments to the payments convention were also approved by the Economic Council on January 11, 1959. Instruments of ratification of these amendments were deposited by the U.A.R. on April 11, 1959; Jordan on April 28, 1959; and Lebanon on April 17, 1960. *Ibid.*, p. 242.

47. The trade agreement and accompanying payments agreement were concluded on January 29, 1956, and came into force on October 24, 1956. *Recueil des Lois Syriennes et de la Législation Financière*, No. 10 (Damascus, October 1956), p. 15. The specified duration of the agreements was for one year from the date of their entry into force, subject to automatic renewal annually unless one of the parties gave three months' notice of its desire to terminate the agreements. The trade agreement reflected the amendments to the Arab League trade convention that were approved by the Economic Council in December 1954, but it did not reflect the amendments to that convention that were approved by the Economic Council on January 25, 1956.

48. If the swing credit was exceeded, the excess was to be paid, unless the parties agreed otherwise, in transferable pounds sterling at the official rate of exchange of the Egyptian pound in respect to the pound sterling at the time of settlement.

49. Such as butter, cheese, pressed dried apricot sheets, artificial fodder, and olive oil.

50. Such as wheat flour, sugar, asphalt, fuel gases, medicines, fertilizers, rubber tires, rayon yarn, cotton yarn of a count of 40 and above, fibrous

cement products, hygienic equipment, tubes, iron or steel products, cables, and batteries. These articles were to be subject to duties equivalent to 50 percent of the import duties in effect in the importing country.

51. Synthetic yarns and fabrics, glass manufactures, tanned skins, shoes, and carbonated beverages were subject to 50 percent of the normal import duties; and tobacco, sugar, and salt were subject to the full amount of such duties. All of the foregoing products were, in addition, subject to import licensing. International Monetary Fund, *International Financial News Survey*, November 7, 1958, p. 153.

52. International Monetary Fund, *Tenth Annual Report on Exchange Restrictions* (Washington, 1959), p. 312.

53. These measures established three categories of products. Category 1 contained various commodities which were produced in both the Egyptian and Syrian Regions and whose production costs were different. Payment for imports of these commodities was to be made through the Syrian account in the National Bank of Egypt at the official rate of L.S. 8.93 for L.E. 1.00. Category 2 contained various commodities which were produced in the Egyptian Region but not in the Syrian Region. Payment for imports of these commodities was to be made in Egyptian pounds, not exceeding L.E. 10 denomination, at the free rate of exchange (usually around L.S. 7.00 for L.E. 1.00). Category 3 contained all other commodities. Payment for imports of these commodities was to be made in part (50 percent) through the Syrian account in the National Bank of Egypt and in part (50 percent) in Egyptian pounds obtained at the free rate of exchange.

54. See *The Economic Development Organization* (Cairo: Dar El-Hana Press, 1960), and *The Yearbook of the UAR (1960)* (Cairo: Information Department, 1960), pp. 250-251.

55. National Bank of Egypt, *Economic Bulletin*, Vol. XIV, No. 3 (Cairo, 1961), pp. 326-333. See also *Foreign Commerce Weekly*, August 14, 1961, p. 8, and September 11, 1961, p. 7; and *The New York Times*, August 10, 1961.

56. The trade agreement and accompanying payments agreement were concluded on June 27, 1956. Instruments of ratification of the two agreements were exchanged on May 27, 1957, and the agreements were put into effect by Egypt on June 11, 1957, and by Lebanon on June 12, 1957. The different effective dates were due to different interpretations by Egypt and Lebanon of the relevant provisions of the agreements. See Lebanon's official journal, *Al-Jarida al-Rasmiya*, No. 28, June 19, 1957, p. 710; and Egypt's official journal, *Al-Waqai' al-Misriya,* No. 88, November 11, 1957, p. 4. The specified duration of these agreements was for one year from the date of their entry into force, subject to automatic renewal annually unless one of the parties gave three months' notice of its desire to terminate the agreements.

57. The trade agreement reflected the amendments to the trade convention that were approved by the Economic Council in December 1954 and some of the amendments to the convention that were approved by the Council in January 1956.

58. Such as olive oil, cottonseed oil, sesame oil, sesame seed cake, oil cakes, natural silk yarns, floss silk yarns, aromatic flower and rose distilled waters, glycerin, fertilizers, molasses, and cereal grain bran.

59. Such as tanned or dyed skins, plywood made of wood of Arab origin, natural essential oils, cement, paints and varnishes, toilet soap, certain rubber shoes, ranges and heaters made of iron or cast iron, brushes, artificial teeth, printing type, electric washers, electric refrigerators, hats, fruit or vegetable preparations, woolen blankets, drugs and medicinals, metal furniture, batteries, tires and inner tubes for automobiles, cereal starch, insecticides, glucose, cement manufactures, chocolate, crackers, cookies, and agricultural pumps, except for their motors.

60. Such as aluminum household utensils, fuel tanks, and water tanks.

61. The conclusion and effective date of the payments agreement was October 11, 1958. The trade agreement, along with economic and technical cooperation agreements, was concluded on November 15, 1958, and came into force on January 17, 1959. The specified duration of the trade and payments agreements was for one year from the date of their entry into force, subject to automatic renewal annually unless one of the parties gave three months' notice of its desire to terminate the agreements.

62. The duty-free list included such articles as butter, olive oil, glucose, various fruit or vegetable preparations, molasses, cereal bran, cement, vegetable oil cake, tar and pitch, drugs and medicinals, animal glue, household soap, fertilizers, various manufactures of leather, certain paper and wood, artificial or natural silk thread, woolen yarns and fabrics, carpets, certain wearing apparel, cotton yarn above number 36 and cotton fabrics made from such yarn, jute fabrics, certain cordage, glass and glassware, certain footwear, certain ceramic products, iron cooking stoves, and various other metal products.

63. This list included such products as cereal flour, biscuits, various chemicals, toilet soap, rubber tires, and jewelry and similar articles made by hand.

64. This list included such products as prepared or preserved fish, sugar manufactures other than those on the duty-free list, tanning and dyeing extracts, aromatic flower and rose distilled waters, matches, artificial silk fabrics made on a Jacquard machine, fibrous cement manufactures, batteries, radio parts, electrical refrigerators, and brushes.

65. A product was to be regarded as of local origin if 50 percent or more of the value of the article consisted of Arab raw materials and local labor. The agreement provided also for most-favored-nation treatment; the exemption, with certain exceptions, of transit trade from duties; national treatment with regard to internal taxation; and the extension of free trade zone privileges in Latakia to Iraqi merchants.

66. International Monetary Fund, *Fifteenth Annual Report on Exchange Restrictions* (Washington, 1964), p. 247. In the meantime, Iraq had concluded, as a concomitant of the continuing vacillation in inter-Arab

political relations, a new trade agreement with Syria shortly after Syria withdrew from the U.A.R. in September 1961. The agreement, which was called an "economic cooperation agreement," was concluded on November 3, 1961, and came into force on December 21, 1961. The agreement provided for the exemption from customs duties, except for the products contained in three lists annexed to the agreement, of Syrian and Iraqi livestock and agricultural, animal, mineral, and industrial products. Products on the annexed lists were to be subject to full duties or to reduced duties equal to 75 percent or 50 percent of the rates of duty prevailing in the importing country. The full-duty list contained such products as cigarette paper, toilet paper, paper bags for cement, metal springs, plastic shoes and tubes, certain metal furniture, alcoholic beverages, salt, and sugar. The list of articles that were to be subject to a 25 percent reduction in customs duties included such products as refrigerators and washing machines; locks, padlocks, nails, metal screens, and pins; various other iron or steel products; concrete and reinforced concrete products; leather shoes; various artificial silk fabrics; woolen mats and rugs; cotton fabrics; certain cotton yarn; waterproof felt; knitwork of all kinds, including wearing apparel, manufactured from any textile except natural silk; other textile wearing apparel and sheeting; and various other textile products, including blankets, handkerchiefs, towels, and tents. The list of articles that were to be subject to a 50 percent reduction in customs duties included such products as cigarettes; various kinds of vegetable oils, including sesame oil; confectionery; varnishes and paints; household soap made from pure olive oil; perfumes and other cosmetics; tanned hides and skins; bags and suitcases of any material; books, notebooks, and similar paper products; natural silk textiles; artificial or natural silk neckties; certain artificial silk fabrics; cotton embroidery; fuel or water tanks of metal; industrial or agricultural tools, including weights, scales, and metal chains; and electric cables and wires. Commercial transactions between the two countries were to be settled in any convertible currency agreed upon by the countries or in Iraqi dinars through a nonresident account. The specified duration of the agreement was for two years from the date of its entry into force, subject to automatic renewal for a like period unless one of the parties gave three months' notice of its desire to terminate the agreement.

67. The trade agreement that was concluded on November 9, 1955, came into force on March 16, 1956. See *Recueil des Lois Syriennes et de la Législation Financière*, No. 3, March 1956, p. 48. The agreement that was concluded on November 16, 1961, came into force on September 10, 1962. The 1961 agreement, like the Syrian-Iraqi agreement of that year, was called an "economic cooperation agreement" and provided for the establishment of a joint committee to consider, among other things, the coordination of industrial planning in the two countries. Arrangements were also to be made to facilitate capital transfers and travel between the two countries and to establish freedom of residence, employment, and economic activity for the nationals of each country in the other country. The specified duration of

the 1955 agreement was for one year from the date of its entry into force, subject to automatic renewal annually unless one of the parties gave three months' notice of its desire to terminate the agreement. The specified duration of the 1961 agreement was for one year from the date of its entry into force, and it was subject to renewal on a yearly basis upon agreement of both parties.

68. The trade agreement with Iraq and an accompanying payments agreement were concluded on May 15, 1957, and came into force on December 20, 1957. The trade agreement with Lebanon and an accompanying payments agreement were apparently not put into effect by Saudi Arabia and Lebanon. The specified duration of the agreements with Iraq was for one year from the date of entry into force, subject to automatic renewal annually unless one of the parties gave three months' notice of its desire to terminate the agreements.

69. The agreement was concluded on February 21, 1958, and came into force on September 21, 1958. See Egypt's official journal, *Al-Waqai' al-Misriya*, No. 50, June 29, 1959, p. 1 (of supplement to No. 50). The specified duration of the agreement was the same as that of Saudi Arabia's agreements with Iraq.

70. The agreement was concluded and came into force in 1963. The specified duration of the agreement was the same as that of Saudi Arabia's agreements with Iraq.

71. For example, the duty-free list of Syrian industrial products annexed to the 1961 agreement with Saudi Arabia included such articles as artificial silk fabrics, cotton fabrics, knitwork of any kind of textile, prepared and preserved fruits or vegetables, chocolate, wooden veneers, cigarette paper, millstones, medicated cotton, medicinal and pharmaceutical products, candles, animal glue, printing type, mother-of-pearl products, industrial or agricultural tools, newsprint, rope, wooden frames for windows, woolen yarn, fishing nets and hooks, edible oils, electric cables and wires, and plywood. All Saudi Arabian industrial products were to be exempt from customs duties when imported into Syria.

72. For example, the reduced-duty list of Syrian industrial products annexed to the 1961 agreement with Saudi Arabia included such articles as starch; confectionery; household soap; various dough products; matches; tanned or dyed hides and skins; leather; leather products; cardboard; cotton yarns; wool or cotton rugs; textile wearing apparel; linen products; artificial silk thread or yarn; various other textile products; glass and glassware; certain paper; metal caps or stoppers; and plastic products.

73. The Egyptian-Saudi Arabian agreement contained only a limited number of agricultural products that were to be exempt from import and export licensing. Likewise, due in part to the fact that both countries were contracting parties to the Arab League trade convention, duty-free or reduced-duty treatment was provided for only a few agricultural products.

74. The conclusion and effective date of the payments agreement was September 5, 1955. See Egypt's official journal, *Al-Waqai' al-Misriya*, No. 82, October 24, 1955, p. 4. The specified duration of the agreement was for one year from the date of entry into force, subject to automatic renewal annually unless one of the parties gave three months' notice of its desire to terminate the agreement.

75. Within the six months following the expiration of the agreement, the creditor country could have its balance collected in either merchandise or services. At the end of that period, it would be entitled to request settlement in a third currency to be agreed upon. It was specifically provided in the agreement that the settlement of the specified current payments would be effected in accordance with the exchange regulations in Egypt and Saudi Arabia. In an exchange of notes annexed to the agreement, Saudi Arabia requested it be understood, and Egypt agreed, that Saudi Arabia would be entitled to utilize any credit balance with Egypt for the settlement of its own indebtedness to third countries having payments agreements with Egypt. In each such case, however, Saudi Arabia would be required to secure Egypt's consent.

76. The protocol specified that the sum of approximately $15 million was to be transferred by Saudi Arabia in five monthly installments of about $3 million each during the last three months of 1956 and the first two months of 1957.

77. Saudi Arabia promised to supply Egypt with its crude petroleum requirements under the following conditions: 50 percent of the price of the shipments (delivery was to be f.o.b. at a Saudi port of shipment) was to be paid in Egyptian pounds under the 1955 payments agreement, as amended, and the balance was to be paid in United States dollars or any other currency acceptable to Saudi Arabia. The amounts in United States dollars were to be deposited by Egypt, upon receipt of the shipping documents, in a United States bank or other bank designated by Saudi Arabia. In an exchange of notes annexed to the agreement, Saudi Arabia promised to authorize the export to Egypt during 1958 of 200,000 tons of crude petroleum.

78. No payments agreements were concluded by Syria and Saudi Arabia in conjunction with their trade agreements of 1955 and 1961. Payments under the 1955 agreement were required to be made in Syrian pounds, United States dollars, pounds sterling, or in any other currency agreed upon by the two countries. Payments under the 1961 agreement were to be made in United States dollars, pounds sterling, or any other convertible currency agreed upon by the two countries. In both agreements, each of the countries promised to permit the transfer of such currencies to the other country for the settlement of current transactions between the two countries.

79. No payments agreement was concluded by Saudi Arabia and Jordan in conjunction with their trade agreement of 1963. Payments under that agreement, which was called, like the 1961 Saudi Arabian-Syrian agreement,

an "economic cooperation agreement," were to be made in United States dollars, pounds sterling, or in any other currency agreed upon by the two countries. Each of the countries undertook to permit the transfer of such currencies to the other country for the settlement of transactions between the two countries.

80. The swing credit, however, was for only three-month periods. At the end of each such period, the debit balance had to be settled in Iraqi dinars from a nonresident account or in pounds sterling transferable into a foreign currency to be agreed upon by the two countries.

81. A trade agreement was concluded on June 25, 1953, which came into force on that date; trade and payments agreements were concluded on May 26, 1956, which came into force on February 14, 1957, replacing the 1953 agreement; and trade and payments agreements were concluded on May 12, 1960, which came into force on June 1, 1960, replacing the 1956 agreements.

82. Trade and payments agreements were concluded on July 2, 1957, which came into force on December 31, 1957; and trade and payments agreements were concluded on March 1, 1962, which came into force on that date, replacing the 1957 agreements. A protocol was concluded in 1963, extending the duration of the 1962 agreements for one year.

83. Trade and payments agreements were concluded on July 31, 1958, which came into force on November 6, 1958; and trade and payments agreements were concluded on July 13, 1959, which came into force on that date, replacing the 1958 agreements. Protocols were concluded in subsequent years extending the duration of the agreements for the period under consideration.

84. A payments agreement was concluded on April 7, 1957, which came into force on April 8, 1957; trade and payments agreements were concluded on November 8, 1959, which were made effective as of July 1, 1959, replacing the 1957 agreement; and another trade agreement (denominated a customs agreement) was concluded on November 8, 1959, which came into force on December 7, 1959.

85. Trade and payments agreements were concluded on April 24, 1963, which came into force on that date.

86. In an exchange of letters annexed to their 1956 trade agreement, Egypt and Libya promised to consider, as a preliminary step toward the establishment of a unified Arab market, the reduction by at least 25 percent of the import duties levied by each on the other's products. On January 8, 1964, the U.A.R. and Algeria signed a protocol amending their 1963 trade agreement so as to provide for the granting by each country of preferential customs treatment to the products of the other country set forth in two lists attached to the protocol.

87. The 1957 agreement with Tunisia provided for mutual clearing accounts in Egyptian pounds, with a swing credit of L.E. 100,000; the 1958

agreement with Morocco provided for mutual clearing accounts in Egyptian pounds and Moroccan francs, with a swing credit of L.E. 125,000, or the equivalent in Moroccan francs; and the 1959, 1962, and 1963 agreements with Morocco, Tunisia, and Algeria, respectively, provided for mutual clearing accounts maintained in United States dollars as the unit of account, with swing credits of $1,500,000, $300,000, and $500,000, respectively. A loan agreement was also concluded by the U.A.R. and Algeria at the time of the signing of their trade and payments agreements. The loan agreement provided for a long-term, interest-free credit by the U.A.R. of the equivalent of L.E. 10 million in United States dollars of account to be utilized in financing imports and services to be rendered by the U.A.R. to Algeria. The loan was to be utilized wholly or partially within two years of the date of the signing of the agreement, and repayment was to be made in twenty equal half-yearly installments. There was no specific swing credit provided for in the 1956 Egyptian-Libyan payments agreement. At the end of each year, the credit and debit balances in the two accounts were to be offset against each other at the fixed rate of exchange of L.E. 0.975 for one Libyan pound, and, as soon as requested, the offset balance was to be entered on the credit side of the relevant account in transferable pounds sterling. However, by the end of 1959 the U.A.R.'s indebtedness to Libya was reputedly over L.L. 2 million, due to increased Egyptian imports of Libyan livestock. Libya complained that it was not in a position to grant credit to any country and sought to obtain settlement of this outstanding balance in transferable pounds sterling in accordance with the provisions of the 1956 agreement. In addition to its complaints concerning the outstanding balance, Libya was also dissatisfied with the U.A.R.'s practice of not granting, on the one hand, export bonuses to U.A.R. nationals exporting to Libya, which was in the sterling area, while, on the other hand, granting a 17 percent bonus in the currency exchange process to U.A.R. merchants selling products to other countries for sterling. Libya complained that because of this, U.A.R. exporters were able to quote lower prices to persons in other countries than they were to Libyan purchasers. As a result of these complaints, the 1960 payments agreement provided for the establishment of mutual clearing accounts, with no swing credit, in pounds sterling rather than in Egyptian and Libyan pounds. Agreement was also reached for the liquidation in pounds sterling of Egypt's outstanding indebtedness to Libya.

88. Sudanese coins had been put into circulation on January 19, 1957.

89. Included among these commodities were such Egyptian products as cotton fabrics, artificial silk fabrics, yarn, footwear, manufactures of leather, toilet soap, tomato sauce, and glassware; and such Sudanese products as live animals, haricot and certain other beans, millet, sesame, spices, gum arabic, cottonseed oil, chickpeas, raw hides, meat products, lupines, and green peas.

90. Sudanese melonseeds, dates, salted fish, and acacia gum for Egyptian perfumery, cardboard boxes and bags, fruits, stationery, and vegetables.

91. The specified duration of the 1959 trade and payments agreement was for one year from July 1, 1959, subject to automatic renewal annually unless one of the parties gave two months' notice of its desire to terminate the agreement.

92. The exchange rate between the Egyptian and Sudanese pounds was to be fixed on the basis of the parity announced by the International Monetary Fund, and in the event of an alteration in the par value of the Egyptian pound the U.A.R. Government, as under the 1957 payments agreement, was to make the necessary adjustments in the balances of the two accounts.

93. The customs agreement, unlike the trade and payments agreement, was for a period of three years from the date of its entry into force and was subject to automatic renewal for additional periods of three years unless one of the countries advised the other of its desire to terminate the agreement.

94. These articles included cotton yarn; artificial silk fibers, threads, and yarns; wool yarn; fishing nets; dyes, paints, and varnishes; certain films; seeds for sowing; cattle; sheep; camels; fresh, prepared, or preserved meat; salted fish; millet; lupine seeds; cottonseed; sesame seed; melonseed; and cottonseed oil.

95. Included among these products were rice; biscuits; rugs and carpets; certain nonalcoholic essences and concentrates; cloth and bags of jute; tubes and tires; wood manufactures; leather manufactures other than footwear; paper, cardboard, and manufactures thereof; preserved fruits or vegetables; rope and twine; tanned or dyed hides and skins; workshop and machine tools; edible or inedible sugar cane syrup; certain dried fruits; starch; yeast; chemical fertilizers; laundry blue; plastic manufactures; asbestos cement manufactures; insulated electric wires; iron and steel; and certain iron or steel products. Cotton threads and silk yarns and threads were to be subject to 60 percent preferences (reductions); bleached or unbleached cotton fabrics, malt, butane gas, and lead pencils to 50 percent preferences; colored or printed cotton fabrics, pure or mixed artificial silk fabrics, and footwear to 50 percent preferences; fountain pens to a 30 percent preference; and glass and glassware, toys, certain medicinal preparations, certain pottery, and certain chinaware to 20 percent preferences.

96. See Appendix II.

97. For example, in 1963 almost 75 percent of the total value of Jordan's imports from the U.A.R. consisted of rice, and most of Lebanon's imports consisted of rice, printed matter, watermelons, a few other fruits and vegetables, and some textiles.

98. For example, in 1963 about 90 percent of the total value of Iraq's exports to Syria consisted of dates, linseed, cottonseed, sheep skins, and wool and other animal hair; about 90 percent of the total value of its exports to Jordan consisted of barley, wheat, dates, date juice, and date cake; about 85 percent of the total value of its exports to Saudi Arabia consisted of barley, cement, and dates; about 90 percent of the total value of its exports to

Lebanon consisted of intestines; dates; barley; sesame seed; linseed; sheep, goat, and lamb skins; wool and other animal hair; and cotton; and virtually all of its exports to Egypt, Yemen, and the Sudan consisted of dates.

99. Although exports of petroleum products from Iraq to Syria and Lebanon did not appear in Iraq's statistics of exports to those countries, they did appear in Syria's and Lebanon's import statistics.

100. Saudi Arabian and Kuwaiti imports of consumer products from countries outside the region increased greatly during this period.

101. Over 75 percent of the total value of Syria's imports from Lebanon during 1963 consisted of fruits and vegetables, and about two-thirds of its exports to Lebanon during that year consisted of livestock, butter, wheat, barley, cotton, and cottonseed. Jordan's exports during 1963 to Syria and Lebanon consisted mostly of fruits and vegetables, raw hides and skins, olive oil, and phosphates. About 60 percent of its imports from Lebanon during that year consisted of apples, oranges, and other fruits and vegetables, and a substantial part of the remainder consisted of Lebanese reexports. About 70 percent of its imports from Syria during 1963 consisted of wheat and other cereals, livestock, fish, fruits and vegetables, and cottonseed oil.

102. Most of the increase in the total value of Jordan's imports from Lebanon during this period was accounted for by larger imports of Lebanese potatoes, oranges, lemons, apples, and tomatoes.

103. As of 1965, no official Algerian trade statistics had been issued for the years 1962 and 1963. For the size and composition of the inter-Arab trade of the individual Arab countries during the 1950's and early 1960's, see their annual official trade statistics.

104. Predominantly oil in the case of Kuwait, Saudi Arabia, Libya, Iraq, and Algeria; cotton in the case of the U.A.R., Sudan, and Syria; and phosphates, cereals, fruits and vegetables, and wine in the case of Morocco and Tunisia. Lebanon's chief exports, a large portion of which went to other Arab countries, were apples and citrus fruits; Yemen's chief export was coffee; and Jordan's chief export to countries outside the region was phosphates.

105. There were very large increases during this period in Arab oil exports and oil revenues.

106. The discussion in the following chapter will pertain to the Arab common market agreements concluded during the first half of the 1960's. There was also concluded during that period an African common market agreement to which some of the Arab countries were signatories. The African common market agreement was signed on April 1, 1962, by representatives of the six so-called Casablanca Powers (the U.A.R., Morocco, Algeria, Guinea, Ghana, and Mali). The agreement provided for the removal, within five years from the effective date of the agreement and by a process of gradual, annual reductions, of all of the customs duties and other restrictions imposed on articles produced in and traded between the contracting parties. Member

countries were, however, to be permitted to conclude provisional bilateral agreements in order to safeguard their trade interests in certain manufactured products. Most of the remaining provisions of the agreement were rather general. The contracting parties promised to undertake to give priority to imports of articles from each other and to grant to each other most-favored-nation treatment. They also agreed, subject to no time limitations, to coordinate their customs tariffs and regulations and to establish a customs union among themselves, as well as to coordinate their export and import policies, their policies of trade in fuel and power, and their social legislation. To implement the provisions of the agreement, the Council of the African Common Market was to be formed. Decisions of the Council were to be taken by unanimous vote, with each member country having one vote. Other African countries were to be permitted to adhere to the agreement if they so wished. Articles 20 and 22 of the agreement provided that the agreement "shall be ratified on June 1, 1962 at the latest by the contracting parties in accordance with their respective constitutional procedures," and that the agreement "shall come into force one month after the deposit of the instruments of ratification by two of the signatory states." However, notwithstanding these provisions, the common market agreement, as well as companion agreements providing for the establishment of an African development bank and an African payments union, failed to come into force.

NOTES TO CHAPTER 6

1. *Arab News and Views*, April 1, 1960.

2. The agreement proposed by the U.A.R. had been approved by the Economic Council on June 3, 1957, but none of the Arab countries had signed it.

3. *Chemical Week*, July 8, 1961, p. 24.

4. For the text of this agreement, see Appendix I.

5. For the text of this resolution, see Appendix I.

6. Excepted from this requirement were taxes imposed for services and taxes imposed on both imported and domestic products.

7. Import taxes on such products were to be reduced at the same rate.

8. Import taxes on such products were to be reduced at the same rate.

9. The quantitative restrictions, duties, and taxes that were subsequently fixed were those in existence on November 1, 1964.

10. Lists of the quantitative restrictions that these countries were imposing on agricultural, animal, mineral, and industrial products were submitted at the same time, pursuant to Article 13 of the resolution. The number of articles contained in each of these lists was as follows:

Agricultural, Animal, and Mineral Products

	Import Restrictions	Export Restrictions
Jordan	130	20
Syria	192	28
Iraq	60	35
U.A.R.	195	98
Kuwait	0	0

Industrial Products

	Import Restrictions	Export Restrictions
Jordan	970	0
Syria	908	14
Iraq	791	0
U.A.R.	920	69
Kuwait	0	0

Source: *Le Commerce du Levant* (monthly edition), March 15, 1965, p. 64.

11. *Ibid.*

12. United Nations, Economic and Social Office in Beirut, *Studies on Selected Development Problems in Various Countries in the Middle East* (New York, 1967), p. 26.

13. *Ibid.*, p. 28.

14. See Appendix II.

15. A substantial part of the sharp decrease in exports during 1965 and 1966 resulted from increased Iraqi wheat production. Syrian exports of wheat to Iraq, which amounted to about L.S. 8 million in 1964, virtually ceased in 1965 and 1966.

16. Mostly livestock, fish, eggs, cereals, cottonseed and olive oil, and various fruits and vegetables.

17. Among other things, the two countries concluded protocols in 1964, 1965, and 1966 (as well as in 1967), which amended their 1958 trade agreement to provide for the exemption from duty of practically all of each other's products. The 1964 protocol also provided for the establishment of a new clearing account in pounds sterling with a swing credit (which was subsequently increased to 1.5 million pounds sterling) to replace the account that had been established under the 1958 payments agreement between the two countries. In addition to the foregoing Iraqi-U.A.R. protocols, there were various other bilateral trade or trade and payments agreements concluded by the four common market participants with each other during the period from 1964 through 1967. Jordan and Syria concluded an agreement on April 26, 1965, which amended their 1953 trade agreement to provide for greater preferential tariff treatment for certain products; Iraq and Jordan concluded

a trade agreement on December 9, 1965, which replaced their 1953 agreement and which contained greater tariff preferences than had the earlier agreement; Syria and the U.A.R. concluded a preferential trade and payments agreement on June 8, 1966; and Jordan and the U.A.R. concluded a preferential trade agreement on September 14, 1967. There were also a number of other inter-Arab bilateral agreements concluded during the aforementioned period. For example, in 1964, Saudi Arabia concluded trade agreements with Lebanon, Syria, and the Sudan; and Algeria concluded a trade agreement with Morocco; in 1965, the U.A.R. concluded a trade and payments agreement with the Sudan, which replaced their 1959 agreement; Jordan concluded an agreement with Lebanon, which amended their 1952 trade agreement; Morocco concluded a trade agreement with Tunisia; and the U.A.R. concluded a protocol with Lebanon, which amended their 1956 trade agreement and terminated their 1956 payments agreement; in 1966, the U.A.R. concluded a trade agreement with Morocco, which replaced their earlier trade and payments agreement; and in 1967, Iraq concluded a trade agreement with Algeria and formally terminated its 1951 payments agreement with Lebanon. There were, in addition, protocols concluded during this period which extended or amended certain of the inter-Arab agreements that had been concluded prior to 1964, including the U.A.R.-Tunisian trade and payments agreement of 1962 and the U.A.R.-Algerian trade and payments agreement and Algerian-Tunisian and Jordanian-Saudi Arabian trade agreements of 1963.

18. National Bank of Egypt, *Economic Bulletin*, Vol. XX, No. 3 (1967), Table 3/2a.

19. Kuwait's refusal to ratify the common market resolution brought into question the nature of the authority delegated to the Economic Unity Council by the five contracting parties to the Economic Unity Agreement. The countries that had ratified the common market resolution contended that Kuwait was committed as a contracting party to the Economic Unity Agreement to become, in accordance with Article 12, a formal participant in the common market undertaking. They did not consider the common market resolution as a proposal to the contracting parties for their approval or disapproval. Accordingly, Kuwait's refusal to become a formal participant was considered a violation of the Economic Unity Agreement and rendered uncertain Kuwait's status as a member of the Economic Unity Council.

20. Membership in the Arab League was increased to fourteen countries on December 12, 1967, with the admission of Southern Yemen.

21. Yemen and the Sudan reportedly became participants in the common market undertaking during the first half of 1968. *Le Commerce du Levant* (monthly edition), June 1968, pp. 15 and 28.

NOTES TO CHAPTER 7

1. For a summary of the Egyptianization and nationalization laws from 1957 to 1962, see Charles Issawi, *Egypt in Revolution: An Economic*

Analysis (London: Oxford University Press, 1963), pp. 57-60. See also Bent Hansen and Girgis A. Marzouk, *Development and Economic Policy in the UAR (Egypt)* (Amsterdam: North-Holland Publishing Company, 1965); and Patrick O'Brien, *The Revolution in Egypt's Economic System* (London: Oxford University Press, 1966).

2. In Syria, 107 privately owned firms were nationalized on January 3, 1965. The government assumed complete control of 22 of these firms, 90 percent ownership of 24, and 75 percent ownership of the remainder. Practically all of the important private manufacturing establishments in Syria were affected, including establishments producing textiles, sugar, construction materials, glassware, synthetic rubber, ceramics, and foodstuffs. During 1965, the government also assumed control of about 80 percent of Syria's foreign trade. *The New York Times*, January 4, 1965, and August 24, 1965.

In Iraq, all banks and insurance companies and 30 industrial and commercial concerns were nationalized on July 15, 1964. The nationalized industries comprised cement, asbestos, cigarette, spinning and weaving, steel, paper, leather tanning, flour, and trading companies. Small firms in these fields were left in the private sector, except for cement, asbestos, and cigarettes, which were placed entirely in the public sector. As of the early part of 1965, about 75 percent of the paid-up capital of Iraq's manufacturing establishments was under government control. *Ibid.*, July 15, 1964. International Monetary Fund, *International Financial News Survey*, August 7, 1964, p. 256. *International Commerce*, June 14, 1965, p. 3.

In Algeria, the government embarked on a program of socialization during the year following independence by nationalizing many farms, factories, and other business establishments. As of 1964, the government controlled 22,000 farms covering 6.5 million acres and accounting for about two-thirds of Algeria's agricultural production. It had also assumed control of the cork industry; French-owned newspapers and tobacco and cigarette establishments; most major bus and truck lines; about 100 flour mills, brick and tile works, and other small plants; most of the big hotels and cafes; and many bakeries and laundries. *The New York Times*, January 20, 1964.

3. *The New York Times*, December 27, 1961.

4. Needless to say, the difficulties involved in the conducting of such planned trade have been found to be quite numerous. In the case of the Comecon countries, their different price levels and their rates of exchange have resulted not only in a distortion of the purchasing parity of products traded between them on a bilateral basis but also in complications in effecting an equitable multilateral balancing of payments within the Comecon area. Michael Kaser, *Comecon: Integration Problems of the Planned Economies* (London: Oxford University Press, 1965).

5. A glance at the extent of industrialization in two countries—the U.A.R. and Jordan—will give some indication of these wide disparities. In the U.A.R. during the fiscal year July 1964/June 1965, the last year of its five-

year economic development plan for the period 1960-65, industry accounted for about 22 percent of the national income of approximately L.E. 1,762 million (at constant prices), or about L.E. 392 million. Approximately L.E. 400 million had been invested in industrial projects during the five-year period of the plan (about 27 percent of the total), and income from industry had increased during that period by over 50 percent, in terms of constant prices. Central Bank of Egypt, *Economic Review*, Vol. V, No. 4 (Cairo, 1965), pp. 346-347.

   In Jordan, on the other hand, during 1964, the third year of Jordan's five-year economic plan, industry accounted for about 9 percent of the national product of approximately J.D. 134 million (at current prices), or about J.D. 12.5 million. Jordan's five-year plan had called for a total development expenditure of about J.D. 127.3 million, of which about J.D. 22 million was to have been invested in manufacturing, mining, and the production of electricity. Although income from industry had increased by over 40 percent during the first three years of the plan, it was only about 3 percent of the income provided by industry in the U.A.R. Jordan, Department of Statistics, *Statistical Yearbook 1965* (Amman, 1966), p. 188. United Nations, *Economic Developments in the Middle East 1959-1961* (New York, 1962), p. 175 (Table VI-5).

   6. United Nations Conference on Trade and Development, *Payments Arrangements Among the Developing Countries for Trade Expansion* (New York, 1966), Appendix II, p. 3. In this connection, it is noted that as of the first half of 1965, all of the Arab League countries, except Yemen, belonged to the International Monetary Fund. Their combined quotas totaled the equivalent of $540 million, which the Board of Governors of the Fund had voted to increase to $680 million. International Monetary Fund, *1965 Annual Report* (Washington, 1965), p. 129.

   7. Jordan, for example, during the first half of the 1960's was dependent on annual grants from the United States which averaged about $35 million. United States, Department of Commerce, "Market Profiles for the Near East and South Asia," *Overseas Business Reports*, No. 66-35 (1966), p. 10.

   8. It was estimated in Jordan, for example, that during the fiscal year April 1963/March 1964, about 57 percent of the total revenue of Jordan's ordinary budget for that year would be derived from indirect taxes, with customs duties probably accounting for a substantial portion of the total revenue (customs revenue was not separately specified). Jordan, Department of Statistics, *Statistical Yearbook 1963* (Amman, 1964), pp. 140-141. The corresponding estimate in the U.A.R.'s public services budget for the fiscal year July 1963/June 1964 was that about 38 percent would be derived from customs duties and other duties and taxes on articles, with customs duties constituting about 27 percent of the total. National Bank of Egypt, *Economic Bulletin*, Vol. XVI, Nos. 3 & 4 (1963), pp. 182-183. In Lebanon's ordinary budgets during the early 1960's, the estimates for customs duties

were even higher. The estimate in the 1961 budget, for example, was that about 57 percent of the total revenue would be derived from indirect taxes, with customs receipts supplying about 38 percent of the total revenue. International Monetary Fund, *International Financial News Survey*, August 26, 1960, pp. 472-473. Correspondingly high figures for customs receipts were also present in the ordinary budgets of the first half of the 1960's for Iraq, Syria, Morocco, Sudan, and Tunisia. For Kuwait and Saudi Arabia, on the other hand, customs duties were a minor source of revenue, and for Libya they were becoming a rather minor source.

9. United Nations Conference on Trade and Development, *Trade Expansion and Economic Co-operation Among Developing Countries* (New York, 1966), p. 23.

10. *Ibid.*

11. The proportion of the total national product accounted for by the goods-producing sectors—agriculture, industry, and construction—does not exceed 35 percent, whereas almost two-thirds of the national product is accounted for by services, with trade accounting for about one-half of the value of all of the services, or about 30 percent of the total national income. The ratio of services to goods in Lebanon is probably one of the highest in the world. United Nations, Food and Agriculture Organization, *Lebanon* (Rome, 1959), Chapter I.

12. Article 9. In this respect, it is noted generally that there are international obligations that some of the Arab countries have under the General Agreement on Tariffs and Trade (GATT) that could lead to complications. As of 1965, there were four Arab countries that bore a relationship to the GATT. Kuwait was a contracting party; Tunisia and the U.A.R. had acceded provisionally to the GATT; and Algeria maintained a de facto application of the GATT. Each of these relationships entailed certain rights and obligations under the GATT, including those set forth in Article XXIV of the GATT pertaining to the formation of customs unions—which provides that the external duties and other regulations of commerce that may be imposed at the institution of a customs union or interim agreement leading to the formation of a customs union may not on the whole be higher or more restrictive than the general incidence of the duties and regulations of commerce applicable in the constituent territories prior to the formation of such a union or adoption of such an interim agreement.

13. *International Commerce*, June 14, 1965, pp. 12-18. International Bank for Reconstruction and Development, *The Economic Development of Kuwait* (Baltimore: The Johns Hopkins Press, 1965), pp. 57-58.

14. International Bank for Reconstruction and Development, *The Economic Development of Syria* (Baltimore: The Johns Hopkins Press, 1955), p. 444.

15. Among other things, the agreement provided for a division of certain transit goods between the motor vehicles registered in Jordan (38 percent), Lebanon (22 percent), and the Syrian Region of the U.A.R. (40 percent). For

details of this agreement, see Muhammed A. Diab, *Inter-Arab Economic Co-operation 1951-1960* (Beirut: American University of Beirut, 1963), p. 18. See also *Middle East Economic Digest*, December 18, 1959, and March 11, 1960.

16. J. E. Meade, *The Theory of International Economic Policy*, Vol. II: *Trade and Welfare* (London: Oxford University Press, 1955), pp. 570-572.

17. For a survey of and bibliography on international trade theory, see Gottfried Haberler, *A Survey of International Trade Theory* ("Special Papers in International Economics," No. 1; rev. ed.; Princeton: International Finance Section, Department of Economics, Princeton University, 1961). W. M. Corden, *Recent Developments in the Theory of International Trade* ("Special Papers in International Economics," No. 7; Princeton: International Finance Section, Department of Economics, Princeton University, 1965).

18. Sidney Dell, *A Latin American Common Market* (London: Oxford University Press, 1966), p. 17.

19. *Ibid.*, pp. 17-18. See also Raymond F. Mikesell, *Intra-Regional Trade and Economic Development* (Washington: International Development Advisory Board, 1958). *Economic Consequences of the Size of Nations: Proceedings of a Conference Held by the International Economic Association*, ed. E. A. G. Robinson (New York, 1960).

20. Article XVIII(2) of the GATT.

21. See, for example, United Nations, Economic and Social Council, *Report of the ECA Industrial Co-ordination Mission to Algeria, Libya, Morocco and Tunisia* (New York, 1964), p. 71.

[R]eal industrial growth depends essentially on stimulating activity at key growth points. This in turn means the laying down or expansion of modern industries strategic for economic development. Such industries are mainly large scale in character with a minimum size which is beyond the scope of existing or immediately foreseeable national markets; hence there is an imperative case for sub-regional co-ordination of industrial development.

22. International Bank for Reconstruction and Development, *The Economic Development of Libya* (Baltimore: The Johns Hopkins Press, 1960), pp. 33 and 179-180. It is to be noted, however, that in recent years there has been an influx of persons from the outlying areas into the main cities due to Libya's rapidly rising oil revenues.

23. International Bank for Reconstruction and Development, *The Economic Development of Jordan* (Baltimore: The Johns Hopkins Press, 1957), p. 19.

24. International Bank for Reconstruction and Development, *The Economic Development of Syria, op. cit.*, p. 110.

25. *Ibid.*

26. Issawi, *Egypt in Revolution . . ., op. cit.*, pp. 183-184.

27. Arthur D. Little, Inc., *A Plan for Industrial Development in Iraq* (Cambridge, Mass., 1956), quoted in Kathleen M. Langley, *The Industrialization of Iraq* (Cambridge: Harvard University Press, 1961), pp. 219-220.

28. International Bank for Reconstruction and Development, *Approach to the Economic Development of Saudi Arabia* (Washington, November 1, 1960), p. 73.

29. International Bank for Reconstruction and Development, *The Economic Development of Syria, op. cit.*, p. 370.

30. United Nations, Department of Economic and Social Affairs, *The Development of Manufacturing Industry in Egypt, Israel and Turkey* (New York, 1958), p. 81.

31. In the U.A.R., for example, during 1965-66 at least 25 percent of the productive capacity of the U.A.R.'s nationalized industries was idle, and the principal causes of the idle capacity (accounting for about 57 percent of the total) were those classified as "external," which included shortages of imported raw materials, intermediate products, and spare parts and breakdowns of worn-out equipment needing to be replaced by imports. International Monetary Fund, *International Financial News Survey*, February 9, 1968, p. 39.

32. A charter for an Arab Financial Institution for Economic Development was approved by the Arab League Economic Council in 1957. However, although a number of the Arab countries pledged subscriptions in 1959 to the proposed capital stock of the institution, as of 1967 it had failed to come into being due to the failure of these countries to ratify the charter. For the Arabic text of this charter, see Arab League, *Majmu'a al-Mu'ahadat wa al-Ittafaqiyat al-Ma'quda fi Nitaq Jami'a al-Duwal al-'Arabiya wa ma' Ba'd al-Haiat al-Duwaliya* (Cairo, 1966) (in Arabic), pp. 278-301.

33. It is to be noted, however, that in 1961 the Kuwaiti Government established the Kuwait Fund for Arab Economic Development with an initial capital of K.D. 50 million, which was subsequently increased to K.D. 100 million, and that the Fund has since extended a number of loans to other Arab countries.

34. See United Nations, *Proceedings of the United Nations Conference on Trade and Development* (8 vols.; New York, 1964).

BIBLIOGRAPHY

BIBLIOGRAPHY

OFFICIAL SOURCES

ALGERIA

Administration des Douanes. *Documents Statistiques sur le Commerce de l'Algérie.* (Annual.) Algiers.
Tarif des Droits de Douanes d'Importation. Algiers, 1963.

GREAT BRITAIN

Board of Trade. *Board of Trade Journal.* (Weekly.) London.
———. *Economic and Commercial Conditions in Egypt.* London, 1947.
———. *Economic and Commercial Conditions in Iraq.* London, 1949.
———. *Economic and Commercial Conditions in Iraq.* London, 1950.
———. *Economic and Commercial Conditions in Iraq.* London, 1953.
———. *Economic and Commercial Conditions in Libya.* London, 1952.
———. *Economic and Commercial Conditions in Libya.* London, 1955.
———. *Sudan: Review of Commercial Conditions.* London, 1950.
———. *Sudan: Review of Commercial Conditions.* London, 1952.
———. *Syria: Review of Commercial Conditions.* London, 1953.
Colonial Office. *Report by the Governor-General on the Administration, Finances and Conditions of the Sudan in 1938.* London, 1939.
———. *Report by His Majesty's Government to the Council of the League of Nations on the Administration of Palestine and Transjordan for the Year 1938.* London, 1939.
Department of Overseas Trade. *Economic Conditions in Egypt.* London, 1933.
———. *Economic Conditions in Egypt.* London, 1935.
———. *Economic Conditions in Iraq.* London, 1933.
———. *Economic Conditions in Iraq.* London, 1936.
———. *Economic Conditions in Morocco.* London, 1932.
———. *Economic Conditions in Morocco.* London, 1934.
———. *Economic Conditions in Palestine.* London, 1935.
———. *Economic Conditions in the Persian Gulf.* London, 1935.
———. *Economic Conditions in Syria.* London, 1930.
———. *Economic Conditions in Syria.* London, 1932.
———. *Economic Conditions in Syria.* London, 1934.
———. *Egypt: Review of Commercial Conditions.* London, 1945.
———. *Iraq: Review of Commercial Conditions.* London, 1945.

——. *Palestine: Review of Commercial Conditions.* London, 1945.

——. *Report on Economic and Commercial Conditions in Algeria.* London, 1936.

——. *Report on Economic and Commercial Conditions in Egypt.* London, 1937.

——. *Report on Economic and Commercial Conditions in Egypt.* London, 1939.

——. *Report on Economic and Commercial Conditions in Iraq.* London, 1938.

——. *Report on Economic and Commercial Conditions in Morocco.* London, 1937.

——. *Report on Economic and Commercial Conditions in Morocco.* London, 1939.

——. *Report on Economic and Commercial Conditions in the Persian Gulf.* London, 1937.

——. *Report on Economic and Commercial Conditions in Syria and the Lebanon.* London, 1936.

——. *Report on Economic and Commercial Conditions in Syria and the Lebanon.* London, 1938.

——. *Report on Economic and Commercial Conditions in Tunisia.* London, 1938.

——. *Report on Economic Conditions in Algeria, Tunisia and Tripolitania.* London, 1933.

——. *Report on Economic Conditions in Algeria, Tunisia and Tripolitania.* London, 1935.

——. *Report on the Economic and Financial Situation of Egypt.* London, 1920.

——. *Report on the Economic and Financial Situation of Egypt.* London, 1922.

——. *Report on the Economic and Financial Situation of Egypt.* London, 1923.

——. *Report on the Trade, Industry and Finance of Syria.* London, 1923.

——. *Report on the Trade, Industry and Finance of Syria.* London, 1925.

——. *Report on the Trade, Industry and Finance of Syria.* London, 1928.

——. *Report on the Trade of Syria.* London, 1921.

Foreign Office. *Handbook of Commercial Treaties, & C., Between Great Britain and Foreign Powers.* 1st ed., comp. Gaston de Bernhardt; and 4th ed. London, 1912 and 1931.

——. *Peace Handbooks.*

    The Balkan States. (Vol. III, No. 16 ["Turkey in Europe"].) London, 1920.

    British Possessions, II: The Congo. (Vol. XVI, No. 98 ["Anglo-Egyptian Sudan"].) London, 1920.

    French African Possessions. (Vol. XVII, No. 101 ["French Morocco"].) London, 1920.

Mohammedanism: Turkey in Asia (I). (Vol. X, No. 60 ["Syria and Palestine"].) London, 1920.

Turkey in Asia (II). (Vol. XI, No. 61 ["Arabia"] and No. 63 ["Mesopotamia"].) London, 1920.

Persian Gulf: French and Portuguese Possessions. (Vol. XIII, No. 76 ["Persian Gulf"].) London, 1920.

Spanish and Italian Possessions: Independent States. (Vol. XX, No. 122 ["Spanish Morocco"] and No. 127 ["Italian Libya"].) London, 1920.

INTERNATIONAL ORGANIZATIONS

Arab Information Center. *Arab News and Views.* (Biweekly.) New York.

———. *Basic Documents of the League of Arab States.* (Document Collections Number 1.) New York, 1955.

Arab League, *Majmu'a al-Mu'ahadat wa al-Ittafaqiyat al-Ma'quda fi Nitaq Jami'a al-Duwal al-'Arabiya wa ma' Ba'd al-Haiat al-Duwaliya.* Cairo, 1966.

General Agreement on Tariffs and Trade. *The Developing Countries and the GATT: The New Chapter on Trade and Development.* Geneva, 1965.

———. *International Trade.* (Annual.) Geneva.

———. *International Trade Forum.* (Quarterly.) Geneva.

International Bank for Reconstruction and Development. *Approach to the Economic Development of Saudi Arabia.* Washington, 1960.

———. *The Economic Development of Iraq.* Baltimore: The Johns Hopkins Press, 1952.

———. *The Economic Development of Jordan.* Baltimore: The Johns Hopkins Press, 1957.

———. *The Economic Development of Kuwait.* Baltimore: The Johns Hopkins Press, 1965.

———. *The Economic Development of Libya.* Baltimore: The Johns Hopkins Press, 1960.

———. *The Economic Development of Morocco.* Baltimore: The Johns Hopkins Press, 1966.

———. *The Economic Development of Syria.* Baltimore: The Johns Hopkins Press, 1955.

International Customs Tariffs Bureau. *The International Customs Journal-Algeria.* 8 eds. Brussels.

———. *The International Customs Journal-Egypt.* 6 eds. Brussels.

———. *The International Customs Journal-Iraq.* 2 eds. Brussels.

———. *The International Customs Journal-Jordan.* 2 eds. Brussels.

———. *The International Customs Journal-Lebanon.* 2 eds. Brussels.

———. *The International Customs Journal-Libya.* 2 eds. Brussels.

———. *The International Customs Journal-Morocco.* 7 eds. Brussels.

———. *The International Customs Journal-Palestine.* 4 eds. Brussels.

——. *The International Customs Journal-Saudi Arabia*. Brussels.

——. *The International Customs Journal-Sudan*. 5 eds. Brussels.

——. *The International Customs Journal-Syria*. Brussels.

——. *The International Customs Journal-Tunisia*. 6 eds. Brussels.

——. *The International Customs Journal-United Arab Republic*. Brussels.

International Monetary Fund. *Annual Report on Exchange Restrictions*. Washington.

——. *International Financial News Survey*. (Weekly.) Washington.

League of Nations. *Treaty Series*. Geneva.

Middle East Supply Centre. *Some Facts about the Middle East Supply Centre*. Cairo, 1944.

United Nations, Conference on Trade and Development. *Payments Arrangements Among the Developing Countries for Trade Expansion*. New York, 1966.

——. *Proceedings of the United Nations Conference on Trade and Development*. 8 vols. New York, 1964.

——. *Trade Expansion and Economic Co-operation Among Developing Countries*. New York, 1966.

United Nations, Department of Economic and Social Affairs. *Customs Unions: A League of Nations Contribution to the Study of Customs Union Problems*. New York, 1947.

——. *The Development of Manufacturing Industry in Egypt, Israel and Turkey*. New York, 1958.

——. *Economic Developments in the Middle East 1945 to 1954*. New York, 1955.

——. *Economic Developments in the Middle East 1954-1955*. New York, 1956.

——. *Economic Developments in the Middle East 1955-1956*. New York, 1957.

——. *Economic Developments in the Middle East 1956-1957*. New York, 1958.

——. *Economic Developments in the Middle East 1957-1958*. New York, 1959.

——. *Economic Developments in the Middle East 1958-1959*. New York, 1960.

——. *Economic Developments in the Middle East 1959-1961*. New York, 1962.

——. *Economic Developments in the Middle East 1961-1963*. New York, 1964.

——. *Report of the ECA Industrial Co-ordination Mission to Algeria, Libya, Morocco and Tunisia*. New York, 1964.

——. *Review of Economic Conditions in the Middle East 1949-50*. New York, 1951.

——. *Review of Economic Conditions in the Middle East 1950-51*. New York, 1952.

———. *Review of Economic Conditions in the Middle East 1951-52.* New York, 1953.

———. *Summary of Recent Economic Developments in the Middle East 1952-53.* New York, 1954.

United Nations, Economic and Social Office (Beirut). *Studies on Selected Development Problems in Various Countries in the Middle East.* New York, 1967.

United Nations, Food and Agriculture Organization. *Lebanon.* Rome, 1959.

———. *Selected Problems of Production and Trade in the Near East.* Rome, 1956.

———. *Yearbook of Food and Agricultural Statistics.* Rome.

United Nations. *Treaty Series.* New York.

IRAQ

Al-Waqai' al-'Iraqiya. (Official journal.) Baghdad.

Ministry of Finance. *Customs Code* (Law No. 56 of 1931). Baghdad, 1932.

———. *Customs Tariff (1933).* Baghdad, 1933.

———. *Customs Tariff Law-1955.* Baghdad, 1956.

Ministry of Planning. *Bulletin of Foreign Trade Statistics.* (Annual.) Baghdad.

———. *Statistical Abstract.* (Annual.) Baghdad.

JORDAN

Department of Statistics. *Statistical Yearbook.* Amman.

Ministry of Finance. *Al-Ta'rifa al-Jumrukiya-1962.* Amman, 1962.

KUWAIT

Central Statistical Office. *Statistical Abstract.* (Annual.) Kuwait.

———. *Yearly Summary of Foreign Trade Statistics.* Kuwait.

Kuwait News and Views. (Monthly.) New York.

LEBANON

Al-Jarida al-Rasmiya. (Official journal.) Beirut.

Al-Wathaiq wa al-Nusus al-Mukhtasa bil Alaqat al-Iqtisadiya wa al-Maliya bain Suriya wa Lubnan. Beirut (no date).

Conseil Supérieur des Douanes. *Statistiques du Commerce Extérieur.* (Annual.) Beirut.

———. *Tarif des Droits de Douane.* (Periodical.) Beirut.

LIBYA

Ministry of National Economy. *External Trade Statistics.* (Annual.) Tripoli.

MOROCCO

Ministère de l'Économie Nationale. *Statistiques du Mouvement Commercial et Maritime du Maroc*. (Annual.) Rabat.

PALESTINE

Blue Book 1938. Jerusalem, 1939.
Department of Customs, Excise and Trade. *The Commercial Bulletin*, September 1, 1927.
————. *Customs Ordinance: Rules, Regulations, Orders and Notices Made Thereunder*. Jerusalem, 1937.
————. *Statistics of Imports, Exports and Shipping*. (Annual.) Jerusalem.
Office of Statistics. *Statistical Abstract of Palestine 1943*. Jerusalem, 1944.
————. *Trade Between Palestine and Syria 1927-1937*. (Special Trade Bulletin No. 1/1939.) Jerusalem, 1939.
Palestine Gazette Extraordinary, November 30, 1939, Supplement No. 2.

SUDAN

Department of Economics and Trade. *Annual Report of the Department of Economics and Trade*. Khartoum.
Department of Statistics. *Foreign Trade Statistics*. (Annual.) Khartoum.

SYRIA

Al-Jarida al-Rasmiya. (Official journal.) Damascus.
Haut-Commissariat de la République Française en Syrie et au Liban. *Bulletin Économique*. (Quarterly.) Beirut.
Ministère des Finances. *Statistiques du Commerce Extérieur*. (Annual.) Damascus.
Ministry of Foreign Affairs. *Wathaiq wa Nusus Tatalaq bil Alaqat al-Iqtisadiya bain Suriya wa Lubnan*. Damascus, 1950.
Ministry of Planning. *Statistical Abstract*. (Annual.) Damascus.

TUNISIA

Secrétariat d'État au Plan et à l'Économie Nationale. *Statistiques du Commerce Extérieur de la Tunisie*. (Annual.) Tunis.

UNITED ARAB REPUBLIC (EGYPT)

Al-Waqai' al-Misriya. (Official journal.) Cairo.
Central Bank of Egypt. *Economic Review*. (Quarterly.) Cairo.
Department of Statistics and Census. *Annual Statement of Foreign Trade*. Cairo.

Direction Générale des Douanes. *Code de l'Administration des Douanes.* (Periodical.) Alexandria.

————. *Le Commerce Extérieur de l'Égypte.* (Annual.) Alexandria.

The Economic Development Organization. Cairo, 1960.

Information Department. *The Yearbook of the UAR.* Cairo.

Journal Officiel du Gouvernement Égyptien. Cairo.

Ministère des Finances. *Tableau des Droits Inscrits au Tarif des Douanes.* (Periodical.) Cairo.

National Bank of Egypt. *Economic Bulletin.* (Quarterly.) Cairo.

UNITED STATES

Department of Commerce. *The Anglo-Egyptian Sudan: A Commercial Handbook.* ("Trade Promotion Series," No. 49.) Washington, 1927.

————. *Foreign Commerce Weekly.* Washington.

————. *Handbook of Foreign Currency and Exchange.* ("Trade Promotion Series," No. 102 and No. 164.) Washington, 1930 and 1936.

————. *International Commerce.* (Weekly.) Washington.

————. *International Reference Service.* (Serial.) Washington.

————. *Overseas Business Reports.* (Serial.) Washington.

Department of State. *The Department of State Bulletin.* (Weekly.) Washington.

————. *Havana Charter for an International Trade Organization.* Washington, 1948.

————. *Mandate for Palestine.* Washington, 1927.

Statutes at Large. (Annual.) Washington.

Tariff Commission. *Operation of the Trade Agreements Program.* (Annual.) Washington.

NEWSPAPERS AND MAGAZINES

Al-Abhath. (Quarterly.) Beirut.

Chemical Week.

Le Commerce du Levant. (Monthly edition.) Beirut.

The Economist. (Weekly.) London.

Middle East and African Economist. (Monthly.)

Middle East Economic Digest. (Weekly.) London.

Middle East Journal. (Quarterly.)

The New York Times .

OTHER SOURCES AND ARTICLES

Balassa, Bela A. *Trade Prospects for Developing Countries.* Homewood, Ill.: Richard D. Irwin, Inc., 1964.

Boardman, Francis. "Civilian Requirements from War to Peace: The Middle East Supply Center," *The Department of State Bulletin*, December 23, 1945, pp. 994-999.

Boutros-Ghali, B. Y. "The Arab League 1945-1955," *International Conciliation*, Vol. CDXCVIII (May 1954), pp. 387-448.

Brown, William Adams, Jr. *The United States and the Restoration of World Trade*. Washington: The Brookings Institution, 1950.

Bureau des Documentations Syriennes & Arabes. *Tarif Général Permanent des Douanes de Syrie*. 6th ed. Damascus, 1963.

Burns, Norman. *The Tariff of Syria 1919-1932*. Beirut: American Press, 1933.

Cooper, C. A., and Massell, B. F. "Toward a General Theory of Customs Unions for Developing Countries," *The Journal of Political Economy*, Vol. LXXIII (October 1965), pp. 461-476.

Corden, W. M. *Recent Developments in the Theory of International Trade*. ("Special Papers in International Economics," No. 7.) Princeton: Princeton University, 1965.

Curzon, Gerard. *Multilateral Commercial Diplomacy: The General Agreement on Tariffs and Trade and Its Impact on National Commercial Policies and Techniques*. London: Michael Joseph, 1965.

Dell, Sidney. *A Latin American Common Market*. London: Oxford University Press, 1966.

Diab, Muhammed A. *Inter-Arab Economic Cooperation 1951-1960*. Beirut: American University of Beirut, 1963.

Grew, Richard. "Organization of Trade in the Middle East: Setup and Functions of the Middle East Supply Centre and Its Results Since Being Established in 1941," *Canadian Exporter*, Vol. XIV (November 1944), pp. 12-26.

Haberler, Gottfried. *A Survey of International Trade Theory*. ("Special Papers in International Economics," No. 1.) Rev. ed. Princeton: Princeton University, 1961.

Hansen, Bent, and Marzouk, Girgis A. *Development and Economic Policy in the UAR (Egypt)*. Amsterdam: North-Holland Publishing Company, 1965.

Hassan, Abdel Razek M., and Dakkak, Nasouh El. *United Arab Republic: Some Economic Features*. Cairo: Federation of Egyptian Chambers of Commerce, 1958.

Himadeh, Sa'id. *Al-Nizam al-Iqtisadi fi al-'Iraq*. Beirut, 1938.

Hunter, Guy. "Economic Problems: The Middle East Supply Centre," *Survey of International Affairs 1939-1946: The Middle East in the War*, by George Kirk. London: Oxford University Press, 1952, pp. 169-193.

Issawi, Charles (ed. and trans.). *The Economic History of the Middle East 1800-1914*. Chicago: University of Chicago Press, 1966.

———. *Egypt at Mid-Century: An Economic Survey*. Rev. ed. of *Egypt: An Economic and Social Analysis*. London: Oxford University Press, 1954.

———. *Egypt in Revolution: An Economic Analysis*. London: Oxford University Press, 1963.

Kaser, Michael. *Comecon: Integration Problems of the Planned Economies*. London: Oxford University Press, 1965.

Keen, Bernard A. *The Agricultural Development of the Middle East*. A report to the Director General of the Middle East Supply Centre. London, 1946.

Konikoff, A. *Transjordan: An Economic Survey*. 2d ed. Jerusalem: Economic Research Institute of the Jewish Agency for Palestine, 1946.

Landis, James M. "Anglo-American Co-operation in the Middle East," *The Annals of the American Academy of Political and Social Science*, Vol. CCXL (July 1945), pp. 64-72.

Langley, Kathleen M. *The Industrialization of Iraq*. Cambridge: Harvard University Press, 1961.

Libya Customs Tariff Schedules-1962. Translated by Ibrahim Hafez Ramadan. Tripoli, 1962.

Lichtenberg, Robert M. *The Role of Middleman Transactions in World Trade*. New York: National Bureau of Economic Research, Inc., 1959.

Lipsey, R. G. "The Theory of Customs Unions: A General Survey," *The Economic Journal*, Vol. LXX (September 1960), pp. 496-513.

Little, Arthur D., Inc. *A Plan for Industrial Development in Iraq*. Cambridge, Mass., 1956.

Macdonald, Robert W. *The League of Arab States*. Princeton: Princeton University Press, 1965.

Malloy, William M. (comp.). *Treaties, Conventions, International Acts, Protocols and Agreements Between the United States of America and Other Powers 1776-1909*. 2 vols. Washington: Government Printing Office, 1910.

Meade, J. E. (ed.). *Case Studies in European Economic Union: The Mechanics of Integration*. London: Oxford University Press, 1962.

———. *The Theory of Customs Unions*. Amsterdam: North-Holland Publishing Company, 1955.

———. *The Theory of International Economic Policy*. Vol. II: *Trade and Welfare*. London: Oxford University Press, 1955.

Mikesell, Raymond F. *Intra-Regional Trade and Economic Development*. Washington: International Development Advisory Board, 1958.

O'Brien, Patrick. *The Revolution in Egypt's Economic System*. London: Oxford University Press, 1966.

Pincus, Joseph. *The Central American Common Market*. Mexico City: United States Department of State (Agency for International Development), 1962.

Ramazani, Rouhollah K. *The Middle East and the European Common Market*. Charlottesville: The University Press of Virginia, 1964.

Recueil des Lois et de la Législation Financière de la République Arabe Syrienne. (Periodical.) Damascus.

Robinson, E. A. G. (ed.). *Economic Consequences of the Size of Nations: Proceedings of a Conference Held by the International Economic Association.* New York, 1960.

Royal Institute of International Affairs. *Great Britain and Egypt 1914-1951.* London: Oxford University Press, 1952.

Saba, Elias S. *The Foreign Exchange Systems of Lebanon and Syria 1939-1957.* Beirut: American University of Beirut, 1961.

Sannwald, Rolf, and Stohler, Jacques. *Economic Integration: Theoretical Assumptions and Consequences of European Unification.* Translated by Herman F. Karreman. Princeton: Princeton University Press, 1959.

Spalding, William F. (ed.). *Tate's Modern Cambist.* 28th ed. London, 1929.

UAR Customs Tariff-January 1962. Translated by Tawfik Mohamed Sadek. Cairo: Japan Trade Center, 1962.

Viner, Jacob. *The Customs Union Issue.* New York: Carnegie Endowment for International Peace, 1950.

Wilcox, Clair. *A Charter for World Trade.* New York: The Macmillan Company, 1949.

Wilmington, Martin W. "The Middle East Supply Center: A Reappraisal," *The Middle East Journal,* Vol. VI (Spring 1952), pp. 144-156.

Winant, Fred, and Dawson, John P. "The Middle-East Supply Program," *Foreign Commerce Weekly,* April 1, 1944, pp. 3-7 and 37-39.

Wionczek, Miguel S. (ed.). *Latin American Economic Integration: Experiences and Prospects.* New York: Frederick A. Praeger, 1966.